Abe Lincoln's Secret War Against the North

Abe Lincoln's Secret War Against the North

John Chodes

Algora Publishing
New York

Library of Congress Cataloging-in-Publication Data —

Chodes, John J.
Abe Lincoln's secret war against the North / John Chodes.
pages cm
Includes bibliographical references and index.
ISBN 978-1-62894-111-1 (soft cover: alkaline paper) — ISBN 978-1-62894-112-8 (hard cover: alkaline paper) — ISBN 978-1-62894-113-5 (ebook) 1. Lincoln, Abraham, 1809-1865—Public opinion. 2. Lincoln, Abraham, 1809-1865—Political and social views. 3. United States—Politics and government—1861-1865. 4. United States—Military policy. 5. Militarism—United States—History—19th century. 6. New York (State)—Politics and government—1861-1865. 7. Maryland—Politics and government—1861-1865. 8. Indiana—Politics and government—1861-1865. 9. Missouri—Politics and government—1861-1865. I. Title.
E457.2.C56 2015
973.7092—dc23
2015002044

Printed in the United States

TABLE OF CONTENTS

Introduction

Abraham Lincoln is an American icon. As "Honest Abe" and the "Great Emancipator," today he is viewed as a demigod whose grand virtues far outweigh his miniscule human failings.

Yet he wasn't always viewed this way. During his presidency, he was feared and hated, not only by Southerners, but also by his political rivals, the Democrats, and to a surprising degree, by the rank and file of his on Republican Party. They recognized that he had become a brutal dictator and was turning the USA into a permanently militarized nation.

Today, much of this has been swept under the rug, but through this investigation of three Northern states that opposed Abraham Lincoln's policies, and one state that fervently supported him, the true reality will be kept alive.

Why is this story important for today? Because many of the negatives in 21st-century American society—the centralization of power in Washington, political indifference to the popular will, the continual expansion of the "military-industrial complex"—can all be traced to their starting point: Abraham Lincoln's presidency.

We shall see that the Radical wing of Lincoln's Republican Party was a precursor of the 20th- and 21st-century totalitarian regimes. These Radicals believed in, and fulfilled, their goal of one-party rule. This goal was not shaped by four years of brutalizing war but was inherent in their ideology from the beginning.

Chapter 1. Lincoln's War Against New York

Overview of Pre-War Political and Commercial New York

The port of New York was the greatest commercial center in the world. The city itself, in a small geographical area, contained a larger population than any other metropolis in the United States.

New York City was in the midst of a tremendous boom. Foreign and domestic trade, along with a flourishing shipbuilding industry, made its harbor the nation's busiest. It was America's banking center, the hub of venture capital. Stock speculators were headquartered at Wall Street, along with like-minded men in real estate. In manufacturing, older industries modernized with the newest technologies, and new ones sprung up alongside, following their lead.

All these factors combined to create a massive job market which lured huge numbers of internal migrants and foreign immigrants. The city's population soared from 629,000 in 1855 to 805,000 by 1860.

New York City: Molded By Democratic Party Philosophy

The Democratic Party was king in New York City. Its platform stressed free trade, an unregulated economy, and home rule. This was totally at odds with the Republicans, who, by 1857, controlled upstate. Like their predecessors, the Whigs, Republicans advocated high protective tariffs to keep out foreign goods; and control over business practices and individual behavior. They were furious at the diametrically opposed vision of government held by the Democrats, who demanded limited power for the President and Governors; frequent local, state and national elections to restrict corruption; and frugality at all political levels and non-interference in personal, religious, or moral beliefs.

Democrats believed that all these tenets were embedded in the Constitution. For this reason, they guarded against all changes in this most basic document. Unlike the Whigs and Republicans, Democrats considered governmental power a dangerous commodity. They defined liberty as consisting of individuals who guarded their autonomy against the intrusions of political institutions. But they also acknowledged that the right to rule, and the power that implied, were the objects of all political parties. They saw that once in office, men were not willing to relinquish the authority they accrued from that position.

To balance these contradictory realities, Democrats maintained that the test of true political behavior rested on three inter-related variables. First, the pursuit of power was only legitimate if it did not interfere with people's rights. Second, the need to dominate was only permissible as long as it was tied to moral political behavior. The contest for power demanded the formation of legal machinery that could allow for peaceful conflicts to exist which would not destroy the social fabric nor the parties involved.

Kansas-Nebraska Act Creates the Republican Party

1854: When Senator Stephen Douglas pushed his "Kansas–Nebraska Act" through Congress, it ignited a national political explosion. First, it repealed the Missouri Compromise, which restricted slavery geographically. This new Act, more democratically, placed the acceptance or rejection of slavery in the hands of the citizens of each territory seeking statehood.

The nationally powerful Whigs, who despised giving power to ordinary citizens, fell to pieces. Its northern wing fused into a new political entity: the Republicans. As it was to the Whigs, "power to the people" was the ultimate sin. Containment and control of slavery was the first step toward the extermination of those "sub-human" Southerners who had slaves or accepted its legitimacy.

The Kansas–Nebraska Act also deeply affected the Democrats. In New York they split into three factions. The "Hards" felt that Congress lacked any jurisdiction over the South's right to expand the "peculiar institution." The "Softs" favored Congress setting a formula for slavery's expansion, based on popular sovereignty. This meant the views of the citizens of each territory would prevail. The "Barnburners" were dedicated to slavery's containment and its ultimate extinction. Many of this last group became Republicans. This allowed the Republican Party to gain power in New York State. The fragmentation process foreshadowed the same process nationally, which allowed Abraham Lincoln to gain the presidency. Even before Lincoln,

Republicans carried New York for their presidential candidate, John C. Frémont, and dominated the State Assembly in 1856.

Republicans Destroy New York City's Charter

The Dutch had established the colony of New Amsterdam in 1625. The capital was the town of New Amsterdam at the tip of what is now Manhattan Island. The charter gave it wide latitude of autonomy from interference from the rest of the colony. However, in 1664, the British, at war with the Netherlands, seized this colony for the Duke of York, and renamed the city New York. It became the capital of the province of New York.

The Dutch recaptured this city for one year (1673–74); then they were driven out again. Then the British governor, Thomas Dongan, granted a new charter for the city in 1686, which also gave New York City substantial independence from the remainder of the colony. All this was due to New York's great commercial and military significance.

Albany became the capital city. It grudgingly accepted this charter, which limited upstate legislative interference with most of New York City's political affairs.

Later, in the 1850s, Republicans, as autocrats, only complete power over the entire state could fulfill their Utopian dream of a perfect society. Nowhere is this more apparent than in pre-Civil War New York City.

1857: With a big majority in the Assembly, Republicans pushed through a radical new charter. It not only neutralized home-rule in New York City, but also created a form of one-party rule throughout the state. This, in turn, led to a strange form of mirror-image totalitarian government by the Democrats; most infamously by Mayor Fernando Wood and later by William Marcy "Boss" Tweed.

Previously, the mayor of New York City was the municipality's chief executive, but under the new Republican charter, he was powerless. Administrative chaos reigned. Executive authority was now divided and diffused among a dozen different departments. This was not to provide democratic checks and balances but to give total autonomy to lesser departments so they did not have to report to, or obey, any other agency or the mayor. Each became an independent fiefdom without any outside oversight.

The Republican charter spread executive duties over nine different agencies. The mayor served on all nine but lacked any input. He was just another member, with no higher voting power. What all this meant was that, instead of forming a bureaucratic structure answerable to the mayor, the city government was driven in the contrary direction: institutionalized fragmentation.

The new charter went further. Previously the commissioners of health, fire, and police were appointed by the mayor, and their jurisdiction was limited to the city. Now the Republican charter had created something called "Metropolitan Districts" which greatly expanded those commissioners' powers — into Westchester and even upstate, which were Republican strongholds. Those commissioners were no longer beholden to the local Democrats. This brought Radical ideology into the city, which had been impossible before.

Even key city administrators were elected or appointed by upstate officials or citizens. Members of the City Corporation Council, the City Recorder, the Comptroller, Surrogate Court judges, and eighteen other major judges of the various court systems, owed their loyalty to Albany.

The metropolitan district tactic also stripped the mayor of any authority over the city's charitable, welfare, and educational institutions, as well as the all-important harbor and water front properties.

Most important, the Republican charter denied the mayor any supervision over New York City's budget. He could not oversee the Comptroller's spending, tax collecting, or the holding or selling of municipal property. As vassals of Albany, the metropolitan commissioners were not subject to any interference by local elected officials or local restrictions. They had the unchecked ability to rig local elections.

Furthermore, all this, and one more clause in the new charter, foreshadowed the Radical Republican congressional abuses in the post-Civil War Reconstruction era, such as the "Tenure of Office Act," whereby President Andrew Johnson's ability to appoint and dismiss cabinet members was drastically curtailed. His defiance of this unconstitutional law brought on his impeachment proceedings.

In pre-war New York, there was a parallel law aimed at the city's mayor. He had to wait a year from taking office to make the few remaining appointments that were left to him. This was another element in neutralizing him.

Fernando Wood: One Man Rule vs. One Party Rule

William Marcy "Boss" Tweed is one of the most infamous political figures in American history. He has been pictured in narratives of the post-Civil War period as a ruthless criminal, mostly through Thomas Nast's brutally satirical cartoons in *Harper's Weekly*, which gave Tweed's negative image immortality.

Innumerable books and articles have crucified Tweed as bankrupting New York, by stealing millions of dollars to pay off both friends and opponents, to do his bidding or to keep them quiet about his criminal activities. And Tweed was not even the mayor of New York City. He was the top man in the Democratic Party's Tammany Hall faction. Yet, through graft, he controlled the city's organs of government.

Tammany Hall became the upholder of Jeffersonian political philosophy, standing for reform on behalf of the common man. It gained its strength by bringing immigrants into the fold by getting them jobs.

The accepted story of Boss Tweed's career is misleading. He was not a political criminal by choice. He was driven into this role by necessity; it was forced upon him by the pre-war Republicans who had completely crippled the city's Democratic administration. They forced Tweed to create a "shadow government" outside the normal legal channels.

But — William Marcy Tweed had a predecessor; less famous, but incorrectly infamous also. He was the two-time mayor Fernando Wood. Wood was mayor when the Republicans first crafted their destructive charter. It was Wood who first envisioned the antidote: a clandestine political "machine." Wood initially spent millions to bribe his Republican enemies so that the city could maintain home rule.

Like Tweed, Fernando Wood has been universally vilified. One of his historian detractors said this about him: "A young Philadelphian, Fernando Wood, combining his attributes of a powerful physique, congenial manners, and absolute unscrupulousness, was ordained from the start to be a success as a Tammany politician. Not only was he twice elected mayor of New York City but he was also the handsomest man that ever sat in the mayor's chair."[1]

The author and statesman John Bigelow said: "But from the throne of thievery, wearing a crown of corruption, and wielding the scepter with an underworld alliance, he ruled New York for a decade; the first of the absolute bosses, for three-quarters of a century thereafter were to hold uninterrupted domination. He died with half a million dollars." (By today's standards, half a billion dollars.) [2]

Fernando Wood claimed that the new city charter was the source of New York City's problems: "The object of government is simple. It is to govern in the public interest, for aiding the many without threatening the few." [3]

Since the Albany legislature was not interested in such aims, Wood advocated a grass-roots movement to once again secure home rule. The example lay in the past, when public spirited people revised outdated charters and submitted them for the voters' approval. When this proved impossible, due to Republican interagency, Wood saw that he would have to play a new kind of politics and institute one-man rule, with unlimited power, to correct "every municipal wrong" and foil "judicial, executive, or legislative tyrants and unjust laws." [4]

Wood saw himself as the sole representative of the city's entire electorate. Any infringement upon his autonomy destroyed popular rights. He viewed Republican centralization of power as having turned New York City into a

1. Jerome Mushcat, "Fernando Wood: A Political Biography" (Kent State University Press, Kent and London , 1990) p. 6.
2. Ibid., p. 20.
3. Allan Franklin, *The Trail of the Tiger, Tammany 1789 to 1928* (New York: privately printed, 1928) p. 42
4. Jerome Mushcat, p. 23.

"subjugated city," which had robbed voters of their constitutional guarantees, by passing "outrageous" laws and plunging citizens into "such a feeble state of vassalage as to be bereft of any voice in the selection of our masters." [1]

These were the first shots in the audacious war against Albany. Wood, in walking a fine line between home rule and anarchy, told the federal attorney Thomas Sedgwick: "I am determined to test the Police Bill and take offensive action." This was to bring the police department back into the city's jurisdiction.[2]

Fernando Wood Wants New York City to Secede From Albany

Years before the South seceded from the United States, which produced four years of fratricide, Fernando Wood was a Congressman. This was in the 1840s. When he lost his bid for re-election, he bitterly announced to his supporters that he was entirely out of politics.

Before his departure from the House of Representatives, he had come under the spell of John C. Calhoun; the famed South Carolinian, who greatly influenced Wood's later political life. Calhoun was the architect of secession as an antidote to expanding federal power. He was not only a Congressman but had previously had been Secretary of War under James Madison and Vice President to John Quincy Adams and Andrew Jackson. It was assumed he would succeed Jackson as President, but this was not to be. Calhoun completely disagreed with Jackson's preference for centralizing federal power, which was giving Washington a dominant influence over the states.

As such, Calhoun became the pre-eminent spokesman for the South, trying to reconcile the problem of Washington injuring the agricultural South at the expense of the industrial North. Calhoun was also a powerful advocate for free trade, which influenced Fernando Wood. Calhoun defied the national Congress when it passed, in 1828 and 1832, progressively higher protectionist "Tariffs of Abomination." He bravely stood up to Uncle Sam, contending that the Constitution gave the states the right to nullify federal laws that were destructive to their sovereignty. South Carolina threatened to secede from the Union over these tariffs, which almost produced war with Washington. Calhoun won, and the taxes were reduced.

When Wood left Congress he called on Calhoun and asked for a patronage job, as a dispatch agent. Calhoun obliged, and granted Wood that position at the State Department. Wood's responsibilities included sending official dispatches to overseas U.S. consuls and diplomatic documents to the White House. This kept his name alive politically, and reminded New York Democrats that he had political contacts in Washington.

1. Ibid., p. 72.
2. Ibid., p. 80.

Calhoun's influence on Wood became evident on January 7, 1861. By this date, five Southern states had seceded from the Union. Comparing the prolonged conflicts that existed simultaneously between the South and Washington, and New York City and Albany, Mayor Calhoun made the following speech before the New York City Council:

New York Sympathizes with the South

"With our aggrieved brethren of the Slave States, we have friendly relations and a common sympathy. We have participated in the warfare upon our constitutional rights as well as their domestic institutions. While other portions of our State have unfortunately been enmeshed with the fanatical spirit which activates a portion of the people of New England [hatred of the South], the city of New York unfalteringly preserved the integrity of its principles in adherence of the compromises of the Constitution and the equal rights of the people of all the States... Therefore, New York will endeavor a continuance of uninterrupted Intercourse with every section."

New York City's Rights Trampled By Albany

"It is a folly to disguise the fact that, judging from the past, New York City may have more cause of apprehension from the aggressive legislation of our own State than from external dangers...For the past five years our interests have been repeatedly trampled upon. Being an integral portion of the State, it has been assumed, and in effect, tacitly admitted on our part, by non-resistance, that all political and governmental power over us, rested in the State legislature. Even the common right of taxing ourselves for our own government has been yielded, and we are not permitted to do so without this authority, which has led to anarchy and utter confusion."

New York Was A Free City-State, Now A Conquered Province

"No candid mind can, after a perusal of the original grants; (the charters) fail to perceive the extent of the usurpations that have been made on the municipal rights and civil liberties of New York. These early charters contemplated the establishment of a municipal corporation that would, in its free and ample privileges, pre-eminence and jurisdictions, vie with the great cities of Europe, and would be worthy of that commerce which unrivalled natural advantages could not fail to attract, to our shores...It has been the settled policy of all civilized countries to encourage the growth and stability of their commerce by giving the cities which are the seats of municipal charters as to secure their dignity and respect in the eyes of the world. Governments, the most despotic, have tolerated there, as in no other place, liberty, in order to foster trade.

"The municipal rights of London, of Hamburg, and the free cities of Germany, have always been regarded as inviolate. The same sanctions were intended to apply to the civic privileges of New York. She was to contain within herself an organic vitality and self-government which should develop and expand and extend so as to insure for herself her future grandeur and importance...The element of good government and economical administration has failed, through the encroachments and invasions which have been carried on for so many years, and our city occupies the position of a conquered province, entirely dependent on the will of a distant and indifferent and alien government [at Albany] ... It is not alone that the inalienable right of self government has been wrested from us, but our taxes have largely increased, while the protection of life and property has decreased.

Shall New York City Secede From The State?

"How shall we rid ourselves of this odious and oppressive connection is not for me to determine. It is certain that dissolution cannot be peacefully accomplished. Deriving so much advantage from its power over the City, it is not probable that a partisan majority will consent to a separation; and the resort to force and violence and revolution must not be thought of for an instant. We have been distinguished as an orderly and law-abiding people. Let us do nothing to forfeit this character...

Much, no doubt, can be said in favor of the justice and policy of separation. It may be said that secession or revolution in any of the United States would be subversive of all Federal authority; that if part of the States form new combinations and governments, other States may do the same...Then it may be said, why should not New York City, instead of supporting, by her contributions in revenue, two-thirds of the expenses of the United States, become equally independent? As a free city, with but a nominal duty on imports, her local government could be supported without taxation upon her people. Thus we could live free from taxes and have cheap goods nearly duty free. In this, she would have the whole and united support of the Southern States.

"It is well for individuals or communities to look every danger square in the face and meet it calmly and bravely. As dreadful as the severing of the bonds that have hitherto, united the States, has been in contemplation, it is now a stern and inevitable fact. [Five Southern states had already seceded.] We have now to meet it with all the consequences, whatever they may be.

"If the Confederacy (The United States) is broken up, the government is dissolved, and it behooves every distinct community, as well as every individual, to take care of themselves.

"Disunion has become a fixed and certain fact. Then why may not New York disrupt the bonds which bond her to a corrupt and venal master, to a people and a party that has plundered her revenues; attempted to ruin her commerce, and taken away the power of self-government...Amid the gloom which the present and prospective condition of things must cast over the country, New York, as a free city, may shed the only light and hope for a future reconstruction of our once blessed Confederacy.

New York: Secession "Peacefully If We Can"

"Yet I am not prepared to recommend the violence implied in these views. In stating this argument in favor of freedom, peacefully if we can, forcibly if we must, let me not be misunderstood. The redress can be found only in appeals to the magnanimity of the people of the whole state. The events of the past two months (the secession of five Southern states) have no doubt effected a change in the popular sentiment, of this state on national politics. Thus, change may bring us the desired relief, and we may be able to obtain a repeal of the Isms to which I have referred, and a consequent restoration of our corporate rights."[1]

Wood did not achieve his goal for an independent New York City, but the former governor of the Empire State, Horatio Seymour, still a nationally prominent figure, would follow up on many of these ideals and force a major military confrontation with President Abraham Lincoln.

New York on the Edge of War

Horatio Seymour would once again regain the governorship during the most critical phase of the Civil War, and his defiance of Lincoln's policies would lead to the President's decision twice invade New York State.

Seymour was one of the leading statesmen of the era, culminating with his being the Democratic presidential candidate against Ulysses S. Grant in 1868. He narrowly lost.

Seymour's speeches before, during, and after the war clearly demonstrate that what we know about Abraham Lincoln, the Civil War, and Reconstruction, are completely at odds with reality. At the Democratic Party's state convention in Albany, when the war was just months away, Seymour made the following speech on January 31, 1861:

1. This speech by Fernando Wood appeared in the *New York Times*, January 8, 1861.

Frantic Washington: A Madhouse

"The mighty fabric of our government is about to crumble and fall because the virtues which reared and upheld it have departed from our counsels. What spectacle do we see today? Already five states have withdrawn from the United. Revolution has already taken place. The term 'secession' divests it of none of its terrors... All virtue, patriotism and intelligence seems to have fled from our National Capital; it has been well likened to the conflagration of an asylum for madman. Some look with idiotic imbecility, some in sullen silence, and some scatter firebrands which consume the fabric above them, and bring upon all a common destruction. Do you not see there the senselessness displayed with regard to personal passions and party purposes; while the glory, the honor, and the safety of the country are forgotten? The same pervading fanaticism has brought evil upon all the institutions of our land...The growing burdens of debt and taxation, the gradual destruction of the African in the free states, which is marked by each recurring Census, are all due to the neglect of our duties, caused by the complete absorption of the public mind by a senseless, unreasoning fanaticism. The agitation over the question of slavery has thus brought greater social, moral, and legislative evils upon the people of the Free states than it has upon the institutions against whom it has been excited....

"The South does not ask to extend Slavery. They say it exists in the territories. The Republicans assert that slavery shall not extend. They show a distrust of their own constitutional constructions and historical statements by demanding Congressional interferences and restraints; and under the cry of 'No Extension,' they are in fact agitating for repeal; and restrictions which are of no significance unless slavery has a legal existence, which they deny.

"Our Fathers [the creators of the Constitution] disposed of similar by compromise. Adjustments have been made from time to time. The condition of our affairs forces upon us the alternative of compromise or civil war. Let us contemplate the latter alternative. We are advised by the conservative state of Kentucky, that if force is to be used, it must be exerted against the united South. It would be an act of folly and madness, in entering upon this contest, to underrate our opponents, and thus may subject ourselves to the disgrace of defeat in an inglorious warfare. Let us see if successful coercion by the North is less revolutionary than successful secession by the South.[1]

1. Thomas Cook and Thomas Knox, editors, "Public Record of Horatio Seymour" (New York, I.W. England, at the offices of the New York "Sun," 1868) p. 23.

The War Begins

In April 1861, the war between the Union and Confederate states commenced with the bombardment and surrender of Fort Sumter, in the harbor at Charleston, South Carolina. Initially there was a wild outpouring of enthusiasm and patriotic zeal. Volunteers by the thousands and hundreds of thousands joined the Union army. Abraham Lincoln and his Republican administration and those who had eagerly joined the military thought the "rebellion" would be crushed in short order.

But after the crushing defeat by the Confederates at Bull Run, and the horrifying annihilations at Fredericksburg and Manassas, and the slaughter and retreat from Richmond, the mood in the North changed dramatically. It was obvious that the Southern enemy had great skill and ability. This was going to be a long war of attrition, and that many Northern homes would be filled with mourning.

As a result, voluntary enlistments dropped dramatically. In 1862, Congress passed a bill that empowered President Lincoln to put the troops of each state under the United States' military jurisdiction. Prior to this, under the Constitution, each individual state shared the responsibility with the federal government for bringing men into the national army. Referring to this law of "dubious legality and confusing arithmetic," historian James McPherson concluded that the federal government "did not hesitate to use this power to reach across state boundaries and institute a quasi-draft." [1]

Then, on March 1, 1963, Congress passed, and Lincoln signed, an "Enrollment Act." This established a nationalized conscription. The federal government was now in complete control of bringing men into the Union army. This enormous increase in Washington's power had serious consequences throughout the North. It defied this clause of the Constitution: "Congress shall have the power for organizing, arming, and disciplining the militia, and for governing such part of them as may be employed in the service of the United States; reserving to the States respectively the appointment of the officers." In nationalizing the draft, this right was taken away. [2]

New York's constitution paralleled the United States document: "New York's militia law makes all the officers elective; captains, subalterns, and non-commissioned, by ballots; field and general officers, by ballot of the commissioned officers." [3]

President Lincoln insisted that the War Department select those officers without the consent of the states. Even before the Enrollment Act went into

1. Jack N. Rakeve, "The Annotated U.S. Constitution and Declaration of Independence."
2. Ibid., p. 57
3. Ibid., p. 57.

effect, but anticipating the disastrous results, New York's Governor Morgan (who served just prior to Horatio Seymour) went to Washington to have a face-to-face confrontation with Secretary of War Cameron, and he insisted that their negotiations be recorded.

Governor Morgan: "You have announced the irrevocable determination of the United States to appoint the general officers for the forces furnished for the government of the United States and refuse to receive these forces in the event that such determination should not be acceded to. I deem it my duty to respectfully but firmly protest against this determination. It imposes on the state officers, unless they submit to it, the necessity of violating the laws and constitutions of the State of New York, which has been framed in conformity to the Constitution of the United States." [1]

Governor Morgan concluded with this truth related to the checks and balances built into the United States Constitution: "There is a deep and prophetic jealousy of military power which is embedded in these provisions of the Constitution. The military arm was subjected to the paramount direction of the national authority, but the right arm, whose million sinews are strong in the militia alone, was guarded by rooting it in the local pride and spirit and sovereignty of the states...The President has taken the responsibility of a series of acts, without authorization of law, trusting for justification to the public exigencies and peril, to the sanction of Congress." [2]

Thus, Abraham Lincoln gained the upper hand over the states. His attorney-general, Edward Bates, from Missouri, a notorious Radical Republican, gave his legal opinion favoring Washington: "Giving to the Constitutional reservations in favor of the States the most liberal construction which can be claimed for them, they confer no right on the State authorities to disturb the organization of militia or volunteer regiments in the national service, or to interfere in any way with the control which the President, under the national Constitution, shall exercise over them." [3]

Later, Republican Governor Andrew of Massachusetts wrote to the new Secretary of War, Edwin Stanton, about resorting to a national draft: "The draft will disturb everything. It will raise a thousand questions, will make a paper army; disorganized, ineffective, discontented, valueless." [4]

Shredding part of the Constitution allowed Lincoln to now conduct a reign of terror against civilians that would have been impossible before. He ordered the arbitrary arrest of "traitors; those who opposed his war. Thousands of

1. "War Government: Federal and State, 1861-1865" (Boston and New York: Houghton Mifflin and Company, 1906) p. 186.
2. Ibid., p. 187.
3. United States War Department, "The War of the Rebellion: A Compilation of the Official Records of the Union and Confederacy," series III, vol 2, (Washington, D.C., Government Printing Office, 1860-1701) p. 151.
4. Ibid., p. 445.

civilians, thus accused, were unconstitutionally tried by military tribunals, not civil courts, and thrown into secret places of confinement. Their property was often confiscated. Antiwar-newspapers, almost all Democratic, were closed at bayonet point." [1]

Federal Draft Leads To Battle of New York

Even before the Enrollment Law, disillusionment with Lincoln and his dictatorial war showed itself in the Congressional and gubernatorial elections. In November 1862, Republicans lost many seats in Washington, as well as in the state assemblies. This included New York, where Democratic Horatio Seymour ascended to the governorship.

Before he was sworn in, Seymour made this comment at a Democratic meeting in Utica. He expressed regrets that the war had not been averted despite all the efforts to do so, but he realized it was inevitable. "First, and above all, we are to show obedience to constituted authorities...The President of these United States can rely on our support, for we have a due sense of loyalty and obedience, and we shall not weaken his policy; he will not be embarrassed by us [the Democrats] so long as he keeps within the limits of his constitutional rights." [2] But it was obvious that Mr. Lincoln had already exceeded those rights.

Mr. Seymour contended that it was not the abolition of slavery but the rights of states that caused the South to secede. This was directly opposed to the view of Lincoln, who argued that slavery was the cause of the conflict, and without it, the rebellion could never have begun and could not continue. Mr. Seymour felt that to make the Southern states accept the abolition of slavery was an invasion of their Constitutional rights and that state rights were equally sacred to those of the general government.

Continuing to clarify the sanctity of state sovereignty, Horatio Seymour said: "The people of the North are uniformly opposed to Slavery, not from hostility to the South, but because it is repugnant to our sentiments. In conformity with our views we have abolished slavery here, and having exercised our rights in our way, we should be willing to let other communities have the same rights and privileges we have enjoyed. We are bound to act upon our faith in the principles of self-government; The Republican organization proposes an assault upon the Southern states by a system of agitation and excitement, directly at war with the purposes of the Constitution. They constantly discuss questions belonging to their states, to the entire neglect of their own local affairs. They organize their party on the ground that all and every difference of opinion about their own concerns are to be overlooked,

1. "War Government, Federal and State," p. 180
2. Alexander J. Wall, "A sketch in the life of Horatio Seymour" (New York: New York Historical society, 1929) p. 22.

provided they agree in their views about an institution [slavery] which does not exist in their own states... [Lincoln's constituency was almost exclusively in the Northeast] and does not exist in states which they admit they have no Constitutional right to interfere." [1]

Horatio Seymour then showed the evils of a war against fellow Americans who had greatly aided the North in the past: "Can we so entirely forget the past history of our country, that we can stand upon the point of pride against states whose citizens battled with our fathers and poured out with them their blood upon the soil of our state, amid the highlands of the Hudson, and the fields of Saratoga? I ask the old men within the sound of my voice, to what quarter did you look for sympathy during the last war with Great Britain [the War of 1812] when New York was assailed upon the shores of Erie and Ontario, and when the disciplined troops who had successfully fought against Napoleon in the Peninsula War, invaded us with cooperating fleets by the channel of Lake Champlain? Was it not the states of the South? [2]

The Enrollment Act

When the Enrollment Act was passed, President Lincoln sent the following letter to Horatio Seymour:

> You and I are substantially strangers, and I write this chiefly that we may become better acquainted. I, for the time being, am the head of a nation which is in great peril; and you are at the head of the greatest state of that nation. As to maintaining the nation's life and integrity, I assume and believe there cannot be a difference of purpose between you and me. If we should differ as to the means, it is important that such differences should be as small as possible; that it should not be enhanced by unjust suspicions on one side or the other. In the performance of my duty, the cooperation of your state, as of the others, is needed; in fact, indispensable. This alone is sufficient reason why I should wish to have a good understanding with you. Please write me at least as long a letter as this. Of course, saying in it, just what you think fit. [3]

On April 17, 1863, Governor Seymour wrote President Lincoln:

> I have delayed answering your letter for some days, with a view of preparing a paper. I wished to state clearly the aspect of public affairs from the standpoint I occupy. I do not claim opinions I hold are entertained by one-half of the population of the Northern states.
>
> I have been prevented from giving my views in the manner I intended by the pressure of official duties, which at the present stage of the

1. David Croly, *Seymour and Blair, Their Lives and Services* (New York: Richardson and Company, 1868) p. 49.
2. Thomas Cook and Thomas Knox, p. 30.
3. Alexander Wall, p. 28.

> legislative session of this state, confines me to the Executive chamber until each midnight. After the adjournment, which shall soon take place, I will give you, without reserve, my opinions and purposes with regard to the condition of our unhappy country. In the meantime, I assure you that no political resentments, or no personal objects, will turn me from the pathway I have marked out for myself. I intend to show to those charged with the administration of public affairs, a due deference and respect, and to yield to them a just and generous support in all measures they may adopt within the scope of their Constitutional powers. For the preservation of the Union, I am ready to make any sacrifice of interest, passion or prejudice.[1]

One of Horatio Seymour's biographers said this about that letter: "Whatever the cause of Governor Seymour writing this cold, guarded letter to President Lincoln, has not been explained. This incident led to bitter criticism of the governor for his lack of cooperation with the president. Men of opposite political beliefs are not always prone to friendly association, and Lincoln was then criticized as any man would be, under similar conditions." [2]

Soon afterward, Governor Seymour became less guarded and confronted Lincoln directly on the issue of the unconstitutional national draft which destroyed state sovereignty: "The rights of the states must be respected. A consolidated government in this vast country would destroy the essential home rule rights and liberties of the people. The sovereignty of the states, except as they are limited by the Constitution, can never be given up. Without them, our government cannot stand." [3]

Then Seymour went one step further. This occurred when a nationally prominent Democratic Congressman, Clement Vallandigham, was arrested for making an anti-Lincoln, anti-war speech in his home state of Ohio. He assailed Lincoln's autocratic powers "as inexorable in its character as that of the worst despotisms of the Old World of ancient or modern times. When an attempt is made to deprive us of free speech and a free press, the hour shall have come when it will be our duty to find some other efficient redress." [4]

Vallandigham was convicted by a military tribunal, like so many other civilians, which was unconstitutional, and deported into the Confederacy. This action immediately prompted national anti-Lincoln rage. Governor Seymour said this about Vallandigham's conviction: "If this proceeding is approved by the government and sanctioned by the people, it is not merely a step toward despotism, it establishes a military despotism." [5]

1. Ibid., p. 29.
2. Ibid., p. 29.
3. Thomas Cook and Thomas Knox, p. 28.
4. New York *Herald*, March 8, 1863.
5. New York *Herald*, March 19, 1863.

Going further, Governor Seymour commented on the illegal kidnapping of civilians to remote locations or countries:

> It is a high crime to abduct a citizen...I shall investigate every alleged violation of our statutes and see that the offenders are brought to justice. Sheriffs and District Attorneys are admonished that it is their duty to take care that persons within their respective counties are not imprisoned, nor carried by force beyond their limits, without due process or legal authority. The removal to England of persons charged with offenses, away from their friends, their witnesses and means of defense, was one of the acts of tyranny for which we asserted our independence. The abduction from the state for offenses charged here, and carrying them many hundreds of miles to distant prisons in other states, territories or countries, is an outrage of the same character, upon every principle of right and fair justice. The General Government has a judicial system, in full and undisturbed operation. Its own courts, held at convenient points in this and other loyal states, are open for the hearing of complaints. If the laws are not ample for the punishment of offenses, it is due to the neglect of those in power. [1]

Horatio Seymour then focused on the suspension of newspapers that opposed the war:

> The suspension of journals and imprisonment of persons has been so glaringly partisan; allowing some of the utmost licentiousness of opinion and punishing others for their fair exchange of the rights of discussion. Conscious of their gross abuses, an attempt has been made to shield the violators of law, and suppress inquiry into their motives and conduct. This attempt will fail. Unconstitutional acts cannot be shielded by unconstitutional laws; such attempts will not save the guilty. [2]

Abraham Lincoln, in stages, declared martial law over all the Northern states, although most of the warfare was confined to the Confederacy. Once again, this was unconstitutional. Horatio Seymour:

> This claim of power under martial law is not only destructive to the rights of states, but it overthrows the legislative and judicial departments of the General Government. It asserts for the President more power as head of the army, than as representative ruler of the people. This claim has brought discredit upon us in the eyes of the world. It has strengthened the hopes of rebellion. It has weakened the confidence of the loyal states....Loyalty is less secure than rebellion, for it stands without means of resistance against outrages or to resent tyranny. Amidst all the horrors that have been enacted under martial law in the history of the world, and amidst all the justifications for its usage, it has

1. David Croly, p. 89.
2. Albany *Argus*, January 8, 1863.

> never been held that it could be extended over peaceful states. It has never before been claimed that the power of the military commanders were superior to the powers of the government.[1]
>
> All these factors accelerated the impulse for a violent military showdown between New Yorkers and Abraham Lincoln and his regime. Fernando Wood ratcheted up the probability of a confrontation still higher when he said that the United States was in the midst of two revolutions: "One, with the sword, at the South, and the other, at the North, by Executive and legislative usurpation... Taking advantage of the popular enthusiasm on behalf of the Union, it has, under the pretext of furthering this holy object, gradually fastened the chains of slavery upon the people. [2]

Unconstitutional arrests and attacks on free speech put New Yorkers on a collision course with Lincoln, but the nationalizing of the draft and its indifference to state sovereignty provoked war. Governor Seymour's reaction was immediate and threatening: "This will prove unfortunate as a policy." He asked Lincoln not to put the draft into effect until its legality could be determined. "I will not dwell upon what I believe would be the consequences of a violent, harsh policy before the constitutionality of the act can be tested. You can scan the immediate future as well as I." [3]

Lincoln refused to wait. Without any political announcement or even a personal message to Governor Seymour, the draft was instituted. The Albany newspaper *The Argus* commented on the secrecy of it:

> The draft has not been ordered by proclamation or any public assignment of quotas for the states. The provost marshals are going on with the conscription under secret instructions from the War Department. Why is this? Why is there not a public proclamation of the draft and of the quotas of each state? Secrecy implies unfairness; and the people want to know that there is a fair and equal dealing among the states, and that New York is allocated the deduction promised her when she sent forward her militia regiments for the emergency. [The emergency was the battle at Gettysburg.] There is something in the manner in which the Conscription Act has been enacted, which to us in unintelligible except under the theory that it has been the intention of the Administration to make it unpopular. There has been no public proclamation or call for men. No public quotas have been assigned to the states or districts. No opportunity has been given to challenge the accuracy or fairness of the lists, and whether or not the enrollment

1. Albany *Argus*, January 8, 1863
2. Sidney David Brummer, *Political History of New York State during the Period of the Civil War* (New York: Columbia University and Longmans, Green and Company, Agents, 1911), p. 320.
3. Ibid., p. 328.

> officers have been partisan. This has left a suspicion of partiality and favoritism. We do not believe that any-civilized government ever undertook a law of this importance, in such a clandestine and underhanded way; under such liability to the suspicion of fraud. It has never before been attempted in this country...This is one of the strangest blunders connected with this war. [1]

Abraham Lincoln's bureaucrats finally sent New York its draft quota. The Albany *Argus* found its fears were well grounded. The quota provoked Governor Seymour to write several furious letters to the President: "If the comparison is made between cities of the different states, the disproportion of men demanded from New York and Brooklyn [both Democratic cities] is startling. While in these, 26% of the population is enrolled, in Boston [a Republican city], only 12.5%, or less than half the ratio, is liable to be drafted." [2]

Lincoln backed down. The quotas were more equitably distributed, but the conflict had reached the point of no return. The New York Democratic Party passed a resolution concerning the Conscription Act: "It is subversive to the rights of state governments and is designed to make them dependencies and provinces, to be ruled by military satraps, under a great, consolidating, usurping central despotism." [3]

Then, J.M. McMasters, the editor of the *Freeman's Journal*, wrote: "The time for deliberation has gone and the time for action has come, by fighting. Not by street fighting, not by disorganized opposition. They should organize by tens and hundreds, by companies and regiments, and they should send to their governor [Horatio Seymour] for their commissions as soon as their regiments are formed." [4]

War began when Horatio Seymour refused to release New York troops until the constitutionality of the Conscription Act could be determined. Lincoln demanded them instantly, and he sent federal troops into New York State to enforce induction.

The Battle Begins

On Saturday morning, July 11, 1863, the actual drawing of draftees began. At 5 a.m. it was already hot and overcast. A long column of citizen soldiers moved from the Lower East Side across Broadway to 9th Avenue, armed with iron bars, bludgeons and bats. Armed women were among them. Small groups split off and smashed into hardware stores to get handguns and rifles.

1. Alexander Wall, p, 75.
2. James B. Fry, *New York and the Conscription of 1863: A Chapter in the History of the Civil War* (New York: G.P. Putnam's Sons, the Knickerbockers Press, 1885) p. 57.
3. *New York Herald*, April 3, 1863.
4. Sidney David Brummer, p, 306.

Another column poured down Lexington Avenue to the Bull's Head Hotel on 43rd Street, the office of the American Telegraph Company. From here messages could be sent to Washington, warning of the uprising. The office was destroyed.

Another formation swarmed over the Harlem and New Haven Railroad tracks, which paralleled the American Telegraph's transmission lines. They were cut. Communications with the outside world and the police precincts went dead. Now Lincoln's military commanders could not quickly summon aid.

Simultaneously, the citizen-militia entered the railroad yards and depots, stopping all service. They moved against the major police stations, isolating them.

Police headquarters on Mulberry Street was placed under siege. The 23rd precinct station house on East 88th Street was burned. The 16th Precinct on East 22nd Street, wrecked. The 5th Precinct on Baxter Street, surrounded. Much further uptown, the Harlem River Bridge was burned to stall federal reinforcements.

This insurrection against the federal government's unconstitutional acts has largely been misrepresented as a "draft riot" to disguise the magnitude and nature of the opposition to Lincoln's policies. But, even at the time that this military operation was developing, major Republicans saw and recorded the truth about the Battle of New York. Gideon Welles, Lincoln's Secretary of the Navy, wrote in his diary: "There is, I think, indubitable evidence of concert in these riotous movements, beyond the accidental and impulsive outbreak of a mob or mobs. [Robert E.] Lee's march into Pennsylvania [Gettysburg], the appearance of several rebel steamers off the coast, the mission of A.H. Stephens [the Confederate Vice President] to Washington, seem to be part of one movement, have one origin, are all concerted schemes between the rebel leaders and Northern sympathizer friends." [1]

The New York *Tribune*, a Republican newspaper, reported that "no person who carefully watched the movements of this mob, who noticed their careful attention to the words of certain tacitly acknowledged leaders who observed the unquestionably preconceived regularity with which they proceeded from one part of their infernal program to the next...can presume to doubt that these men were acting under leaders who had carefully elaborated their plans."[2]

Sunday, 6 a.m. Another large body of New Yorkers massed along Second Avenue. One section moved against the Union Steam Works, on 22nd Street, a weapons factory that made small arms for the federal government. Thousands of rifles were in that building. A second attack was aimed at 21st Street, the

1. James McCague, *The Second Rebellion: The Story of the New York City Draft Riots of 1863* (New York: The Dial Press, 1968) p. 107.
2. Ibid., p. 107

New York State Armory. Small arms and artillery were stored there. The police held the armory; ten thousand New Yorkers charged them. The police retreated. To block reinforcements to the armory, the 18th Precinct on 22nd Street was also assaulted, its officers routed. Further downtown, New York's militia headed for the City Hall area and the offices of the *Tribune*. Simon Gay, the managing editor, saw the approaching force and said: "This is not a riot but a revolution!"[1]

The New Yorkers wrecked the *Tribune's* facility, but the police counter-attacked, drove them out, and the newspaper printed its next edition.

Fifty thousand New Yorkers were now in the streets. To divide police and army strength away from the main battle area in New York City, other attacks were staged in Brooklyn, Staten Island, and the Bronx. On Staten Island, there was an assault on the military drill room at the Tompkins Lyceum. A detachment of 200 took 30 rifles. A second drill room near Stapleton Landing was sacked and more weapons taken. Then a railroad car barn at the Staten Island Railroad was burned at the Vanderbilt Landing depot. This was to slow federal and police reinforcements.

Two companies of New York's 5th Regiment were diverted from lower Manhattan to Staten Island, along with two federal companies and 300 policemen. At Clifton, as they disembarked, one company was fired upon by citizen snipers concealed in the surrounding woods. They fired back. The citizens charged, took the soldiers weapons, crushed one's head, disemboweled a second, and bayoneted others.

In Brooklyn, military activity pinned down a considerable portion of the police force, when they were desperately needed in lower Manhattan. The Metropolitan Police District, which encompassed both cities, had about 2,000 men. At least half remained in Brooklyn as long as the threat existed there. One such attack was on two huge floating grain elevators in the bay off Atlantic Basin. The elevators had been loading grain as food for the Union armies. They were set on fire at night. The flames were visible to all of Brooklyn. This gigantic blaze drew firemen and police away from the major battle areas.

A huge crowd gathered. It seemed they were just fascinated by the fire, but they attacked the pier where the elevators were docked "like Zouaves charging an enemy's breastworks." [2]

Firemen, police, and security guards only survived by escaping on small boats in the river. The Brooklyn Navy Yard was a logical target. Four howitzers were placed at one gate, four cannons along the Flushing Avenue wall, and more artillery covered the main. Soldiers and sailors were withdrawn from other locations to reinforce this critical base. It was not assaulted. In the

1. Ibid., p. 105
2. Brooklyn *Eagle*, July 16, 1863.

Bronx, at Morrisania, and the West Farms sections, citizen-militia burned the enrollment offices. At Westchester Square they demolished the telegraph offices and at William Bridge and Melrose, they ripped up the rails of the New Haven and Harlem Railroad.

Police and Troops Counter-Attack

The initial clash between New Yorkers and the Union army occurred on the first day. Fifty "Invalid Corps" troops met the New Yorkers on Third Avenue. The Invalid soldiers bad been wounded in earlier battles and were unfit for front line service. At first they fired blanks at the New Yorkers. This did not stop them. They switched to live rounds. Six New Yorkers fell, but the rest surged forward, killing several soldiers and taking their weapons. Because of the cuts in communications, it look thirteen hours for two companies of regular *U.S.* infantry, stationed in the harbor, to arrive in the city. Mayor Opdyke sent an urgent telegram to Secretary of War Stanton, asking that all New York regiments return to the city from Gettysburg, where they had just been fighting.

At the Steam Works weapons factory, 150 New York State militia-men who were still loyal to the federal government confronted the citizens. It seemed that the loyalists would not fire on their own people. But they did: grape-shot from artillery, six rounds. The street was littered with the dead and dying.

The police supported the loyal militia by attacking the Steam Works from a different direction. They charged forward but were trapped in a hail of bullets and bricks from snipers on rooftops. The police poured into these buildings. They rushed to the roofs. In hand-to-hand fighting, both sides were hurled to the street below. The citizen-militia retreated from the Steam Works, regrouped, and attacked again. The loyalists and police gave ground. The citizens took the factory and it became their headquarters.

Later the police, with loyalist reinforcements, once again rushed forward, gained a foothold on the first floor, and in room-to-room, floor-to-floor combat, slowly took back the Steam Works.

There were many shipyards along the East and Hudson Rivers, most of them engaged in the building of military vessels for the navy. The New Yorkers attacked Webb and Allen, one of the largest, where the *Dunderberg*, an iron-clad ram, was near completion. The 7th New York Regiment defended the facility. Their concentrated fire drove back the citizen militia.

Simultaneously, a column of citizens attempted to seize the ferry terminal on Fulton Street to deny this landing site to Union reinforcements. It was already defended by federal troops. Here the citizens were also beaten off.

The police headquarters at Mulberry Street was still under siege. Thomas Acton, head of the Metropolitan Board of Police Commissioners, ordered all police reserves to relieve the blockade, along with a company of Zouaves. The howitzer batteries were readied. But the citizens learned quickly. On the order to fire, they flung themselves flat on the pavement or scattered into doorways on both sides of the street. In the interval between rounds of canister screaming harmlessly down First Avenue, an answering rattle of musketry began to grow from windows and rooftops; these sharpshooters concentrated their fire on the Union officers. Their troops were trapped and because they did not have the training to fight their way out or clear the buildings, they died. The citizens routed the Zouaves, captured the artillery, and turned it on the Union troops.

Then, two companies of police struck the citizen army in the rear at 4th Street and Broadway. With more hand-to-hand fighting, they surged back and forth. The New Yorkers retreated up Broadway, "which looked like a battle-field, thickly strewn with prostrate forms." [1]

On the third day, the 47th New York Regiment reached the battle from Gettysburg. Edwin Stanton informed Mayor Opdyke that another five regiments had been relieved and would be forwarded to New York "as fast as transportation can be furnished." [2] Stanton had chosen New Yorkers to kill New Yorkers.

At noon of the third day, after having been driven back from Webb and Allen, the civilian militia retreated until they reached barricades of cobblestones along 9th Avenue. There the Police and Union army combined to dislodge them. Connecticut troops poured a withering fire that allowed the police to overwhelm the defenders.

At this point Governor Seymour came into the city and found that he not only had to try to force the Union army to withdraw, but he also had to deal with the Republican leaders. They were intent on inciting the New Yorkers to greater violence. This would allow General Wool, who commanded the Department of the East, to declare martial law — which would end Democratic rule and civil law in New York. It would be replaced by military justice, administered through the Republicans. Martial law would depose Horatio and require a military governor to control all future elections.

To further discredit the Democrats and legitimate martial law, Lincoln's men placed tons of weapons inside a Negro orphanage. Then they leaked the information to the New Yorker's leaders. Federal troops were stationed inside the orphanage to protect that materiel.

The New Yorkers attacked the orphanage. It was sacked and two black children were killed. It was made to look like their deaths were racially

1. James McCague, p. 148
2. Ibid., p. 148.

motivated murder, but in fact the orphans died in the cross-fire as the New Yorkers tried to take the weapons stored there.

When General Wool refused to declare martial law, the *Tribune* called him "an imbecile." Wool was immediately replaced by General Dix who was much more compliant, but the battle ended before he could initiate such an extreme measure.

As the tide turned and federal troops pushed the citizen-militia back, Governor Seymour, with a cavalry escort, entered City Hall Park. It was filled with infantry. Seymour spoke to the New Yorkers, asking them to stop fighting. He realized that the battle was lost and to continue meant needless slaughter and permanent federal control of the state. "My friends, I come from a high regard for the welfare of those who, under the influence of excitement and supposed wrong, are in danger of not only inflicting serious blows to the good order *of* society, but also to their own interests.... I beg of you to listen to me as your friend and friend of your families." [1]

Governor Seymour told the citizens that he had sent his personal Adjutant General to Washington to stop the draft. The New Yorkers threw down their weapons and scattered into the wreckage of the city.

Union Victory

After four days the battle was over. Union troops remained in control of the city. More soldiers were brought in as part of the continuing army of occupation. Secretary of War Stanton sent this telegram to General Dix: "We are sending you 10,000 infantry and three batteries of artillery. These are picked troops, including the regulars. If you need cavalry, we can, perhaps, send you 500." [2]

This tremendous battle did not make Lincoln more willing to compromise on conscription. He announced that the draft would continue immediately, under General Dix, who provoked another confrontation with Horatio Seymour. Dix telegraphed the Governor that since the enrollment "will probably be resumed in this city at an early date, I am desirous of knowing whether the military power of this state may be relied upon to enforce the execution of the Order, in case of forcible resistance to it... [so that] I need not ask the War Department to put at my disposal for the purpose, troops in the service of the United States."[3]

Seymour wrote back that he had appealed to Lincoln not to resume conscription until its constitutionality could be tested. Lincoln refused to postpone it.

1. Ibid., p. 145.
2. Thomas Cook and Thomas Knox, p. 25.
3. Morgan Dix, *Memoirs of John Adam Dix*, vol. 1 (New York: Harper and Brothers, 1883) p. 86.

August 14th was the day the draft was resumed. Dix requested more federal troops. Seymour once more refused to comply, warning that enforcement would "excite popular resistance" and clarifying that New York State authorities would not carry out this national law. Conscription proceeded under the bayonets of this large army presence.

Later, General Dix wrote: "It has never been known how many perished in those awful days." There are reasons for this vagueness. The United States army disguised its casualties, since this as supposed to be a "riot" and not an official battle. Their dead and wounded were added to the lists for Gettysburg and past and future engagements to prevent the magnitude of the Battle of New York from being discovered. Yet, by indirection we can get a rough estimate of the carnage.

General Dix added: "According to the lowest estimates, some 1,200 of the rioters must have been killed and five to six times that number wounded; but they hid their losses as far as possible and disposed of their dead in silence and darkness."[1]

First, these numbers are absurdly low. At the New York State Armory alone, where the building was set ablaze during the fighting, "Fifty barrels filled with human bones were carried off to Potter's Field." [2]

And yet, even if we take Dix's numbers at face value, he is saying that 8,400 New Yorkers were casualties. Then, as a rule, an attacking army suffers three times as many killed and wounded as the defenders. That means the Union army and police lost 25,300 men. The combined total of 33,000 is higher than the great slaughter at Antietam and close to that at Gettysburg.

This battle radically altered the political climate in New York. When the war ended, as we shall see, an attempt was made to shred its Constitution, as if New York was a conquered Confederate state that had to be taught a lesson through "reconstruction."

Second Invasion of New York

A year later, in August 1864, Abraham Lincoln was informed by his Republican leaders that his November re-election prospects were hopeless. Horace Greeley, editor of the New York *Tribune*, one of the major Republican newspapers, wrote Lincoln that if the election were held in August, the Democrats would carry New York with a 100,000 majority.

General Benjamin Butler was one of the most controversial officers in the Union army. He had political ambitions as a Republican. In the final stages of the national campaign, Butler divided his time between fighting and writing speeches for Lincoln, which were read at political rallies.

1. Ibid., p. 86.
2. Ibid., p. 75.

For a New York convention, Butler wrote that those voters who supported the Democrats would be acting in a way "more detrimental to the country and beneficial to the rebellion than if they placed themselves actively in arms, side by-side with the rebels in the field."[1]

As a reward for his loyalty to the Republican cause, Butler was called to Washington for a new military assignment. The presidential election was only weeks away. He met with Edwin Stanton, the Secretary of War. Stanton wanted a stronger military presence in New York, particularly at the voting polls, to guarantee a Republican victory for Lincoln, who was opposed by a Democrat, General George McClellan. Stanton also hoped to depose Horatio Seymour and replace him with Reuben Fenton, the Radical Republican. Butler would command that force.

Choosing Butler for this operation indicated the contempt that the Lincoln administration held for New York. It was viewed as another rebel stronghold to be crushed.

Earlier in the war, Butler had stirred considerable resentment, even in the North, when he was in charge of federal troops in occupied New Orleans. He was replaced because of his behavior. His first widely publicized act was the summary execution of William Mumford who pulled down the United States flag from the New Orleans mint. Then Butler generated more bad press when he rounded up many New Orleans residents and exiled them to barren Ship Island in the Gulf of Mexico.

Butler growled and scowled, swaggered and bulldozed. He suppressed newspapers; then came his infamous "Woman Order." The women of New Orleans, to show their defiance of the occupying Yankees, began the practice of pouring the contents of chamber pots on the members of Butler's staff as they walked beneath their windows. Butler decreed: "Hereafter, when any female shall, by word or gesture or movement, insult or show contempt for any officer or soldier of the United States, she shall be regarded, and held liable to be treated as a woman of the town [a prostitute] plying her avocation."[2]

This had negative repercussions in the Northern press. England's newspapers denounced his actions. British Prime Minister Palmerstone protested. And further, Butler's excessively harsh confiscations and trade restrictions aroused objections from foreign governments. All this resulted in Butler being called "Beast." Secretary of State William Seward replaced him. Back home in Massachusetts, Butler said: "I have not erred too much in harshness ...There is no middle ground between loyalty and treason." [3]

1. Louis Taylor Morrill, "Ben Butler in the Presidential Campaign of 1864" (*The Mississippi Historical Review*, vol. xxxiii, No. 4, March 1947) p. 565.
2. Louis Taylor Merrill, p. 538.
3. Ibid., p. 540.

When Butler arrived in Washington for his new assignment, Stanton gave him an overstated report about conditions in New York to disguise the truth that Butler's role in that city was to steal the election for Lincoln by raw force and terror.

In his memoirs, Butler described his meeting with Stanton, who said:

> "Read these papers, General." I carefully read the paper...In substance they stated that there was an organization of troops to be placed under the command of Union General Fitz John Porter; there was to be inaugurated in New York a far more widespread and far better organized riot than the draft riot in July 1863; that the whole vote of the city was to be deposited for McClellan... that the Republicans were to be driven from the polls; that there were several thousand rebels in New York who were to aid in the movement; and that Brigadier-General John A. Green, who was known to be the confidential friend of the governor [Horatio Seymour] was to be present, bringing some forces from the interior of the state to take part in the movement.
>
> Butler asked Stanton: "What do you want me to do?"
>
> Stanton replied, "I want you to go down there and take command of the Department of the East, relieving General Dix; and I will have sent to you from the front a sufficient force to put down any insurrection."
>
> Butler continued: "He then asked me what troops I wanted, and I said: 'About 3,000 will be enough, but a larger force may be better for overawing an outbreak.' Stanton said: 'I suppose you will want your Massachusetts troops sent!'"
>
> Butler: "Oh," I said, "not Massachusetts men to shoot down New Yorkers. That won't do. I have as faithful, loyal, good soldiers in my New York regiments as there are in the world, and I can fully rely on them."

Butler moved into his New York City headquarters at Hoffman House on November 4th. The election would be on the 8th. Butler wrote:

> That day Major-General Sanford, commanding the divisions of state militia in the city of New York, called upon me and said that he proposed, on the day of the election, to call his divisions of militia to preserve the peace. I told him that could not be done without his reporting to me as his superior officer... He did not agree with that. I then told him that I did not need his divisions, and that I did not think it advisable to have the militia called out; that if they were called out, they would be under arms, and in case of difficulty, it may be not quite certain which way all of them would shoot...He was very obstinate about it, and said he would call out the militia. "Well," I said, "if there are to be armed forces

> here that do not report to me, and are not under my orders, I shall treat them as enemies.
>
> And from the reported doings of Governor Seymour in the center of the state in organizing new companies of militia, which I believe to be a rebellious organization. I may find it necessary to act promptly in arresting all those whom I know are preparing to disturb the peace here on Election Day. [1]
>
> Then Butler issued a harsh military order designed to intimidate voters. The Albany *Argus* editorialized: "We will not characterize, as it deserves, the conduct of the administration in sending to New York on the eve of the election, a man like Butler...His career in the army is calculated to arouse bitter indignation." [2] Many Republicans doubted the wisdom of sending Butler into New York.

The Military and Fraudulent Voting

In April 1863, Governor Seymour addressed the Albany legislature concerning "the question of the method by which those of our fellow citizens who are absent in the military and naval service of the nation may be able to enjoy the right of suffrage. The constitution of this state requires the elector to vote in the district in which he resides; but a law can be passed whereby the vote of an absent citizen may be given by his authorized representative."[3]

Instead, the Republican legislature passed a law that the members knew to be unconstitutional. It was designed to force a veto by Horatio Seymour, thus making it seem as if he was opposed to soldiers voting. In fact, Seymour did veto it, saying: "The bill is in conflict with vital principles of electoral purity and independence... The bill not only fails to guard against abuses and fraud, it offers every inducement and temptation to perpetuate them by those who are under the immediate and particular control of the General Government. That government has not hesitated to interfere, directly, with local elections, by permitting officers of high rank to engage in them in states of which they are not citizens." [4]

In March 1864, a constitutional amendment was passed by the people, after being accepted by Governor Seymour, enabling soldiers to vote in the field. In September 1864, as the presidential election approached, Seymour instructed commanders to give their troops the absentee ballots, but the Republican

1. Benjamin Butler, *Butler's Book; Autobiography and Personal Reminiscences of Major-General Benjamin Butler* (Boston: A.M. Thayer and Company, 1892) p. 754
2. Albany *Argus*, November 8, 1864.
3. David Croly, p. 134.
4. Ibid., p. 126.

Secretary of State of New York, Chauncey Depew, refused to distribute the forms to the officers. Seymour was forced to appoint a committee to do it.

Then Lincoln's aides seized the agents who were transporting the New York soldiers' ballots, charged them with fraud, and either held the ballots until after the election or secretly changed the forms to show a Republican choice. The agents, Colonel Samuel North, Major Levi Cohen, and M.M. Jones, were brought before a secret military tribunal which charged them with being "Confederates and employees of Governor Seymour" engaged in fraudulent election practices.

Thousands of other ballots deposited in the mails were detained in the post offices until after the presidential election. To prevent detection of this crime, the postmarks were altered. In some instances, when soldiers returned home to vote in person, they discovered their Democratic ballots had become Republican votes. The *Albany Argus* editorialized: "In the history of outrage and crime which makes up the Lincoln administration, there is no darker deed than this. It reveals the terror and desperation of the Washington junta." [1]

Horatio Seymour appointed three prominent Democrats as commissioners to proceed to Washington to inquire about the arrests and voting deceptions. They reported that there were irregularities. Jones, North, and Cohen were later acquitted.

The Fall of New York City

Ben "Beast" Butler prepared for the election in his usual efficient way. He commandeered dozens of ferryboats and positioned them in Jersey City's slips. Fifteen thousand seasoned troops were loaded aboard. At a given signal they would be launched for a massive amphibious assault against New York's shoreline, directly across the Hudson River. Gunboats flanked the attack route. Infantry had been steadily infiltrated into the city over the previous two weeks to cover the polls and all other locations where the citizens might rise up as they had the previous year.

Horatio Seymour made one more desperate effort to keep the voting honest by threatening Butler's Union Army presence, saying that "The power of this state is ample to protect all classes in the free exercise of their political duties." Sheriffs and other officials were directed to take care that every voter should have a free ballot, and they were required to see that "no military or other organized force shall be allowed to show themselves in the vicinity of the places where the elections are held, with any view of menacing or intimidating citizens attending thereon. Against such interference they must exercise the full force of the law." [2]

1. Albany *Argus*, October 28, 1864.
2. Sidney David Brummer, p. 437.

Butler paid no attention to this threat, but the order to send in the water-borne attack never materialized. New York's citizens had been sufficiently broken up and imprisoned and terrorized in the aftermath of the 1863 battle. Large-scale resistance did not occur. General Ulysses S. Grant sent this telegram to Stanton about the expected and pre-ordained Republican landslide in New York: "The election has passed quietly; no bloodshed or riot...It is a victory worth more to the country than a battle won. Rebeldom and Europe will so construe it." [1]

Yet the results, despite all the chicanery and military terror, were not as overwhelming as Lincoln would have hoped for. In fact, so close were the contests that for several days after the election the Albany *Argus* claimed a Democratic victory. In the end, Lincoln edged McClellan by fewer than 9,000 votes, and Reuben Fenton defeated Horatio Seymour by 7,000. As we shall see, with Fenton at the head, and backed by a Radical Republican Assembly, New Yorkers were to learn that political rebellion had a high price.

Lincoln's Andersonville: Elmira New York

The name "Andersonville" has an infamous meaning to most Americans. This prisoner-of-war camp in Andersonville, Georgia, held 40,000 Union soldiers during the Civil War. About one quarter of them died from starvation, exposure and disease.

Television documentaries, articles, a Pulitzer Prize novel, and a Broadway play on the trial and execution of Andersonville's commandant Henry Wirtz, have all contributed to the view that Southerners are barbarians.

All this changed in the 1950s when secret War Department documents from the Civil War were declassified. Northerners, who believed themselves to be morally superior, were stunned to learn of a POW camp at Elmira, New York, that was far more horrifying than Andersonville. It contained not only Confederate soldiers but also New York civilians who had participated in the Battle of New York or whose only crime was to oppose Lincoln's war. They died from exposure, starvation, and systematic mass executions. The civilian deaths are not mere speculation. Today, the Elmira camp is a national cemetery. Many of the graves list the POW's name, regiment, and state. But about one in five of the tombstones simply read "Citizen." These are the unidentified New Yorkers.

Official records show that 25% of the 13,000 inmates died, but other official documents indicate that the death rate was much higher. These extreme fatality statistics are directly attributable to Abraham Lincoln's policies

1. Ibid., p. 771.

toward Elmira. There are also indications that Elmira was chosen for this death camp as a result of the Battle of New York.

Elmira's Earlier History

Elmira is located just north of the Pennsylvania border, in Chemung County. In 1860 it was a village of 8,800, an important hub in New York's transportation grid. The Chemung Canal was Elmira's connection to the Erie Canal, where goods moved to all parts of the state. Later, railroads linked it to New York City, Chicago, and the Midwest.

With the surrender of Ft. Sumter, there was a resounding patriotic call to duty in Elmira. Partisan politics, at least for the moment, were pushed aside. Throngs of men converged on the recruiting stations.

Abraham Lincoln called for 75,000 volunteers. New York's governor, Edwin Morgan, designated Albany and Elmira as military depots. Recruits overwhelmed Elmira and it became a garrison town. Ten companies of troops were anticipated but forty arrived. Finding places to quarter them proved a monumental problem. A barrel factory was converted into a barracks. Churches, storehouses, and private homes became temporary shelters. Then the army built official housing for 2,000 troops. It was called "Barracks No. 3."

After basic training these men were put on open cattle cars for the long journey to the South. Anticipating a quick victory, Governor Morgan ordered the closing of Barracks No. 3, but the battle at Bull Run shattered that illusion. Abraham Lincoln saw the reality and called for an additional 500,000 men. New York's quota was 25,000. Immediately Barracks No. 3 was re-opened.

Lincoln Nationalizes Elmira

Barracks No. 3 served as a state military facility until July 1863. Then, with the war going badly for the North and volunteers dwindling, as was discussed before, Congress empowered President Lincoln to put all state troops and officers under federal control. Elmira was nationalized. This was unconstitutional.

Then, in early 1864, six months after the Battle of New York, Secretary of War Stanton ordered Commissary-General of Prisoners Colonel William Hoffman to find, in New York, a prison camp location for Confederates. Hoffman informed Stanton that "there are quite a number of barracks at Elmira, which are not occupied, and are fit to hold rebel prisoners." [1]

Elmira was about to become an integral part of the 19th century's version of Stalin's gulag archipelago. This Lincolnian POW system, which dotted the North, was politically placed in those states that had defied him: The Gratist Street Prison in St. Louis, Camp Lookout in Maryland, Camp Douglas

1. United States War Department, *The War of the Rebellion, etc.*" vol. 7, p. 146.

in Chicago, Camp Morton in Indianapolis, Camp Rock Island in Illinois, Alton, also in Illinois, and Johnson's Island, in Sandusky, Ohio. "The tragic period of the Civil War concentration camps was inaugurated with Elmira prison." [1]

Elmira was officially named Camp Chemung, and it opened in July 1864. Its first commandant was Lt. Colonel Seth Eastman, a West Pointer with thirty-five years of military service. Previously, Eastman had been military governor of Cincinnati and presided over the military tribunal that convicted Clement Vallandigham, the Ohio Congressman who condemned President Lincoln for using the war as an excuse for converting the USA into a military dictatorship.

Camp Chemung had an absolute maximum capacity of 5,000 prisoners. Soon, 13,000 POWs and civilian "traitors" crammed the facility. When Eastman arrived, two crises had already developed. No hospital had been provided for the sick and wounded prisoners; and a pond for drinking water and another, called Foster's Pond — the camp latrine, had merged, polluting the fresh water. Within days many of the inmates were seriously ill or dying.

It was almost a month after Camp Chemung opened before the War Department assigned a Chief Surgeon, Major Eugene F. Sanger. His placement at Elmira is significant, indicating that New Yorkers were targeted for revenge because they had risen up. Sanger had served as Chief Surgeon under "Beast" Butler during the occupation of New Orleans. Sanger was in charge of the "medical facilities" on barren Ship Island, where "traitorous" civilians were sent. Many of them died.

Sanger was a good surgeon, but his personal characteristics affected his medical judgment. "A deluded martinet, self-righteous and vindictive," point to his responsibility for the thousands of deaths at Camp Chemung. [2]

Sanger had been wounded at Port Hudson, Louisiana. His left leg had been amputated below the knee. With his vindictive personality, he sought vengeance on all Southern soldiers for his disability.

Within two months of the opening of Camp Chemung, hundreds of inmates had died from the mixing of human waste with their drinking water. Attempts to get War Department authorization to construct another reservoir for drinking failed to get approval for months; this is now viewed as a deliberate tactic. Camp Chemung overflowed with prisoners. More arrived every day. Not one inch of space existed inside the barracks. Tents accommodated the new "guests."

1. Lonnie R. Spear, *Portraits in Hell: Military Prisons in the Civil War* (Mechanicsville, PA: Stackpole Books 1997) p. 241.
2. Michael Horigan, *Elmira: Death Camp of the North* (Mechanicsville, PA,: Stackpole Books, 2002) p. 57.

Prisoner Exchange

July 22, 1862. At Maxwell's Landing, on the James River in Virginia, Major General J. Dix, the same officer who commanded Union forces in the Battle of New York, met with Major-General Daniel Hill of the Confederacy. They signed the "cartel," an agreement to exchange prisoners of war worked out by the opposing armies but not by the antagonistic governments. This document specified that once prisoners were released, they could not rejoin the military. The Confederacy then proposed a formal pact between Jefferson Davis and Abraham Lincoln, but the United States President refused. To agree to it would mean official recognition that the South was a legitimate separate nation.

In April 1863, Lincoln ended the prisoner exchange program. General Ulysses S. Grant publicly said that this was because the Confederacy had allowed released prisoners to join their units. Privately, he believed that holding Southern men would quickly exhaust the Confederacy's manpower. The North, with an overwhelming advantage in population, would not experience a shortage of troops. A war of attrition would work in the USA's favor. Secretary of War Stanton agreed.

The End of Prisoner Exchange Leads to Retaliation

In December 1863, a House of Representatives committee released the 30-page "Report No. 67." It stated that there was evidence that "the rebels" planned to kill all Union prisoners. The same Colonel Hoffman who promoted Elmira as a location for a POW camp wrote this to Stanton: "I respectfully suggest, as a means of compelling a less barbaric policy toward the Union prisoners in their hands, to allow only half rations for rebel officers in our custody." [1]

President Lincoln, the army, and many Northerners, thirsted for revenge. The *New York Times* editorialized for retaliation, convinced that Confederates were "plagued with moral infirmities." Henry Raymond, the editor, said: "A chapter will be written by some future historian, on the horrors of Andersonville, which will equal in fearful interest, the records of the Bastille." This editorial called the policy of withholding food as "brutally, savagely cruel." Raymond concluded: "Retaliation is a terrible thing, but the slow wasting away of life of our brethren and friends in those horrible prisons, is a worse thing." [2]

The belief that the South deliberately starved Union prisoners is incorrect. Unlike the North, where soldiers and civilians were well fed, the Confederacy was subjected to a two-sided blockade. On the Atlantic coast, the U.S. navy prevented food from entering Southern ports. The Mississippi River was

1. United States War Department, *The War of the Rebellion, etc.*, vol. 7, p. 146.
2. The *New York Times*, March 31, 1864.

patrolled by gunboats. Food from the western side could not reach the east. Southerners were being starved. Even Ben "Beast" Butler acknowledged that fact: "If Union soldiers at Andersonville are starving," he informed Stanton, "their Confederate guards are also on half or quarter rations." [1]

Still, Stanton enthusiastically endorsed retaliation. Colonel Eastman, Elmira's commandant, notified Stanton that rations for his POWs could be substantially reduced. That same day, Stanton submitted "Circular No. 4," which was Eastman's recommendation for cutting rations. Retaliation was now national policy. Food at Elmira was restricted to bread and watery soup. Circular No. 4 was then issued to all prison camp commanders by Colonel Hoffman. He ordered all food and clothing sent by relatives be restricted to those listed as sick.

Report No. 67 and Circular No. 4 were a lethal combination. In 1908, in recalling the restrictions on food, Confederate POW R.B. Ewan wrote: "Many hundreds of boxes of provisions were brought to the camp, but unless we were in the hospital, the ham, cheese, bread, and pie, were put back in the wagon and hauled out to fill other stomachs." Prisoner Anthony Kelly wrote in his diary: "This brought on an epidemic of scurvy." [2]

Chief Surgeon Sanger had pangs of conscience. He went over camp commandant Eastman's head and wrote an official memorandum to Brigadier-General John Hodson. This document displayed both his arrogance and sense of guilt over his morbid duties. First, Sanger wanted a transfer out of Elmira. That reflected his sense of guilt. Then he boasted: "I have now been in charge of 13,000 rebels, a very worthy occupation for a patriot, and I think I have done my duty, having relieved 386 of them from all earthly sorrows, in one month." [3]

Sanger's disturbing revelation is corroborated by prisoner Walter D. Addison, who wrote, years later, that while in the hospital, he observed that opium pills were dispensed to patients, "no matter what the nature of their disease. One occasion, several prisoners were dying. Sanger directed Dr. Van Ness to administer opium to them. In a short time they breathed their last. No investigation ensued. No reprimand. Dr. Van Ness continued his position." According to Addison, there was a desire to kill the Confederate prisoners: "All in authority in Elmira seemed to be of this opinion." Anthony Kelly agreed. "In six weeks Sanger made more orphans and widows than the siege of Troy." [4]

Kelly also charged that Sanger refused to sign any report that stated the cause of death was related to malaria, because: "In the medical department there were opportunities to plunder. Vast quantities of quinine were

1. United States Official Records, etc., Vol 7, p. 175.
2. Michael Horigan, p. 87.
3. Eugene F. Banger Papers, Records of the office of the Adjutant General Regimental Correspondence, 1861–1865, Maine State Archives, p. 120.
4. Horigan, p. 129.

prescribed, then stolen. The price, $8 an ounce [over $300 in 21st century terms] tempted the cupidity of the physicians beyond all resistance." [1]

In late 1864, both Singer and Eastman requested to be relieved of their duties. Both said that they were very ill and could not continue. In reality, Sanger was removed after writing a scathing report which implicated Eastman and the newly appointed commander, Franklin Tracy.

Colonel Tracy started out as a volunteer officer who gained high military rank through his political connections. He had been a Republican in the New York Assembly. As such, he headed the 109th New York Regiment. At the Battle of the Wilderness he won the Congressional Medal of Honor. Then he was assigned to Elmira because he was loyal to Stanton.

Immediately upon his arrival, Tracy had a major conflict with Sanger since the latter had mentioned him in the damning medical report. Tracy dismissed Sanger. Tracy had blocked Sanger's efforts to improve hospital conditions, and then demanded an investigation of Sanger's administration of the medical facility.

This provoked Sanger to send another report to Tracy: "The ratio of disease and death has been unprecedentedly large and requires an explanation from me, to free the medical department from censure." [2]

Sanger said that there were 2,011 admissions to the prison hospital between August and September 1864, and within that time period, a death rate of 24%.

Throughout Eastman's time as commander and in the early stages of Tracy's, Sanger submitted nine communiqués to them, all unanswered, "calling attention to Foster's Pond and its deadly poison [the human waste flowing into the drinking water] and the existence of scurvy to an alarming extent." [3]

Alarmed that this information might reach his superiors, Tracy made a belated effort to address the problem; but without War Department authorization he could not begin. He never received it. To circumvent that indifference and prevent an army investigation, Tracy used prison labor instead of army personnel to separate the two ponds.

Sanger had another serious complaint, this time about "the great delay in filling my requisitions for the hospital," and "the sickness and suffering occasioned thereby." This led Tracy to put Sanger under house arrest, then to dismiss him.[4]

Stocker, New Chief Surgeon

December 22, 1864. Major Anthony Stocker became the new Chief Surgeon. Before the war he was a prominent Philadelphia physician. Prior to

1. Ibid., p. 130.
2. United States, Official Records, etc., Vol. 7, p 1093.
3. Ibid., Vol. 7, p. 1093.
4. Ibid., Vol. 7, p. 1096.

that, a military surgeon in the Mexican War. In May 1861, Stocker received another commission as an army doctor, and was placed under General Mead's command. Shortly thereafter, Mead had Stocker arrested, charging him with unsatisfactory performance of his duties "in relation to the care of the sick." Later, the charges were dropped.

August 1863: Stocker was arrested again, related to the hospital under his direction. In the court-martial trial, he was cleared.

If Stocker made an attempt to correct the horrific conditions at Elmira, he left no record of requests for improvement, despite the fact that over 1,200 POWs and civilians died during the first three months of his taking over the hospital.

Attempts To Investigate Conditions At Elmira

Soon after the House of Representatives Report No 67 was published — that was the first attempt to promote retaliation — the United States Sanitary Commission requested an inspection of Camp Chemung. This request was rejected by Stanton. The Sanitary Commission, an independent philanthropy supported by private funds, was dedicated to "preserving and restoring the health and securing the general comfort and efficiency of troops; to the proper provisions of cooks, nurses and hospitals." [1]

This included similar concerns in Union POW camps but the Sanitary Commission required the cooperation of the War Department's Medical Bureau. Instead, there were endless confrontations between these two entities that involved egos, jealousies, and political intrigues. In December 1864, a Dr. Turner of the Sanitary Commission arrived at Elmira, without War Department permission, in hopes of inspecting the prison.

Colonel Tracy, in a telegram to the War Department, wrote: "Deeming it important that the inspection should be made and the report published for the purpose of correcting the impression that the prisoners are cruelly treated, I concluded to admit him with the understanding that no report is to be made until my action is approved by you." [2]

Three days later, a General Wessels informed Tracy that an inspection by civilians was "highly improper, and the publication of a report cannot be permitted, unless under the direction of the Department of War."[3]

Special Order 336

In October 1864 it began to snow. Colonel Tracy issued his most controversial edict: Special Order 336. "Whereas, the fresh beef now furnished

1. United States, Official Records, etc. Vol. 7, p. 1180.
2. Ibid.
3. Ibid.

to this point is unfit for issue [to the prisoners] and inferior in quality, therefore, officers are hereby designated to reject such parts as appear unfit for issue."[1]

Most of the meat was rejected and sold to local markets. This came on top of the previous ration reduction. It meant that most prisoners were down to bread and water. The most serious losers were those hospitalized, who, up to this point, ate better than the other inmates, with some meat in their diet. The winter cold increased in intensity. Thousands of the prisoners were quartered in open tents, since the barracks were filled beyond capacity.

Tracy ordered the construction of additional barracks for those living in the elements, but they were poorly built and not insulated, and offered no greater protection than the tents.

During this period, a Captain Mugger of the army's Medical Department, arrived at Elmira. He reported: "The past week produced 112 deaths. 1,666 prisoners are entirely destitute of blankets."[2]

All Aid Rejected

On January 6, 1865, a winter storm struck Elmira. All train service was suspended. Freezing winds ripped through Camp Chemung. Noah Walker, who owned a clothing store in Baltimore, sent the camp packages of garments from the inmates' relatives. The War Department returned all the packages. Not to be denied, Walker tried to send the clothes through an independent relief agency which was located in nearby Watkins Glen. Stanton wrote back to this agency with a description of the inconceivably complex procedure that the bureaucratic maze required to get the apparel into the camp. The head of the relief agency gave up and wrote, "The brutal Stanton turned a deaf ear to the prisoners' suffering."[3]

Then another effort was made at a much higher level. Judge Robert Gould, who had been the Confederate agent during the prisoner exchange program, took up the cause of bringing about an agreement between the United States and Confederate governments to supply food and clothing to prisoners on both sides. Gould wrote to Stanton, who sent the letter to Ulysses S. Grant and then to Lincoln, who had it delivered to Robert E. Lee. Lee agreed to the plan and Grant apparently accepted it.

It was Judge Gould's idea that the South should provide a large shipment of cotton to the North. It would be sold in New York and the money realized would be used to purchase coats and blankets for the prisoners. The simplicity of the plan raised hopes for its success, but a series of delays deliberately

1. National Archives, "General and Special Orders," Vol. 3, p. 287.
2. United States, Official Records, etc., Vol. 7, p. 1185.
3. "Treatment of Prisoners During the War," Southern Historical Society Paper I, No 4, April 4, 1876, p. 294.

orchestrated by Stanton eliminated any possibility of the clothing reaching the inmates before the end of the winter.

Months passed before the cotton was finally sold. By that time the cotton market had declined sharply and only a fraction of the hoped-for aid could be purchased. To make matters worse, instead of the original intention of focusing on Elmira alone, the reduced help was diffused among ten Northern prison camps so that only a minute amount reached each location. Three boxes of clothing were delivered to the thousands of freezing inmates at Camp Chemung.

Mass Burials for POWs and Civilians

The way the dead at Elmira were buried raises many questions about how many died there. In mid-July 1864, when Camp Chemung first opened, the United States government purchased half an acre of Elmira's Woodlawn Cemetery to bury those who died while incarcerated. Union officers asked those Southern captives with carpentry skills to build coffins. The incentive was better food and better treatment. Soon the demand for coffins outstripped their ability to make them.

The burial of the dead was managed by John W. Jones, a runaway slave from Leesburg, Virginia. He was paid $2.50 per grave. Nine coffins were piled into each grave. Jones was aided by inmates who volunteered for this burial detail. They also received better food and treatment.

The burial section was between the Chemung River and Foster's Pond. The name, regiment, state, and date of death were written on a piece of paper and placed in the dead man's armpit. Years later, Jones reflected on the mass graves: "Each body was put in a box, then I dug a trench, large enough to contain nine of them." A wooden headboard, above ground, gave the same information that was placed in the coffins for all nine men. [1]

Prisoner Marion Howard revealed forty years later why there is a discrepancy between the official and true death rate: "We buried our men on what we called 'free ground.' The place was low and marshy, and the water [from the Chemung River] often rose to a depth of three feet where we buried our dead. We had to take a pick and make a hole in the coffin on each side, so it could fill with water and sink." [2]

Filling the coffins with water made the dead men's I.D. illegible. And the flood water often washed away the above-ground markers. Those without identification were not counted as having died.

John Jones was a religious man. He believed that those he buried were Christians, as he was, and the mass graves were degrading and a sin. He

1. Horigan, p. 92.
2. Ibid., p. 194.

reburied, in individual graves, those who could be identified, and he devised a codex so that relatives could find the exact location of their loved ones. Jones' re-burials, the codex, and the creation of Camp Chemung as a national cemetery, are based on known bodies.

The war ended in April 1865. On the morning of July 11, the last 246 prisoners assembled for the two-mile trek through the dusty streets of Elmira to the railroad station. They were transported to Baltimore. From there they were on their own.

One of the last men out was James Huffman. He started the long, painful journey to his home in Virginia, arriving there seven days later, "to find destruction, waste and poverty. There was no money; the start must be made from the bottom. I went to work with a will." [1]

Initially, Camp Chemung was scheduled to be torn down. Instead, it was converted into a military center devoted to the mustering out of Union soldiers. In February 1866 the camp was completely destroyed.

Final Official and Real Death Rate

Elmira's official death rate was about 3,000; 24.5% of the inmate population. This represents only those who could be identified. Adding the unknown dead probably brings the total to 35%. All other Union camps had a combined fatality percentage of 11.7%.

June 1874: Congress established "Woodlawn National Cemetery" at Elmira.

1997: Elmira's Southside High School students placed a plaque at the cemetery, which reads: "Confederate soldiers were buried here with kindness and respect by John W. Jones, a runaway slave. They have remained in this hallowed ground by family choice because of the honorable way in which they were laid to rest by a caring man."

Republicans Reconstruct New York Like the South

In April 1865, Abraham Lincoln was assassinated, and then the war ended. His disciples, the Radical Republicans, continued his policy of retribution against "collaborationist New York."

New York's post-war history has generally been glossed over as a mirror image of Southern carpetbag corruption, personified by William Marcy "Boss" Tweed, and his multi-million dollar bribes and scams. The more intriguing and realistic story is how the Radicals tried to turn New York into a colony of Washington, and failed, because of Tweed.

1. Ibid., p. 194.

Radicals and Radical Social "Reform"

In 1864 Republican Reuben Fenton "defeated" Horatio Seymour for the governorship, with the help of "Beast" Butler, the stationing of the U.S. army at the polls, and the switching of thousands of the ballots of soldiers in the field from Democratic to Republican.

Fenton was 45, a four-time Congressman from Jamestown, and very much a Radical. And yet, Fenton had been elected to Congress in 1852 as a Democrat. Contrary to that party's platform, which gave each state the right to choose or repudiate slavery, he was a virulent abolitionist. In 1856, Fenton bolted from the Democrats and became president of the first Republican convention in New York, and then he was re-elected to Congress.

As governor, Fenton, with his anti-home rule and Jacobin philosophies, believed in revolutionary social change for both South and North. His programs, paralleling Congressional reconstruction in the defeated South, included federal control of voting rights for blacks and the exclusion of whites, as well as Albany's greatly expanded hold over the business practices and personal behavior of New York's citizens. The city's health, fire and police departments were put under increased jurisdiction from Albany, along with local housing regulations. By 21st-century ideals, this sounds progressive, and a legitimate role for government, but this was not the case in the 19th century. Radical Republican objectives in these areas were less inclined toward social reform than to destroy the Democratic Party that they had begun in the 1850s. These so-called reforms led to the incarnation of Boss Tweed.

The Radicals' leading newspaper, *The Tribune*, called for a "completely new departure" and proclaimed that Albany had the right to step in and fill the needs of the people whenever New York City's Democratic authorities demonstrated their inability to do so. The New York *Times* presented the issue more truthfully: "Nothing less than the uprooting of the whole Democratic system springing from City Hall could rescue the people."[1]

The Policies of Fire Protection

New York City had a volunteer fire department. Virtually all major cities in the USA and in Europe followed such a plan. The Radicals introduced a bill into the State Assembly which called for a paid, professional fire department. Supposedly this new plan would cut taxes, because the "volunteers" were actually supported by the city already. The 4,000 firemen's equipment, and food and board at the fire houses, were in the city's budget. Under the Republican plan, only 1,000 men would be required to do the same job.

But the volunteer system was tied to the Democratic Party. These firemen doubled as ward organizers. On election days the Democrats depended on

1. The *New York Times*, December 3, 1864.

them to get out the vote. Also, the "bunking system" allowed the volunteers to live in the fire houses at public expense to be on hand in emergencies and provided a means of rewarding the party faithful with free room and board for a year, in return for delivering their wards.

Indicative of the intimate tie between the Fire Department and the Democratic Party was the rise of the most powerful Democrat in the city during the postwar era: William Marcy Tweed. He helped organize the "Americus" fire company as a young man and discovered that the ladder up through the fire department stood so close beside the one which led up through the Democratic Party machinery that he had no trouble transferring his power from one to the other.

As part of their take-over plan, the Radicals spread the sensational lie that the fire houses "were little more than bawdy houses" in order to sway the Assembly. This was similar to the tactics used in the occupied South, where rumors were spread of blacks being tortured or killed by whites. These greatly exaggerated terror stories were used to maintain or increase the U.S. army's presence in the former Confederacy to keep it a conquered territory indefinitely. [1]

In New York, hypocritical concern with "immorality" reveals the Utopian social preoccupation of the Radicals. They dreamed of transforming a flawed world into a perfect one.

The Firemen's Bill passed the Assembly in March 1865. Three weeks later Albany's Radicals introduced another piece of legislation that was intended to neutralize the Democrats. It was entitled "An Act to Establish Metropolitan Sanitary Districts and a Board of Health, to preserve the Public Health and to prevent the Spread of Disease Therefrom." This proposal precipitated a legislative battle that raged for two full sessions.

With their usual exaggeration, the Radicals frightened New York's population with overblown stories of health horrors; that the metropolis was the filthiest city in the Western world; that the slaughterhouses, which supposedly spread fatal diseases to humans, were cheek-to-jowl with residential dwellings; that the waste from 50,000 horses filled the streets and was never cleaned, which attracted flies, vermin and rats; that the majority of tenement apartments had no plumbing, and their outhouses regularly overflowed, creating another appalling health threat. All this was greatly overstated.

But there was a germ of truth to it. The already existing Board of Health was not functioning as originally intended. The Radicals ranted that this was

1. See John Chodes, "The Union League, Washington's K.K.K." (Tuscaloosa, AL, The League of the South Institute for the Study of Southern Culture and History, 1999)

due to Democratic corruption; private contractors took government money to correct these problems but never did their job.

In fact the Republicans, from the 1850s, in their successful attempt to neuter the Democrats and create one-party rule, had revoked all authority within the mayor's office and all other major agencies so that most of the city's business came to a grinding halt.

Boss Tweed: Democrats Counter One Party Rule

As the Republicans reconstructed New York into a one-party state, the Democrat, William Marcy Tweed, used the Radicals' own tactics against them. He has been portrayed as the quintessential corrupt politician, but in the context of Radical power in the city he appears more as a Robin Hood than a monster.

Tweed has been more realistically described this way: "For all his bulk [he weighed over 300 pounds], he is a man hidden in the shadow of Thomas Nast's leering cartoons in *Harper's Weekly*. In Nast's portraits, Tweed is a lecherous, corrupt and powerful Falstaff. What is missing from the image is an explanation of Tweed's personal powers; his ability to ingratiate himself with men of respectability, and with low politicians, his breadth of political imagination, and his vindictiveness." [1]

Tweed united the elements of a divided society the only way they could be united, by paying them off. Attracted to the scorned profession of a politician, he acted with scorn for conventional social ethics. His climb to political power is a classic success story. Even his setbacks stood him in good stead.

William Marcy Tweed was born April 3, 1823, the son of a chair-maker. At fourteen he headed a gang, the "Cherry Streeters." At twenty-one, he was foreman of the volunteer fire company, "Big Six." He used this as a stepping stone to a political career.

1852: Alderman from the 7th Ward. The Board of Aldermen was called the "Forty Thieves." Within a year Tweed was elected to Congress and served two terms.

1857: School Commissioner for New York City. Here, he was in the belly of the beast. He served the Republican commission system as an insider and learned about craft first hand, as his position related to building and supply contracts for all city schools.

Then Tweed was elected to an even more lucrative spot: the Board of Supervisors for the County of New York. This large geographic area was one of the infamous Metropolitan Districts, which encompassed urban and rural zones and diffused Democratic power. Tweed and the other supervisors

1. Seymour Mandelbaum, *Boss Tweed's New York* (Chicago: Elephants, Paperbacks, 1990) p. 67

received their "fair share" of the enormous cost over-runs of the endlessly under construction County Court House.

Tammany Hall would soon be led by Tweed, and Tammany would emerge as the dominant political organization in the city. Tweed's political savvy enabled the Democrats to finally break the Radicals' hold on the city. But that would be in the future. Before that moment arrived, the Radical Republicans tried to expand their influence. For instance, to rationalize their further takeover of the street cleaning, health, and fire departments, they contended that street cleaning contracts were being given out as political rewards, and were subject to kick-backs, rather than as genuine business arrangements for which the contractors would be held accountable.

The *World* newspaper gave a more realistic picture of why there were breakdowns in public services: "It cannot be denied that our health laws and organizations are a maze of contradictions and incongruities. We have a Board of Health, but it is only in name, for the mayor, who alone can convene it, cannot summon the members together. Then we have commissioners who have equal power and jurisdiction on the Board of Health. [These bureaucrats were placed there by the Albany Republicans to block the Democrats.] Then there is the City Inspector, with all the machinery for sanitary inspections, without the power to accomplish this purpose." [1]

Cholera spread through Europe at this time, but not in epidemic proportions. Although it did not enter the United States, the Radicals whipped up a panic and the Health Bill easily passed the Assembly. The Republicans were not shy about preventing it from becoming a bipartisan law. The Radical Assemblyman, Mr. Low, said: "We should not sugar coat this bill by dividing the commissioners between the two parties. We should have the courage to make it a commission to represent the Dominant party." [2]

Immediately, all the slaughter-houses were forced to move to upper Manhattan, north of the center of population, "for health and safety reasons," although it was never proven that slaughter-houses were a source of diseases like cholera.

This move was put into effect even though there was only one death in the city from cholera. Immediately Governor Fenton declared a "State of Emergency" which gave the health commissioners greater dictatorial powers.

Now they had the extraordinary ability to physically remove individuals from their homes if they were perceived to be a threat to other inhabitants of the building, and place them in a hospital. The vague wording of this bill could interpret "threat" to include "traitor" or "disloyal." Now hospitals

1. James C. Mohr, *Radical Republicans and Reform in New York During Reconstruction*, (Ithaca and London: Cornell University Press, 1973) p. 64.
2. Ibid., p. 92

could be used as locations for incarceration. Remember, the Civil War had just ended.

This sweeping power put New Yorkers under a form of martial law, since no trial or hearing was required for a person's removal. And, as under martial law, this new health code allowed for random house-to-house inspections of those suspected of being "diseased," a euphemism for disloyalty.

Labor

Up to this moment in American history, both state courts and the United States Supreme Court had clearly indicated that it was unconstitutional to regulate by law the hours of employment in private businesses. Most previous labor laws were aimed at government employment.

Now Governor Fenton and his Radicals proposed a maximum eight hour work day for all employees in New York State. If passed, this would mean a massive increase in Albany's bureaucracy and its control over the city.

Even many Radicals felt this law would be impossible to enforce, or would be nullified by the courts, since employment had traditionally been guided by the principle of freedom of contract, where workers were free to negotiate wages and conditions with their employers.

Despite this, the Eight Hour Bill passed the Assembly. The Democrats could not block it. Governor Fenton said: "The State now has a legitimate role to play in solving the great problem of social economy." [1]

The Eight Hour Bill was a precursor of Socialist ideology, as represented by this comment by one of the Radicals who dreamed of an America where every man becomes a capitalist in the sense that classless cooperation would replace individual exploitation. "Institutional reform and positive legislation, rather than violent class revolution, will bring this about." [2]

With the success of the eight-hour day, the Radicals took another step toward control of everyday life of the citizens, and the dissolution of the Democrats.

At the war's end, thousands of Union soldiers drifted into the city along with large numbers of immigrants from Europe. This created a housing shortage and a sharp rise in rents. According to the Radical press, this forced many families to find shelter in the tenement slums, where they never would have resided in normal times.

For the Radicals this was a golden opportunity to control yet another aspect of society. They proclaimed that the natural laws of supply and demand worked to the detriment of society and the State must step in to curb the

1. James C. Mohr, p. 120.
2. Ibid., p. 123.

greedy landlords. The New York *Times* linked continued inaction by Albany toward the housing problem as "gambling with Satan."

Once again the manufactured threat of a cholera epidemic was raised, this time to enable Albany to get a stranglehold on private residences. The Republicans called the tenements "King Cholera's five-story throne." They said: "Sheltered all over the city are pestilential hells, which are commonly known by the mild and insignificant title of tenement houses. They are nothing more or less repulsive plague-spots, reeking with filth and rank with poison and disease. Truthfully, it can be said, all those who are qualified to speak, will verify the statement, that all the diabolical, horrid, atrocious, fiendish, and even hellish systems of money-making ever invented by the mind of man, the tenement house system of this city, is the most horrible, and the sum of all that is enormously repulsive, fearful and devilish." [1]

In addition, education, like in the defeated South, was transferred from local, private control, to Albany, where curriculum content became a matter of politically-motivated social engineering. The direction of elementary and higher education in private and religious schools changed dramatically as a result of governmental intervention and subsidies. God in the classroom was downgraded. Literary classes were discarded. History, especially as it related to the recent war, became highly politicized. Schooling lost its respect for the wisdom of the past. Education became utilitarian. Private and parochial schools that dared to continue to teach classical ideals were subject to legal sanctions.

Democrats Regain the City

Tammany Hall, soon to be led by William Marcy Tweed, gradually emerged as the dominant political organization in the city. Tweed enabled the Democrats to finally break the Radicals' hold on New York. By 1868, Tammany's candidate, John T. Hoffman, a former mayor of the city, became governor. Mr. Hall became a Tammany mayor. For the first time in twenty years, Democrats captured the legislature.

Still, the Radical Republican commissioners for fire, police, and health departments remained in place. The Radicals had used the police to close saloons on the Sabbath, which had restricted local Democrats from collecting their cut of sales. Now, under Tweed's bribes, that grip was released and liquor money flowed back into the Democratic coffers seven days a week.

New York City had 85 newspapers. They represented a dozen different languages and ethnic groups. The larger publications were subsidized by rival political parties, thus presenting their points of view as to platforms. But Tweed, the master at understanding man's greedy nature, outspent his

1. *World*, November 12, 1865, p. 1

rivals and bought off the opposition to give the Democratic perspective. This united the fragmented population behind him.

Tweed used tax dollars to place city government advertising in both large and small periodicals that smiled favorably on "The Boss." "Bought" stories that appeared in out-of-town newspapers were reprinted in New York, via under-the-table money, to create the impression that the entire nation admired and backed the new direction of New York's Democratic leaders.

Tweed also rallied opposition and Republican groups to his side by subsidizing their operations. He won favor with the large Catholic population by giving educational aid to their schools, without interfering with their religious curriculum. With more bribes and pay-offs, Tweed reorganized the city government. This required additional money to leading Republicans who, until they received the cash, had been intent on retaining their stranglehold over the city. More large sums flowed to influential citizens who were anxious to bring order out of political chaos. This led to public opinion that supported Tweed. His implied motto was "something for everyone."

Many city Democrats feared the political consequences, but Tweed believed that ever more money was needed to keep his opponents at bay. For instance, many real estate men and landlords had been driven to the brink of bankruptcy by the Tenement Law, which required them to take full responsibility for bringing apartments and buildings up to the standards of this draconian legislation.

Using more pay-offs and muscle, Tweed forced Albany to weaken the Tenement Law so that now the city and state would pay for half of the costs.

The United States Constitution and the vision of the Founding Fathers were dedicated to limiting the size of government, whether at the state, federal, or local level. Democrats were committed to that principle. But to break the Radicals, Tweed was compelled to vastly expand City Hall's jurisdiction. New York City's harbor was the first area to experience this. More millions flowed to and from political friends and foes alike to allow a huge building program for new docks, which gave City Hall unlimited borrowing power to improve the sewage system, pave the streets, and build bridges.

Despite all this, the city government was still partially neutralized due to the 1857 Republican charter. Tweed's next challenge would be his greatest: to create a new charter which would allow local government to work in an orderly way. Tweed later admitted that it required millions in bribes just to get the charter passed.

When it was finalized, the destructive commissions instituted by the Radicals were abolished. City departments with locally elected officials replaced them. Now the mayor once again could appoint these department heads.

As Superintendent of Public Works, Tweed was responsible for the harbor, street paving, water supply and sewage projects. He had an amazing ability to bribe his way into half a dozen official positions. Simultaneously, in addition to all his other titles, Tweed was also a state senator, Grand Sachem (top man) of Tammany Hall, and Chairman of the Democratic–Republican General Committee. This last position was a perfect role for him, where he could meet his opponents face-to-face and make deals with them. As yet, Tweed was not criminally tainted by all this.

In another ingenious plan, Tweed extended Democratic clout upstate, which had been solidly Republican. Jay Gould, the famed or infamous railroad tycoon, paid Tweed a huge fee for his help during Gould's highly publicized court battle with Cornelius Vanderbilt, owner of the New York Central Railroad, over control of the Erie Railroad. Tweed used his considerable monetary influence over the judges involved in the case and secured a law altering the method of selecting the Erie's Board of Directors, in Gould's favor.

In return, Tweed was elected to the Erie Board and received Gould's political aid to bring upstate Republicans into the Democratic fold, all along the railroad's route.

Tweed's Fall From Grace

In 1867, New York City's indebtedness was $30 million (30 billion in 21st-century terms). By 1871, when Tweed fell from power, that debt had tripled. This was largely financed through city bonds by local banks, Tammany men were the officials for those banks. No attempt was made to raise funds through national financial institutions, where this immense borrowing could lead to investigations. Additional millions came from overseas investors, secretly, as knowledge of such large debt issues would cause alarm.

Then disturbing reports about the size and management of the debts began circulating during the political campaign of 1870. Just prior to the election, Tweed called in six leading citizens, including John Jacob Astor, and allowed them to glance at the financial ledgers. After a hasty inspection, these six men issued a reassuring statement that provision had been made for the massive loans; the city's accounts were in order.

Despite this, negative rumors grew more persistent and in the spring of 1871, a Berlin financial newspaper editorialized that only the reputation of a major German underwriting company that was involved with the selling of New York bonds allowed the city to continue to sell them on the Berlin Stock Exchange.

Then, catastrophe. New York County's auditor, who was on Tweed's payoff list, was killed in an accident. His place was filled by James O'Brien, an enemy of Tweed, who couldn't be bribed.

Now O'Brien had access to the secret and accurate copies of the city and county accounts. He gave this "scoop" to the Republican New York *Times*, which published a long list of the frauds. Before the list became public, Tweed offered George Jones, the *Times* publisher, five million dollars, in cash, to suppress the evidence of graft. Jones refused to accept the money.

Then bankers denied any further credit to the City. The Berlin Stock Exchange stopped trading New York bonds. All this took place, conveniently for the Republicans, just before state elections. A committee from the Chamber of Commerce, comprised of many Republicans, reported. "Your committee regards as futile, any attempt to borrow large sums while the city is controlled by the present management." [1]

This exposé gave the Republicans a chance to regain power within the city. They moved quickly to destroy Tweed, holding a "reform" meeting at Cooper Union and resolved that: "The wisest and best citizens [Republicans, of course] should run the city government...City officers should be elected in such a manner as to secure the representation of the minority [Republicans] as well as the majority." [2]

Tweed's enemies flocked to the reform movement. Even major Democrats saw him as a great liability. Samuel Tilden, the head of New York state's Democrats, who had been on Tweed's gravy train, said: "I fear that the impression will be spread throughout the country that the evils and abuses in the local government of the city of New York are general characteristics of the Democratic Party, and would occur in the federal government if our party should come to power in Washington." [3]

A rebellion swelled up among the city Democratic rank and file. Immigrant Germans felt that they had been denied their share of patronage under Tweed because a considerable number of Irishmen had moved into positions of power. The Germans saw Tweed's dilemma as undermining their status. Both groups used their muscle to depose Tweed. His hold on power was slipping fast. A huge crisis loomed.

Then Judge George Bernard, formerly Tweed's loyal ally, ordered an injunction to restrain the Comptroller from issuing additional bonds or making any more payments, including government workers' salaries. City workers panicked and protested in front of City Hall. The Comptroller's office was ransacked. His records were stolen. Tweed pressed the Comptroller to resign, hoping a sacrificial lamb would reduce the hysteria. But Samuel Tilden convinced Mr. Connolly, the Comptroller, to remain in office, so Tweed could not replace him with one of his friends.

1. Seymour Mandelbaum, p. 80,
2. Ibid., p. 80.
3. Ibid., p. 81.

The crisis eased as Judge Bernard's injunction was modified. The city workers would get paid. Then it was modified once again so that the city could borrow millions more. But Tilden supplied the coup-de-grace to Tweed. He filed an affidavit directly tracing crooked city contracts to Tweed's account. The next day Tweed was arrested.

Reformers, Republicans, and many Democrats created a coalition to annihilate Tweed. They were not dissuaded by his desperate slogan: "No one goes outside the party to purify it, any more than one goes outside the Church." [1]

On Election Day, the inconceivable happened. While all those in the "Tweed Ring" were defeated, "The Boss" was re-elected to the state Senate. For the moment, Tweed escaped retribution, but his problems were far from over. He was pursued with intense vigor through a long and torturous road of indictments, hung juries, convictions, prison terms, unduly shortened by technicalities; flights to California, Spain and Cuba followed, with re-arrests, civil suits, and finally, more imprisonment, in default of a judgment; he was sent to Ludlow Street Prison, where he died.

Yet Tweed's legacy of renewed Democratic control of the city remained. By the mid-1870s the Tammany ticket once again swept New York City, now containing many honorable men, who, like Tweed, believed that the city should not be controlled by Albany.

The Radical Constitutional Convention

In 1846 a convention was held to amend New York's constitution. This was in keeping with the tradition that every twenty years the state's organic laws would be reviewed, and those sections that were no longer effective in maintaining good government would be changed to promote the democratic process for the citizens.

1866 was the 20th year, but such changes were not automatic. It required the approval of the majority of all eligible voters to allow the governor to call such a convention. A vote was held and a majority agreed to the convention. But that was only a majority of those who had voted, not a majority of the eligible voters. Thousands of voters had not gone to the polls. Thus, by law, no convention could take place.

But Reuben Fenton, ever the Radical governor, was committed to reconstructing New York, just as his Radical brothers in Congress were committed to transforming the defeated Southerners. Fenton had no intention of letting the illegality of the convention stop him dream of a new social order for his state.

1. Ibid., p. 83.

January 1867: As soon as Fenton's annual message to the Albany legislature was read, all doubt about the illegality of the constitutional convention disappeared. The Radicals pushed ahead with "reform" no matter what.

Fenton ordered the Assembly to set up a special election for delegates for it. Disguising his true intentions, he sketched out in general terms why New York needed to revise its organic law: the Civil War debt, antiquated taxes, and overlapping court jurisdictions. Fenton neglected to state the most dramatic issue: Negro suffrage reform. Never was the phrase "conspicuous in its absence" more appropriate. Every legislator and every newspaper-reading citizen knew that Negro voting rights was of paramount importance to the Radicals, just as it was a top priority for the South.

The existing constitution required a $250 property qualification for every man of color in order to vote. This effectively disenfranchised most of New York's black citizens. No such requirement was imposed on white voters. Fenton hoped to eliminate this disparity.

Democrats objected to the way the Radicals planned to present this to the voters. Henry C. Murphy, the leader of the Democratic convention delegates, favored a separate submission to the voters. This meant that the bulk of the proposed changes would be accepted or rejected by the citizens, but that the equal suffrage section needed a second vote to pass or fail. Democrats believed that the second vote would defeat the equal franchise clause without destroying the truly needed revisions that both sides agreed upon.

This viewpoint was not racist. Murphy's rationale revolved around his prediction that if the equal voting rights section was adopted as part of the whole, it would embolden Congressional Radicals to more actively pursue the same course in the South and other Northern states. This would destroy state sovereignty where suffrage was constitutionally denied to the federal government.

But this did occur in 1868, when the 15th Amendment nationalized voting. Realistically, the Democrats were pessimistic about their chances of holding back the Radical juggernaut, which also intended to continue its policy of turning New York into a one-party state.

The disparity of the delegate count was grounds for this pessimism. When the convention began its work in June 1867, it contained 96 Republicans and 64 Democrats. With such a substantial margin, the Radicals busied themselves with "reform" to dominate New York permanently.

Mr. Francis, a Republican, tried to make the case for returning the city to be a fiefdom of Albany: "Mr. President, as one of the Committee on Cities, I wish to say that I disagree with the previous report, that it proposes to establish within the state, under the name of City Governments, local sovereignties, superior to, and above, and beyond the control of, the state itself; thus practically applying to the State of New York, the same obnoxious doctrine which the rebels of the South sought to enforce for their states, with respect to the Union. This whole idea of city independence from federal authority. It belongs in the same petulant family, and carried out in practice would involve the state in perplexities, dangers, and possible future calamities, even as we have seen in the disastrous results worked out in the collision of states with the sovereignty of the Union. Whence do cities derive their power of government? Why, their very organization is from the state." [1]

Appointed vs. Elected Officials: Commissions

There were other issues that were equally disturbing to the Democrats. Prior to 1857, most major political officials were elected, but in that year the Radicals' new charter transferred that power to the governor, who appointed them as "commissioners." Mostly republicans. Now the Radicals wanted this to be the case permanently, in the revised Constitution. The following demonstrates the Radical's bias against elected officials, since they could be Democrats: "District Attorneys shall be appointed by the governor, in seeing to the enforcement of all penal laws. From the nature, of the position, he is brought into contact with those whose favor is valuable, or ill will is difficult to be resisted, while he holds his office by popular vote. We know that the popular vote is almost invariably controlled by a few leading politicians."[2]

The New York *Times* added this: "Mr. Hadley presented the report of the Committee on the Organization and Powers of Counties, Towns, etc. This committee believes that there is a demand for increasing the powers of Boards of Supervisors [Commissioners] in relation to the internal affairs of their respective counties and they therefore recommend the following: there shall be in each of the counties of the state, a Board of Supervisors who shall possess and exercise the power to legislate [these would be unelected legislators] in relation to the local and internal affairs of their respective counties and towns.[3]

Mr. Folger, another member of the committee, said that the objective of the proposition was to prevent corrupt legislation (but unelected commissioners would inevitably be more corrupt because they are not kept in line by voters).

Then the New York *Times* presented another issue in a biased, radical way: "At present we have the state divided into 32 senatorial districts; each one operating independently of the other. By the new constitution that is proposed,

1. The *New York Times*, September 6, 1867.
2. Citizens' Association of New York, "The Constitutional Convention of 1867: Alterations The Fundamental Law Of The State" (New York: George F. Nesbitt & Company, 1867) p. 3.
3. The *New York Times*, August 15, 1867.

there will be only eight districts. (This will make uniform all local laws, and destroy home rule.)[1]

The *Times* continued: "It is certain that the small district system for all officers has worked badly in our large towns and cities. In many instances the worst class of people [Democrats] have been sent to Albany, whose proper place would be in Sing-Sing prison. They have made fortunes by selling their votes in the state capital, as members of the legislature.

Some years ago we had a Board of Councilmen for this city, made up of 60 members; and of these, about one-third were the immediate representatives of policy dealers, keepers of bawdy house, and others of scarcely less repulsive occupations. One half of this one-third could neither read nor write. Had sixty men been voted in by general ticket throughout the city, not one of these rascals would have a ghost of a chance of election. But, to return to the legislature; the small district system has worked quite as dangerously there. We can point out localities where the whole Assembly and even senatorial districts are under the domination of thieves and swindlers. We do not apply these illustrations to the whole state; but as far as New York City, Brooklyn [Democratic zones] and other cities are concerned, we speak only of a manifold truth; that the small district system has worked with mischief." [2]

> Another proposal graphically showed the extreme bias against home rule for individual cities: "The undersigned, dissent from those who confer upon the mayor, the sole power of appointing all the officers of cities, including the Boards of Administration, commonly called Commissioners. Such a power is entirely foreign to the genius of republican institutions [that is true, if "republican" began with a capital "R!"] and unknown, in fact, in any department of our government, state or federal. [At least, since the Radicals took over the United States Congress and state Assemblies.] In the city of New York it would constitute a patronage in a single person, greater than that of the entire government of most states of the Union, and create an autocracy which, if it did not, by reason of the ineligibility of the mayor for re-election, enable him to secure his place indefinitely, could nevertheless enable him to name his successor and perpetuate his rule, or to place himself in any other position within the power of the electoral body to bestow, In the hands of an ambitious man, such a power would be fraught with the greatest danger to the interests of the community." [3]

1. Citizens' Association of New York, p. 2.
2. The *New York Times*, August 5, 1867.
3. Ibid.

Radicals Continue War-Time Loyalty Oaths

In the occupied South, Democrats were ejected from political positions they had been legally voted into, through Republican sponsored loyalty oaths. They were so all-encompassing that even the most loyal person could not pass them if challenged. These same oaths came North. "By the constitutional convention section for the choosing of delegates, the influence of the Civil War was manifested in the provision which required a voter, if challenged to establish his loyalty by taking an oath that he had not voluntarily borne arms against the United States, nor aided in the late rebellion, nor held any office under authority, real or pretended, in hostility to the United States, nor voluntarily supported any such authority and that he was not a deserter and did not leave the state to avoid the draft during the late rebellion."

In June 1868, the Court of Appeals declared this provision of the convention act unconstitutional; that the legislature could not add to qualifications fixed by the constitution. [1]

No Habeas Corpus In Peace-Time

The following is a residual after-effect of New York being under martial law for years, during and after the war. Under military domination, speed of enforcement, cost-cutting, and rapid confiscation of "traitors' property" was considered mandatory, at the expense of civil rights: "When the Habeas Corpus section came up for consideration, Mr. Martin Verplanck offered an amendment that no person should be arrested without due process of law." Explaining the amendment, he said he wished to prevent arrests "except where the complaint has been made on oath before a magistrate and a warrant issued, or in cases authorized by the common law, and to prohibit the legislature from authorizing the arrest of the citizen in any other case." He referred to instances of arrests that he thought unlawful. Mr. Smith favored the amendment because it would prevent unlawful arrests in the Metropolitan Police Districts. The amendment was rejected. [2]

Military Trials in 20th Century

The fact that military trials were still being conducted for civilians into the 20th century is confirmed by a pamphlet written in 1915, related to another constitutional convention: "There has appeared some criticism of the failure of the convention to provide for the supremacy of the civil courts over military tribunals." [3]

1. *Constitutional History of New York*, p. 243.
2. Ibid., p. 289.
3. Citizens Union of the City of New York, "The Proposed Constitution: summary of important changes" (Albany, 1915) p. 5.

Elimination of Senate Aids Autocracy

The Radicals attempted to create permanent one-party rule by reducing the classic separation of powers between the state Senate and House of Representatives, hoping to fuse these two bodies into one. They falsely presented that their roles were similar: "The constitutional convention met to consider the report of the Committee on the Organization of the Legislature. Mr. Van Colt [a Republican] said he would like to take a voice vote of the convention on abolishing the State Senate. Upon what principle were the two houses of the legislature organized? Why should two Houses be organized, to go through the forms of legislature alike? [They were created to be completely different. Representatives respond to their constituents in limited districts. Two senators divide the entire state. Their responsibilities are far more sweeping.] Each House passes upon every measure in a similar manner." [1]

Fortunately, this proposal was defeated.

Black Suffrage

As the price of defeat, the former Confederate states had to accept new constitutions imposed by the Radical Republicans in Washington. Equal voting rights for the former slaves was a mainstay of this constitution. This seemed to apply only to the South, but the Radicals sought to make it national. As stated before, the existing New York Constitution required a $250 property qualification for a man of color to vote — a pretty high barrier.

Partisan politics, not pure motives, played a key role. In reality, only about 11,000 blacks would be added to the voter rolls in any event. This number seems insignificant when more than 720,000 votes had been cast in the previous governorship race. But then, Reuben Fenton's margin of victory over Horatio Seymour had been about 8,000 in 1864. Since the Radicals overconfidently presumed that every Negro would vote Republican out of gratitude, those 11,000 could not be ignored.

The Republicans pretended to demand universal male suffrage, but their true plan was to curb white Democrats in the following way, as outlined by the New York *Times*: "The limitation of suffrage in municipalities is probably the best starting point in the direction of efficient reform. The evils which afflict the local administration in New York City are mainly the products of universal white suffrage. The mob is in the ascent. Intelligence, wealth and character have no potency in the Common Council. Its property at their mercy, its income material for their wasteful management. Taxation and representation go together in the political world, so why should not taxation be the measure of representation in the narrower sphere of a municipality by investing taxpayers with electoral power. [This reverses the Negro property

1. The *New York Times*, August 7, 1867.

qualification; no property, thus no taxation, means no ability to vote. In New York City, the majority of Democrats were workingman who did not own property.] Thus a strong guarantee is obtained against the election of irresponsible administrations and the corruption and extravagance now in vogue. That has furnished the justification for the interference with local government, which has already taken place, and will unquestionably constitute a valid argument for further interference, if the city continues to be subjected to the domination of demagogues." [1]

As time went by, Northern voters turned against the Radicals and their brutally inflexible agenda of eternal revenge against the South and the Democratic North. As a result, moderate Republicans backed down in their demand for Negro voting rights at the expense of the whites. They saw it was leading to political suicide. So they proposed, along with the Democrats, a separate submission for this issue.

The rapid change of perspective was due to defeats in what had been overwhelmingly Republican states. They were crushed in Connecticut, which was expected to ratify the so-called equal suffrage clause of its constitution.

Another disaster was narrowly averted in Republican Ohio. General (and future President) Rutherford B. Hayes squeaked through as governor. In 1864, a Republican had won this position by 40,000 votes.

Republican Vermont and Maine lost many votes to the Democrats. Nationally, Republicans lost more ground. All these results were sobering. New York's Radicals reacted swiftly. They passed a resolution to adjourn the constitutional convention until the state elections were over. With their large majority, it passed. But the Democrats wanted the convention to complete its work before the elections. Their idea of reform was far different. It was to free New York City from the Metropolitan District commissions.

After November the convention re-convened, but did not end its deliberations until November 1869. By that time the Republicans had lost the Assembly.

In 1868, the 15th Amendment passed the national Congress which was controlled by the Radicals. This nationalized voting rights for the entire United States, but it could not become law until ratified by each state separately. It was rejected twice, but finally, in 1871, equal voting rights came to the Empire State. With the Radicals in the minority, whites were not stripped of their rights.

Black Suffrage and The Enforcement Act

During the spring of 1870, Congressional Republicans readied a bill ordained to cause havoc for New York City Democrats. Congress passed the

1. The *New York Times*, June 11, 1867

Enforcement Act, which supposedly protected the constitutional rights of freed blacks, provided for in the three Reconstruction amendments (13th, 14th, and 15th). The 15th gave blacks the right to vote, but was illegally used to deny that right to Democratic whites, and to deny them political office.

The Lawrence Committee was created by New York's Radicals to investigate alleged Tammany voting frauds, where newly naturalized immigrants became Democratic voters. To block this, Radicals used the powers of the Enforcement Act. Nationally, most of the frauds were committed by Republicans, who used federal troops to guard polling places and terrorize voters into placing their ballots in their box. The Enforcement Act authorized federal marshals, all Republicans, to supervise all elections, appoint Republican deputies and use federal troops to "maintain decorum" (at the point of a bayonet).

The Radicals greeted the Enforcement Act as "a godsend" in New York. Horace Greeley, editor of the *Tribune*, predicted that federal elimination of fraud in New York and other strongholds of the Democracy guaranteed that party's permanent defeat. The New York *Times* editorialized that it would mean the end of Tammany Hall.

Democrats were outraged. They denied the need for such a law. Republican John I. Davenport was the Enforcement Act's United States Commissioner for the Southern District of New York, which included New York City. Before the 15th Amendment, each state could choose any method they wished to naturalize immigrants to join the ranks of voters. The 15th Amendment made that right ambiguous, so that now Davenport criminalized the Democrats' naturalization process, although it was still legal.

Davenport: "There is evidence of the boldest, most gigantic and corrupting crime against free institutions, ever perpetrated on the face of the globe." He described how a lawyer witnessed the "illegal" way in which immigrants were processed to vote. The most obvious question is, if these procedures were criminal, why would the Democratic officials allow an unknown outsider to witness them?

The following statement by Davenport is misleading and was made to give the impression that illicit actions were taking place; naturalizing immigrants without them being present. Yet his words clarify that this was simply the bureaucratic paperwork phase, and so was in no way outside the law: "This lawyer visited a room in the basement of City Hall [the word "basement" implies unlawful actions] belonging to the sheriff of the county; and he saw four squads, of four men each, engaged in clerical work, the several squads being under the charge of one of their number, who acted as a foreman. Each foreman, having before him a list of names and addresses, would keep three members of his squad employed filling up blank applications for naturalization in the names of persons he would call off from the list. As rapidly as the clerk would fill in an application, he would sign their name." (This is also misleading; he was placing the name, not forging the signature, and for a witness, signing the name of the immigrant, to check the work, as will become obvious in the next paragraph.) "No applicants or witnesses were present." (None were necessary. That comes in the next phase.)

Davenport now traps himself into giving a more realistic picture of how the system worked: "Finding him fast becoming interested in what he had discovered, the attorney next visited the Supreme and Superior courts. In the former court, where Judge Barnard presided, the sessions were held in the evening, nominally from seven to nine o'clock, and sometimes until eleven." (Davenport sees this as a scam in itself, but Judge Barnard had important judicial duties to deal with during the day.) "He saw the batches of men brought into the court, averaging 150 in a batch. As they came before the bench, they would be divided into groups around four or five bibles. The bibles would be held up and the men would either touch them or stretch their hands toward them.

"The clerk would then call out their names at the same time, handing to the judge an application, upon the back of which the magistrate, without any examination of the paper, would affix his initials." (There was nothing to examine. That process had taken place in the previous phase. The judge was merely legalizing the men by swearing them in.) "The fiat for naturalization; no question being asked of any person, either applicant or witness." (Not necessary. All the information had been gathered previously.)

The following demonstrates that everything was legal, Davenport's contention to the contrary: "When this procedure was through with, the men actually being naturalized by order of the court, Judge Barnard would administer the following oath: 'You, the several applicants, swear that you are 21 years of age; that you arrived in this country before attaining that age, and have resided five years in the United States, and for the last year, in the State of New York.' The same person often appeared as a witness for a score of applicants." Again Davenport makes that sound like a fraud, but the scores of applicants could have been relatives or friends. [1]

In the fall of 1870, state elections were held. Under ordinary circumstances, the Democrats would have won handily, but the Radicals threw all the machinery of the Enforcement Act against them. They believed that Tammany Hall and all Democrats would be neutralized, but the Act and its implications were so obviously illegal, that it backfired.

Davenport appointed 772 "supervisors" for New York City alone. Then George Sharpe, the United States Marshal, placed additional deputies at the polls, "to keep order just like in the South."

1. Allen Franklin, p. 13.

Then election registration began. Davenport's supervisors arrested five Democratic candidates, including John McLoughlin, a member of Tammany's General Committee. Immediately the Republican's prosecuted him, as an object lesson, and he received a two-year prison sentence prior to Election Day. In the South, this was business as usual.

The Republicans went one step further to make the message of intimidation even clearer. The week before the polls opened, Radical newspapers listed the names of more than 15,000 Democrats who they claimed were illegally registered, and warned them that jail awaited those who dared to vote.

Next, the Republicans spread rumors that the disgruntled Democrats would provoke riots. The municipal police were dispatched to guard the polls. An additional 1,000 federal troops, with fixed bayonets, added an extra sense of fear and violence. If that wasn't enough, the state militia was called up, on stand-by readiness. All this took place in New York, not Mississippi, Louisiana, or Georgia.

This reign of terror created a tremendous negative reaction. The citizens defied all these threats and swept the Republicans out of power in the legislature, the mayoral and gubernatorial offices.

Results of Constitutional Convention

Now the citizens would vote on the constitution. The Republicans had no choice but to sub-divide the constitution to prevent the entire document from being defeated.

The sections on taxation, the judiciary, and equal suffrage were presented to the public separately. Under this fragmented form, New Yorkers rejected tax reform and expanded Negro voting rights. The judiciary section passed. It was now part of the organic law of the state.

As such, it would be of interest to learn of the flaws in the 1846 constitution that required a change, as understood by former New York State Supreme Court Justice J. W. Edmunds: "Our existing judiciary system is the product of a Committee in Convention, of some of the ablest men in the state. Yet, twenty years of experience of its working as provoked an almost, if not quite universal opinion, that it had radical defects. 1. The election of judges, at the same time as local elections. The consequence of this has been the mingling of the judiciary with the political parties of the day. 2. Another evil was the smallness of the districts, in which a Supreme Court judge is chosen. It is only necessary for the candidate to have a local reputation, and not extensive, throughout the state." [1]

1. The *New York Times*, September 1.3, 1867.

The new constitution maintained this practice: "The existing judicial districts of the state are continued."[1]

Also: "Five of the judges shall reside in the district, which is New York City, and to be chosen by electors in their district." [2]

In relation to the duration of terms of Supreme Court justices, Judge Edmunds said this about the present system:

> A judge's term is for eight years, yet every two years he beholds one of his associates going through the ordeal of a popular election and is thus reminded of his impending fate. He has angered many a man by deciding a case against him. And he knows how much more active is anger than gratitude, and has abundant reasons to know:
>
> 'That no man who ever felt the halter draw,
> has a good opinion of the law.'
>
> His decisions affect his hope for re-election. Thus, the judiciary is not independent. Yet, it is not the mode of selecting judges (appointed or elected) but the shortness of their term that is the trouble. I am persuaded then, that the plan of the Committee on the Judiciary at the Constitutional convention, should devise a plan for the long term, and then, with the ineligibility to be re-elected. This will restore the independence of the judiciary, and will restore the public confidence in the judiciary. This will erase the evils we have witnessed under the present constitution, where we have seen, in the City of New York, almost every judge, while in office, has been heralded in the newspapers, as a candidate for President or Vice President. Not from their own choice, but from compulsion. It is the party leaders who demand it. The remedy is long terms and separate elections. [3]

The new constitution did increase the terms of Supreme Court justices to fourteen years but the hope for separate elections did not materialize. Judge Edmunds also made this significant comment related to the State Supreme Court: "It is now proposed to have four Supreme Courts in the state. The inevitable affect of such a system is to destroy uniformity of decisions, or, in other words, to impair that 'certainty which, in the law, is the mother of repose.' Anyone at all familiar with the actions of courts, will be able to realize a lamentable conflict of adjudication, and how impossible it will be to know what the law is. We should have one Supreme Court for the whole state." [4]

Unfortunately, the new Radical constitution maintained the political chaos that Judge Edmunds recognized: "The legislature, at its next session, shall divide the state into four judicial departments, and each of the

1. Luther Caldwell, "Amended Constitution of the State of New York" (Albany: Weed, Parsons and Company, Printers, 1868) p. 22.
2. Ibid., p. 22.
3. The *New York Times*, September 13, 1867.
4. The *New York Times*, September 23, 1867

departments into two districts, to be bounded by county limits (paralleling the Metropolitan District plan). The city and county of New York shall form one district. There shall be thirty-four justices of the Supreme Court. Ten in the Department of New York, and eight in each of the others." [1]

1. Luther Caldwell, p. 24.

Chapter 2. Lincoln's Invasion of Maryland

Maryland Remains Loyal to Union

Knowingly defying the Constitution, Abraham Lincoln, immediately after the firing on Fort Sumter in April 1861, ordered the invasion of Maryland, a Union state that had no intention of seceding to the Confederacy. Although a slave state, Maryland was loyal. Despite its small size, it was strategically critical as it bordered on Washington, D.C.

A large United States army moved from Boston to Baltimore. Martial law was instituted. Civil liberties were erased. Citizens and politicians who opposed Lincoln and his actions were incarcerated in undisclosed places. The President instituted one-party rule, as Lincoln's Republicans attempted in New York.

Many modern historians claim that Maryland intended to join the South, but Lincoln's swift attack held it in the Union. This is an erroneous picture of events of that time.

When Abraham Lincoln was elected President, he found very little support in Maryland, receiving only 2,200 votes out of 92,441 cast.[1]

In 1860, the Negro population was split between 87,189 slave and 84,842 free.[2]

Upon his election, five Deep South states seceded, fully aware that Lincoln and his Republican Party were committed to eradicating their culture and their "peculiar institution."

1. Harold R. Manakee, "Maryland in the Civil War" (Baltimore: Maryland Historical Society), p. 4.
2. Ibid., p. 12

Ever the consummate politician, Lincoln denied this threat. At his inaugural address, he deceptively said: "I have no purpose, directly or indirectly, to interfere with the institution of slavery in the States where it exists. I believe I have no lawful right to do so, and have no inclination to do so."[1]

The Republican Party evasively stated in its platform: "Resolved, That the maintenance inviolate of the rights of the States, and especially the right of each State to order and control its own domestic institutions according to its own judgment exclusively, is essential to that balance of power on which the perfection and endurance of our political fabric depend; and we denounce the lawless invasion by armed force of the soil of any State or Territory, no matter what pretext, as among the gravest of crimes." [2]

With these guarantees, even after the surrender at Fort Sumter, the border states remained faithful to the Union. That is, until Lincoln called for 75,000 troops to "crush the insurrection." These states were appalled at this aggression against fellow Americans. This generated a second wave of secession.

Abraham Lincoln believed that Maryland would be the next to go. He called for federal troops to invade, on the pretext that they had to go through Maryland to reach the Capital to prevent a Confederate assault on Washington. Maryland's governor, Thomas Hicks, the legislature, and the majority of the citizens, clearly indicated that there was no desire to cut their ties with the United States. Maryland was more like a Northern state. Slavery only existed in a few counties. Non-slave farming and industrialization dominated. Baltimore, one of America's largest cities, was a major manufacturing center, closely linked to the commerce of the North.

Before Fort Sumter Lincoln Prepares for War

Lincoln's inauguration was viewed as a declaration of war by the South. Violent abolitionists, who hated the South, were placed in every department of the federal government. Long before the initial clash at Fort Sumter, Lincoln stealthily ordered army units recalled from outlying posts and brought them to main military centers. Warships from the Mediterranean fleet were ordered home. Washington, D.C. became a major military training center. Lincoln promised a peaceful evacuation of Fort Sumter, but tried to reinforce it. Frantic activity was observed in dockyards and armories throughout the North. Arsenals were busy day and night manufacturing weapons. Troop transport vessels with amphibious landing craft prepared for immediate action. All this occurred before the first shots were fired.

On the 27th of November, 1860, a memorial signed by ex-Governor Pratt, and other prominent citizens, was presented to Hicks, requesting him to

1. John C. Nicolay and John Hay, editors, *Complete Works of Abraham Lincoln* (New York: Tandy and Themes Publishing Co.) Vol. III, p. 175.
2. First Inaugural Address of Abraham Lincoln, at http://avalon.law.yale.edu/19th_century/lincoln1.asp, accessed March 24, 2015.

summon the legislature to a special session, in view of the gravity of the national situation. Hicks replied, in his first public statement on the subject, contending that such a session would only increase the excitement which was all too prevalent in Maryland.

Many of those who advocated that special session insisted that they did not want Maryland to secede, but rather wished an opportunity to act as mediators between North and South.

When the governor of Mississippi telegraphed Hicks announcing the withdrawal of the state from the Union, Hicks said: "Mississippi has seceded and gone to the devil."[1]

As a further indication of Hicks' pro-Union stance, on January 25th, 1861, he wrote to General Winfield Scott, asking if 2,000 rifles could be had from the United States government to "meet the emergency, if it should arise." Scott approved the request.

April 12, 1861: Fort Sumter surrendered.

April 15: Lincoln called for 75,000 volunteers to quell the insurrection. This call-up spread consternation in Maryland, even among Republicans and Union men. The cherished hope of neutrality in the struggle, or at least the simple adherence to the Union, was rendered impossible when Maryland was expected to submit four regiments of infantry to the war effort.

The position that Hicks held was no longer tenable. Two courses were open to him, both somewhat in conflict with his previous record: either to break away from the Union on the grounds that sufficient provocation was offered for this by coercion, or to swallow his scruples in regard to coercion, and support the federal administration.

Hicks had previously declared himself in favor of an "Unconditional Union Party" which would totally support Lincoln's policies. But when he realized how seriously fraught with consequences that would be in a war, he hesitated. This hesitation was by no means peculiar to Hicks, for throughout the country, and especially in the border slave states, many of the most pronounced adherents of the Union shrank back when called upon to advocate coercive measures.

Governor Hicks foresaw the gruesome consequences of disunion. Massive armies from both sides would sweep over his state's landscape, devastating its cities, agriculture, and population. So, despite tremendous agitation, Hicks remained levelheaded. He issued a proclamation that assured the people of Maryland that it would remain neutral in the conflict.

Upon learning of Kentucky's military quota, Governor Magoffin said he would "furnish no troops for the wicked purpose of subduing her sister

1. George L. Radcliffe, *Governor Thomas Hicks of Maryland and the Civil War* (Baltimore: The Johns Hopkins Press; Johns Hopkins University Studies in Historical and Political Science, Series XIX, Nos. 11-12, 1901) p. 35.

Southern states." Indecision led that state to be invaded by both Confederate and Union armies.

Governor Letcher of Virginia wrote Lincoln: "This is not within the purview of the Constitution." Virginia seceded. Governor Ellis of North Carolina said: "I can be of no party to this wicked violation of the laws of the country." North Carolina seceded.

Governor Claiborne Jackson of Missouri said: "Your requisition, in my judgment, is illegal, unconstitutional, and revolutionary, and its objective, inhuman and diabolical." Jackson pledged his loyalty to the United States, but his state was still overrun by the U.S. army.

Neutrality, for Governor Hicks, also meant that when South Carolina's Governor Gist wrote Hicks about "concerted action" on behalf of the Confederacy, he replied that he was against "any measure looking toward secession." Hicks added that he prayed "that my right arm might rot from its socket if I ever raised it against my Southern brethren." [1]

In a letter just after the first Deep South states withdrew from the United States, Hicks wrote to a Prince George County resident: "If the Union must be dissolved, let it be done calmly, deliberately, and after full reflection on the part of the united South. After allowing a reasonable time for action on the part of the Northern states, if they shall neglect or refuse to observe the plain requirements of the Constitution [the right to secede], then, in my judgment, we shall be fully warranted in demanding a division of the country." [2]

Yet Hicks' comments did not infer the disunion involved Maryland. During his inaugural speech, Thomas Hicks said: "Maryland is devoted to the Union and all the states. Maryland never listened to the suggestions of disunion from the Southern states, and has refused to join with the misguided people of the Northern states in their assault on slavery." [3]

Excitement in Baltimore was growing so strong that on the day following Lincoln's call for troops, a telegram was sent to Hicks urging him to come to Washington, where he had an interview with Lincoln, General Winfield Scott, and Simon Cameron, Secretary of War. Hicks presented to them the intense opposition of the people of Maryland to any attempt to secure by force the return of the Southern states. Hicks was assured that the four regiments required of Maryland would not be taken out of the state, except for the defense of Washington.

But after his return to Baltimore, he had misgivings as to the conclusions reached by his interview in Washington. He telegrammed Lincoln for a definitive statement, and the reply was the same as at the interview.

1. George Radcliffe, p. 31.
2. Ibid.
3. Ibid.

The Constitution Permits Secession

Abraham Lincoln's policy of provoking war was evident even before his inauguration. On several occasions he said that secession was illegal, giving himself the rationale to commence military action. Yet, all the original thirteen states had stipulated, as a condition of their signing of the United States Constitution, that this was a voluntary union and that they could withdraw at any time if their sovereignty was violated.

In ratifying the Constitution, Virginia added this proviso: "That the powers granted under the Constitution, being derived from the people of the United States, may be resumed by them, whenever the same shall be perverted to the injury or oppression, and that every power not granted thereby remains with her." This means the right to withdraw from the United States if Virginia's sovereignty is imperiled.

New York's proviso stated: "That the power of government may be reassumed by the people whenever it shall be necessary to their happiness." [1]

Yet Abraham Lincoln defied the constitutional truth and said: "No state can lawfully get out of the Union; resolutions and ordinances to that effect are legally void...Secession is the essence of anarchy." [2]

Outbreak of War Against Maryland

As Thomas Hicks filled out the requisition forms to deliver Maryland's four regiments to the United States army, he learned that Baltimore's streets were filled with angry citizens demonstrating against Maryland's men being used to attack the South. He notified Secretary of War Cameron that "it would be prudent to decline responding affirmatively to the requisition." [3]

Now Northern soldiers prepared for war against Maryland. On April 18, the Massachusetts 6th Regiment boarded a 35-car train in Boston which would take them through Baltimore to Washington.

Just before leaving, Benjamin Butler, later General "Beast" Butler, described earlier, addressed the 6th Regiment: "Soldiers, our Commander-in-Chief [Lincoln] has assigned us to lead the advance guard of freedom...Let us say to the good people of the Commonwealth [Massachusetts] that we will not turn our backs until we show there is but one thought in the North; the union of the states, now and forever."[4]

1. Jefferson Davis, "The Rise and Fall of the Confederate Government" New York: D Appleton; 1881) p. 167.
2. John C. Nicolay and John Hay, editors, Vol. 6, p. 179.
3. Frank Marcotte, *Six Days in April: Lincoln and the Union in Peril* (New York, Algora Publishing, 2005) p. 42.
4. Ibid., p. 42.

Baltimore's mayor, George Brown, telegraphed Lincoln that the Massachusetts 6th should not enter the city under any circumstances. Brown activated the militia to repel this "federal invasion." Lincoln disregarded Brown's warning.

John Dennis was a Private in the Massachusetts 6th. He later described the journey down to Baltimore: "We arrived in New York City and it looked like the whole population had come out to welcome us. All along the route through New Jersey the enthusiasm kept up. The people of Philadelphia were not lacking in kind words and deeds toward us...News came by telegraph that the secessionists in Baltimore were preparing to resist our march through their city...When the train left Philadelphia on its way to Baltimore, Colonel Jones [commander of the Massachusetts 6th] requested a pilot engine to run ahead of the train [as a precaution against track sabotage]...When about 10 to 15 miles from Baltimore, ammunition was issued to us and orders given to load. Colonel Jones passed through the train and gave orders that when we marched through the city, we should not cast our eyes right or left, but to keep straight on unless fired upon by the mob that was likely awaiting us." [1]

The chaplain of the regiment, John Hanson, wrote: "At every station, communications was had with the railroad officials in Baltimore and... assurance was received that there would be no trouble unless the regiment provoked it. Orders were therefore given to the band to confine their music to tunes not likely to give offense, especially avoiding the popular air, 'Dixie.'"[2]

Trains going through Baltimore on their way to Washington had to make a change, since steam locomotives were not allowed to go through the city. Arriving in Baltimore from Philadelphia, a train had to terminate in the President Street Station on the east side of the city. The steam locomotive was disconnected from the train, and horses then pulled the train, a few cars at a time, on a special railroad track across the city to the Camden Station. There another steam locomotive was connected to the re-assembled train. Then, on to Washington.

Friday, April 19th, 10 a.m. The Massachusetts 6th arrived in Baltimore. As the train pulled into the President Street Station, the streets were filled with enraged citizens, but this time they were armed.

The horses pulled the cars. Baltimore's mayor, George Brown, wrote of what he experienced:

> Troops began to arrive at Camden Station. There was a great deal of excitement. A large and angry crowd assembled... At this time an alarm was given that a mob was about to tear up the rails on the railroad to Washington. I ordered my men to protect the track. I was about to

1. Ibid., p. 42
2. Ibid, p.43.

> leave, supposing all the danger to be over, when news was brought to me that some of the Massachusetts men were left at the President Street Station and that the mob was tearing up the track on Pratt Street. Demonstrations were made on one or two of the cars. But nothing like an attack was made until the seventh car started. It was attacked by clubs, paving stones, and other missies. The soldiers were now anxious to fire on the assailants but their officers forbade it, until they should be attacked by fire-arms. One or two of the soldiers were wounded by paving stones and bricks. At length, one man was shot. He asked to fire in return. Orders were then given to lie on the bottom of the car and load their muskets, and rising, to fire from the windows at will. The car was three times thrown off the track [when the wheels encountered obstructions placed on the tracks]. The car finally reached the main body of the regiment. [1]

Several railroad cars carrying the remainder of the Massachusetts 6th were still at the President Street Station. They were ordered to march across the city, because the tracks were so obstructed with debris.

John Dennis also recalled:

> Obeying the order to leave the cars, the soldiers seemed to throw themselves into the arms of the howling mass of hungry rebel wolves. It was with the greatest difficulty that the men could file out of the cars and form a line. When Mayor Brown worked his way through the crowd, he snatched a rifle from the hands of one of the soldiers and deliberately fired right into the crowd. The firing by the mayor acted as a. signal to the officers, and the command to fire was given. The mob returned fire, and here the demons commenced their onslaught, with fifty times the number of our little band. It was here that Ladd, Taylor, Whitney and Needham fell. The first martyrs of the rebellion. Ladd was pierced by more than a dozen rebel bullets. They beat the life out of Taylor with clubs, leaving his blood and brains to mingle with the filth of Pratt Street. [2]

The mob reached 10,000. There were 220 soldiers. The crowd pressed on the flanks and rear of their columns. At one of the bridges on Pratt Street, a barricade with cannon had been placed. The soldiers scaled the barricade. Had they halted there, they would have been annihilated.

As the detachment passed along Pratt Street, gun fire rained down from windows and doorways. They marched under fire for 1.5 miles. Many soldiers were wounded.

1. John W. Hanson, *Historical Sketch of the Old Sixth Regiment* (Boston: Lee and Sheppard, 1866) p. 25.
2. Frank Marcotte, p. 52.

When the Massachusetts 6th finally reached Washington, Abraham Lincoln met them and made another false statement: "Thank God you have come; for if you had not, Washington would have been in the hands of the rebels before morning." [1]

Yet, at this time there was no indication of an offensive plan by the Confederacy against the Capital.

Northern newspapers screamed for revenge. The Boston *Courier* editorialized, "Push on to Baltimore and lay it in ashes." More federal troops, vowing retribution, approached from Philadelphia. Governor Hicks and Mayor Brown sent this desperate telegram to Lincoln: "A collision between the citizens and Northern troops has taken place in Baltimore, and the excitement is fearful. Send no more troops here." [2]

President Lincoln sent back this ambiguous reply: "General Scott said this morning, 'March them around Baltimore, and not through it. By this, a collision of the people will be avoided, unless they go out of their way to seek it.'"

Mayor Brown understood the double meaning of the message and emphatically replied, "Northern troops should not be allowed to pollute the soil of Maryland." [3]

On the night of the 19th, a meeting was held in the house of Mayor Brown, where Hicks was staying. Subsequently, a bitter controversy arose as to what really took place there. Hicks was feeling so unwell that he was obliged to hold the conference in his bedroom. The actions of the federal government in using Maryland as a passageway for troops to be employed against the seceded states was vehemently denounced and the opinion generally shared that similar occurrences must be prevented in the future. Little hope was entertained of prevailing upon Lincoln at the time, if at all, to accede to the public demands of Maryland.

It was then decided that prompt measures were necessary to keep soldiers of the U.S. government from crossing the state. As the most efficient means of accomplishing this end, it was agreed to burn the railroad bridges connecting Baltimore with the North; Hicks' consent was asked. He agreed that troops should not cross the state, but spoke of the seriousness of burning the bridges, and pleaded a lack of authority on his part to give the plan his consent.

Mayor Brown and others in the room said that Hicks seemed persuaded by the arguments and signified that he would offer no objection to the proposed undertaking. But the reply came that his direct order was necessary, since Mayor Brown's jurisdiction did not extend beyond Baltimore. Then, it was claimed Hicks definitely gave the order to burn the bridges.

1. Ibid., p. 59.
2. Ibid., p. 59.
3. Ibid., p. 60.

On May 4th Hicks sent a message to the Senate of Maryland in respect to a request from that body for information on the burning of the Baltimore bridges. In this message Hicks denied that he had given his consent for their destruction. He admitted that he was excited but that he went no further than to say "that the mayor can do as he pleases; that I had no power to interfere with his decision. If this be consent to the destruction of the bridges, then I consented." [1]

In a short time Hicks denounced all measures hostile to the U.S. government as those of rebellion. His short defection was overlooked and soon Hicks was on cordial terms with the Lincoln administration.

On the 20th of May Lincoln sent word to Hicks that he desired to consult with him and Mayor Brown. Hicks telegraphed Brown: "My going depends on you." Brown went but Hicks did not.

Brown spoke to Lincoln about the danger to be incurred in attempting to once again pass through Baltimore. A promise was extracted that, if possible, the troops would march around the city.

Later that day, United States Senator Anthony Kennedy independently had interviews with Lincoln and Seward, General Scott and Cameron. But now the Administration positively refused to bypass any portion of Maryland with troops. Washington could only be approached from the north of the "Old Line State."

Then the Baltimore City Council voted funds for 1,000 rifles to be used against the impending onslaught. For the third time Baltimoreans filled the streets. Now they numbered about 15,000. The Chief of Police handed out the weapons. Artillery units drilled on strategic cross streets.

All this caused Lincoln to press war against Maryland with greater determination. Not only Baltimore but also the State Capital at Annapolis would be over-run and occupied. First, the Massachusetts 8th Regiment, now commanded by Benjamin Butler, moved from Boston to Philadelphia. Here, the New York 7th Regiment, led by Colonel Lefferts, united with Butler's men. With the bridges burned, they searched for an alternative route.

Both Butler and Lefferts had big egos. Lefferts, although a lower ranking officer, refused to be under Butler's command. He had his own plan to go by steamer up the Potomac River, directly to Washington, avoiding battle in Baltimore and Annapolis. Butler called him a coward. His idea was to move from Philadelphia to Perryville on the Susquehanna River, seize a ferry boat that was anchored there, cruise into Chesapeake Bay, and hold Annapolis. There he would gather reinforcements for an assault on Baltimore.

Governor Hicks telegraphed Butler; "Do not land men at Annapolis...Take your men elsewhere." Butler paid no attention to that plea.

1. Ibid., p. 52.

When Lefferts was informed that Marylanders had captured several United States warships, he panicked. His steamer was not armed and could not fight off military vessels. He turned his boat into Chesapeake Bay for the safety of Annapolis. Once again he connected up with Butler. Now, reinforced with Lefferts' regiment, Butler ordered his men ashore.

They poured into the State Capital, and captured and used the Naval Academy, with its defensive wails and artillery, as their first onshore position. Here they met with Governor Hicks and the mayor of Annapolis. Butler later wrote: "Both of them exhorted me to withdraw. They said all of Maryland was ready to rush to arms...I implied that I should stay and go through to Washington, but I had no provisions. I desired to purchase the provisions I needed. Then the mayor said I could not purchase an ounce of provisions in Annapolis. No patriot would sell to Yankee troops. Later he had a change of heart."

Shortly afterward, the Baltimore *Sun* reported:

> A rumor arrived at the city on Saturday, that thousands of troops had reached Cockeysville. At five before eleven o'clock the bell of the town clock sounded the call to arms, and instantly the people ran in every direction. Boys of 14, to hoary-headed men of 70 to 80 years, appeared on the streets on their way to join their respective companies. Within half an hour of the call to arms, the headquarters of several recruiting stations were thronged with people anxious to join in the defense of Baltimore. A large militia company was mustered into service, then they proceeded to receive their arms.

The Eagle Artillery Group marched to the intersection of Gay and Second streets, where they drilled for some time in loading and firing their cannon. Full preparations were made for a conflict and large quantities of grape and canister shot, besides heavy balls, were provided. Among the pieces of ordnance was a 32 pounder pivot gun.

At Annapolis, Butler and Lefferts had more ego-conflicts. Lefferts demanded that they wait for reinforcements before pushing on to Baltimore by road. Butler was just as adamant about moving swiftly before the Marylanders could counter-attack. Again, Butler called Lefferts a coward. They continued arguing but did not move, but their presence did affect Maryland's political atmosphere.

The legislature was fearful of meeting at Annapolis because they would be arrested to prevent the possibility of a secession vote. So Governor Hicks changed the location where the Assemblymen could meet to Frederick, 70 miles to the west.

Meanwhile, General Scott ordered Lefferts to follow Butler's swifter plan: use the railroads and repair the tracks as they moved along. Butler, in a conciliatory gesture, told Lefferts that if he left part of his New York 7th at Annapolis, to hold the city, Butler would give his regiment the honor of reaching Washington first. Lefferts agreed.

With the State Capital under army control, General Scott created a new military district, the "Department of Annapolis." Butler would be its commander, with "ample powers, extending even to the suspension of the Writ of Habeas Corpus, and the bombardment of Annapolis, if necessary." Civil law was erased. [1]

May 3rd: Butler began his assault on Baltimore. First, he captured Relay House, a strategic railway junction, six miles away. Then, without waiting for further orders from General Scott, he marched directly on Baltimore. His opposition became terrified and scattered, and his patrols reported no resistance. Butler arrogantly said: "It was as easy to capture Baltimore as it was to capture my supper." [2]

Once inside the city, Butler told his men; "If any shot is fired from any house, a detail should be put in that house and the building fired, until it is fully burned." [3]Then he set up artillery positions around Monument Square.

When General Scott learned what Butler had accomplished without an order to do so, he was furious. Butler was relieved of his command. He was so humiliated at being put in charge of insignificant Fort Monroe that he threatened to resign, but thought better of it.

In its new temporary location at Frederick, the Maryland General Assembly declared that the war was unconstitutional and that Maryland would not participate in it. It protested against occupation. It would not vote for secession. When the Assembly adjourned, Ross Winans, a prominent secession member, was charged with high treason and arrested.

Lincoln Arrests Maryland Legislature

General Scott received the following letter from Abraham Lincoln: "The Maryland legislature will take action to arm the people of the state against the United States."

Lincoln realized that it would not seem justifiable if the civil police arrested them. It would look too much like the actions of a dictatorship. So he put the burden squarely on General Scott: "I therefore conclude it is only left to the commanding general [Scott]." [4]

Scott, 75, hesitated, and Lincoln compelled him to retire. The responsibility was now placed on the younger, more aggressive General Nathaniel Banks, even though the legislators were mostly loyal Unionists. Secretary of War

1. Frank Moore, editor, *The Rebellion Record* (New York: Arno Press) Vol. I, p.149.
2. Benjamin Butler, *Autobiography* (Boston: A.M. Thayer, 1892) p. 222.
3. Ibid., 225.
4. John C. Nicolay and. John Hay, Vol. 6, p. 68.

Cameron ordered Banks to make a preemptive strike: "The passage of any act of secession must be prevented. If necessary, all or part of the members must be arrested." [1]

This was done before the Assembly made any decision. General Banks marched his troops into the Assembly Hall and at bayonet point arrested 29 members. A loyalty oath was forced on them, but few would take it, on principle, not because they were disloyal.

Assemblyman Lawrence Langston said, while in prison: "I have twice taken the oath to support and defend the Constitution of the United States, during the past year, and I am not disposed to turn a solemn obligation into ridicule by my constant repetition of it." [2]

One Party Rule for Maryland

As in New York, loyalty oaths became the basis for transforming Maryland's democratic government into a totalitarian one-party system. Those running for political office were obliged to take the "iron-clad" oath. Disloyalty was not the criterion. Political opposition was. Most Democrats could never pass the oath, because the wording was designed to demonstrate that their party promoted disunion. This made them all traitors. Government officials, corporate executives and clergymen were compelled to take a similar vow. If they failed to pass it, they could not pursue their professions. For clergymen, disloyalty was defined as their failure to give sermons written by military commanders, who virtually replaced God with Abraham Lincoln's name.

This was the wording of the standard oath:

> I do solemnly swear that I will support, protect, and defend the Constitution and Government of the United States against all enemies, whether domestic or foreign; that I hereby pledge my allegiance, faith and loyalty to the same; any ordinance, resolution, or law of any State Convention to the contrary, notwithstanding; that I will at all times yield a hearty and willing obedience to the said Constitution and Government, and will not directly or indirectly, do any act in hostility to the same, either by taking arms against them; that without permission from the lawful authorities, I will have no communication, direct or indirect, with the States in insurrection against the United States, or with any person or persons within said insurrectionary States, and I will in all things deport myself as a good and loyal citizen of the United States. This I do in good faith, with full determination, pledge to keep this, my sworn obligation, and without any reservation or evasion whatsoever. [3]

1. William Starr Myers, *The Maryland Constitution of 1864* (Baltimore; The Johns Hopkins Press, 1901) p. 55 .
2. "Disenfranchisement in Maryland," *Maryland Historical Magazine*, vol. xxviii, December 1933, No 4 (Baltimore: p. 308).
3. William Starr Myers, p.16.

General Banks brought Baltimore under full military control. Later, under General Dix, and his successor General John B. Wool, and then General Robert E. Schenck, Maryland received the full impact of federal suppression.

Later, General Dix's son wrote: "Maryland was substantially the military base of operations on the Potomac. The loss of Baltimore would have been the loss of Maryland; the loss of Maryland would have been the loss of the national Capital; and perhaps, if not probably, the loss of the Union cause."[1].

General Dix defended his policies with this comment: "There is no city in the Union in which domestic disturbances have been more frequent or carried to more fatal extremes, from 1812 to the present day. Although the great body of the people are extremely distinguished for their moral virtues, Baltimore has always contained a mass of inflammable material, which ignites on the slightest provocation. A city so prone to burst into flames, and thus become dangerous to its neighbors, should be controlled by the strong arm of the government whenever these paroxysms of excitement occur." [2]

The police force of Baltimore virtually became a federal police. Throughout the war, many important people were arrested by the military and languished for months or more in prison without access to the Writ of Habeas Corpus.

General Wool was unpopular, and the clamor for his removal was so insistent that he was replaced by Major-General Schenck of Ohio. But once he assumed command, Marylanders regretted his appointment. His regime was: "rendered particularly odious by his blustering energy and arbitrary arrests and persecutions. Pictures, songs, and writings that were freely permitted in Boston or New York, were rendered treasonable in Baltimore, with a series of arrests for real or alleged petty offenses that would give credit to autocratic Russia. Military trials and imprisonments were conducted which seemed to be desperately calculated to inflict the greatest amount of humiliation." [3]

John Fulton, a Southern Rights advocate, said that martial law had overthrown the constitution of the state. Moreover, "brutal outrages such as had never disgraced the soil of Maryland, and acts of petty tyranny which any man would, a twelve-month before, have been ashamed to order to execute, were perpetuated without eliciting a word of public remonstrance or denunciation from the Union Party [Republican Party]. People were dragged from their home upon the mere order of some contemptible underling of the government. The houses of citizens were canvassed and ransacked in the

1. Morgan Dix, *Memoir of John Adam Dix* (New York: Harper and Bros, 1883) p. 87.
2. Raphael Semites, "Vignettes of Maryland History" (Maryland Historical Magazine, XL, No, 1, March 1945) p. 51.
3. Harold Melvin Hyman, *Era of the Oath; Northern Loyalty Tests During the Civil War and Reconstruction* (Philadelphia: University of Pennsylvania, .1954). p. 88.

search for arms, papers, and flags, and oftentimes without the pretext of an excuse for the outrage being vouchsafed to the occupants. Free speech became an act of treason, which the government agencies punished as they chose, and persons of both sexes and of all ages were over and over again arrested for some casual remark which was disrespectful to the government and therefore deemed to be disloyal. Even the unconscious utterances of the drunken reveler were noted for having in their cups said something that savored of respect for Mr. Jefferson Davis [President of the Confederacy] or Stonewall Jackson.

To those citizens who failed the loyalty oath, whose homes or crops were destroyed by the large-scale warfare that later ravaged Maryland during Robert B. Lee's Antietam and Gettysburg campaigns, their fate was to starve or freeze to death. All aid was denied to them. If friends or relatives tried to help, they were incarcerated. The life-altering repercussions of the iron-clad oath lasted through the war, beyond Reconstruction, and in some locations, into the 20th century.

As a result, Republicans assumed the overwhelming majority of all political positions. A small opposition was allowed, to prove that a dictatorship did not exist.

Governor Hicks Joins Lincoln

Thomas Hicks did all he could to prevent his state from being over-run by federal troops, but when 40,000 Union soldiers occupied Maryland, he submitted to Lincoln's dictates, adopting the same attitude as the Radical Republicans. Hicks: "The loyal states and our army and navy are full of traitors. Many of our office-holders are faithless to the Government, and unless things are watched closely...we shall be whipped." [1]

When Baltimore's mayor George Brown was imprisoned by Lincoln's orders, for burning Baltimore's bridges, Hicks turned against his former ally. Yet, after all, Hicks had approved the plan.

He advised Secretary of State Seward not to release Brown because "that would be suicidal, for he, at once, would get in touch with the South." [2]

When Abraham Lincoln believed that Brown would influence a decision to have Maryland secede, he was imprisoned. Brown described his seizure this way:

> At midnight, I was arrested at my country home, near Relay House, on the Baltimore and Ohio Railroad, by four policemen and a guard of soldiers. The soldiers were placed in front and back of the house, while the police rapped violently on the front door. I opened my bedroom window, and asked the intruders what they wanted. They replied that they wanted Mayor Brown. I asked who wanted him, and they answered,

1. George Radcliffe, p. 43
2. George Radcliffe, p. 71

> "The government of the United States." I then inquired for their warrant, but they had none. Closely guarded, I was driven to Fort McHenry (and imprisoned there for one night)...Next, to Fort Monroe for about two weeks. Finally, to Fort Warren [in Boston harbor]." [1]

He was imprisoned there for more than a year.

Lincoln attempted to obtain an oath of allegiance from Brown; in return he would be allowed to continue as mayor, with the assurance that he would not try to undermine the Union. Brown objected that he had been arrested without a warrant and so should be released without taking a loyalty oath.

The Merryman Case: Lincoln Defies Supreme Court

The United States Constitution provides that "the Writ of habeas Corpus shall not be suspended unless, when, in cases of rebellion or invasion, the public safety may require it."

April 27, 1861: Anticipating rebellion in areas where none existed, Abraham Lincoln telegraphed General Scott before he was forced to retire: "You are engaged in suppressing an insurrection against the laws of the United States. If at any point in the vicinity of Philadelphia and the city of Washington, you find resistance...suspend the Writ of Habeas Corpus." [2]

The only invasion was instigated by Lincoln. The only Northern insurrection was in Baltimore. Philadelphia and the other areas down to the Capital were still at peace.

On May 25th, federal troops arrested John Merryman, who had participated in the Baltimore bridge-burnings. He was taken into custody without a warrant, under the suspension of the Writ, without specific charges, and secretly jailed at Fort McHenry. "By chance," he learned where he was incarcerated and contacted Roger Taney, the Chief Justice of the Supreme Court. Taney ruled that suspending the Writ was unconstitutional. "Congress alone has the power to suspend the Writ...The President's action represents a threat to the liberties of all Americans." [3]

Taney issued a Writ to release Merryman, but under Lincoln's direct order the commander at Fort McHenry disregarded it, as well as the later charge of contempt of court.

Then, on July 2, 1861, when Maryland's "insurrection" had long been quelled and there was no armed activity in the northeast, Lincoln once again extended the areas where the Writ of Habeas Corpus would be suspended. Again, he projected the possibility, not the reality, of insurrection. "If, at any point or in

1. Ibid., p. 73.
2. John Nicolay and John Hay, vol. 6, p. 75
3. "Suppression and Control of Maryland, 1861–1865: A Study of Federal-State Relations During the Civil War Conflict," *Maryland Historical Magazine*; Baltimore: Maryland Historical Society, September 1959) p. 335.

the vicinity of any military line which is now, or shall be used between the city of New York and the city of Washington, you find resistance, you [General Scott] are authorized to suspend the Writ." [1]

Lincoln and England Recognize the Confederacy

Historians of the Civil War often go to great lengths to prove that the Confederacy's attempts to gain diplomatic recognition from the major European powers was futile, and since the denial of official international status prevented military or financial aid, the Southern cause was doomed.

Below I reproduce a secret diplomatic dispatch, written on May 21, 1861, by William Seward, U.S. Secretary of State, revised and approved by Abraham Lincoln. It is directed to Charles Francis Adams, Minister to England and son of John Quincy Adams. He is credited with preventing British recognition of the Southern government, but this dispatch and the implications disprove that. [2]

This document presents a furious Abraham Lincoln virtually declaring war on England for conducting clandestine diplomatic relations with the Confederacy. From its tone, it is clear that Lincoln considered these secret meetings as the initial step toward full legal recognition.

Most diplomatic language is cautious and circumspect, even when two countries are on the verge of war. Lincoln's extremely hostile wording demonstrates that he believed Great Britain had gone beyond the stage of unofficial acknowledgement. This communiqué also reveals that the national policy of most other European nations was to follow England's lead, in terms of diplomatic relations, with the Confederacy.

This secret dispatch is followed by an even more startling revelation. Part II of this story shows that the United States itself granted official legal status to the Confederacy as an independent country, despite continual presidential and congressional statements to the contrary, saying that the war was against an "insurrection" or a "rebellion." This was to prevent both sides from committing atrocities against prisoners of war.

Text of the Secret Dispatch

> Mr. Adams: George Mifflin Dallas [former United States Vice President and former Minister to England] in a brief dispatch on May 2nd, tells that Lord John Russell [British Foreign Secretary] recently requested an interview with him. In that conversation the British Secretary told Mr. Dallas that three representatives of the Southern Confederacy were in London, and that Lord John Russell was not unwilling to see them unofficially. He further informed Mr. Dallas that

1. John G. Nicolay and John Hay, vol vi, p. 258.
2. Ibid., p. 277-279.

an understanding exists between the British and French governments that would lead both to take one and the same course as to recognition. The President [Lincoln] regrets that Mr. Dallas did not protest against the proposed unofficial intercourse between the British government and the missionaries of the insurgents. Intercourse of any kind with the so-called commissioners is likely to be construed as recognition of the authority which supported them. Such intercourse would nonetheless be hurtful to us for being unofficial, and it might be even more injurious, because we have no means of knowing what points might be resolved by it. Moreover, unofficial intercourse is useless and meaningless if it not expected to ripen into official recognition. It is left doubtless here whether the proposed unofficial intercourse has yet actually begun. You [Mr. Adams] will, in any event, desist from all intercourse whatever, official and unofficial, with the British government, as long as this continues of either kind with the domestic enemies of this country. [This is a form of diplomatic break.]

We all know another fact that has not yet been officially communicated to us; namely, that other European states are being apprized by France and England of their agreement, and are expected to concur with or follow them in whatever measures they adopt on the subject of recognition.

As to the blockade [of Southern ports], we will say that by our laws and the laws of nature, and the laws of nations, this government has a clear right to suppress insurrection. An exclusion of commerce from national ports which have been seized by the insurgents, in the equitable form of blockade, is the proper means to that end.... And therefore we expect it to be respected by Great Britain.

We will add that we have revoked the Exequatur of the Russian consul who has already enlisted in the military services of the insurgents. [An Exequatur is a document given to a consul by the country in which he is stationed, authorizing him to perform his duties there.] We shall dismiss or demand the recall of every foreign agent, consular or diplomatic, who shall disobey the Federal authority. [In a parallel action, a high-ranking British officer, in uniform, was an advisor and observer to Robert E. Lee. This reflects a form of official recognition.]

As to the recognition of the so-called Southern Confederacy, a concession of belligerent rights is liable to be construed as recognition of them. [The dictionary defines "belligerency" as existing in a war between nations or in a civil war, if the established government treats the insurgent force as if it was a sovereign power. Part II demonstrates that the United States did grant belligerent rights to the Confederacy.] None of the proceedings will pass unquestioned in the United States. Great Britain is called upon not to intervene and give it body and independence by resisting our measures of suppression. British recognition would be British intervention to create within our territory a hostile State by overthrowing this republic itself. When this act of intervention is distinctly performed, we, from that hour, will cease to be friends, and become once again, as we twice before have been forced to be, enemies of Great Britain. [In both the Revolutionary War and the War of 1812.]

As to the treatment of privateers [privately owned and operated war vessels commissioned by the Confederacy to capture United States shipping] in the insurgent service, you will say that this is a question exclusively our own. We treat them as pirates. They are employed by our citizens, preying on the commerce of our country. If Great Britain shall choose to recognize them as lawful belligerents, and give them shelter from our pursuits and punishment, the laws of nations afford an adequate and proper remedy, and we shall avail ourselves of it [the United States could attack Confederate privateers in British waters, which could be considered an act of war by England], because England is willing to become the patron of privateering when aimed at our devastation. [Great Britain's participation in privateering and building warships for the Confederacy is another example of recognition. The *Alabama*, which was built in Liverpool in 1861–62, captured 69 Union vessels, was aided and protected by British interests. The *Florida*, also constructed and fitted out in Liverpool and launched in 1863, sank or captured 60 United States ships. The *Shenandoah*, purchased by the Confederacy in 1864 in London, seized 38 American vessels. These Confederate Navy raiders were largely responsible for the decline of the United States' Merchant Marine.] We are not insensitive to the great importance of this occasion. We see how, upon the result of the debate in which we are engaged, a war may ensue between the United States and one, two, or even more European nations. War, in any case, is as exceptional from the habits as it is revolting to the sentiments of the American people. But if it comes, it will be fully seen that it results from the action of Great Britain, not our own; that Great Britain will have decided to fraternize with our domestic enemy, either without waiting to hear of our remonstrances and our warnings, or after having heard them. War in defense of national life is not immoral, and war in defense of independence is an inevitable part of the discipline of nations.

The United States Recognizes Confederacy

This section is edited from a pamphlet, "The Dangerous Condition of the Country," by Reverdy Johnson.[1] He served in the Maryland legislature and

1. Reverdy Johnson, *The Dangerous Condition of our Country: The Causes Which Have Led to it, And The Duty of the People* (Baltimore: Sun Book and Job Printing Establishment, 1867.)

United States Senate and won a reputation as one of the ablest constitutional lawyers of his era. Johnson was appointed Minister to Great Britain in 1868.

Here Reverdy Johnson describes how the United States, through its own separate constitutional definitions of "war" and "insurrection," was forced to recognize the Confederacy as an independent sovereign nation:

> The insurrection, before it was suppressed, assumed such proportions, as made it a war, and brought it within the "war powers" vested in that body [Congress] by the Constitution. This is an error. The powers to declare war, and the powers to provide for the suppression of insurrection, are in their very nature, distinct powers. The one [declaring war] looks exclusively to hostilities with foreign nations; and the other [suppression of insurrection] to disturbances at home, and they are so treated in the Constitution. Congress is vested with the authority to declare war, raise and support armies and provide and maintain a navy.
>
> If these powers were intended for cases of insurrection, the conferring upon Congress, or any other authority for that end, would be mere surplusage [irrelevant or unnecessary words]. And yet, in the same section of the Congress vesting these; the power is expressly given to call out the militia to suppress insurrection.
>
> The insurrection became so formidable that, upon the grounds of humanity, as well as to give the government the means to assist in the suppression, belligerent rights were granted to the insurrectionists. If our government had executed those captured by its forces [which could be done legally if they were outlaws, guerrillas, rebels, pirates, or insurrectionists] the Confederate authorities would have retaliated. Such a result would have answered no good purpose toward the suppression of the rebellion, and would have not only lacerated the feelings of the public, but also shocked the public sentiments of the world.
>
> Congress therefore, and the President, wisely and with the best motives, recognized the belligerent rights of the insurrectionary government. And such concessions at the same time gave to Congress the authority to exclude neutral nations from all intercourse with the South [because the war was now between two distinct sovereign nations].
>
> As far as such nations are concerned, Congress properly claimed the rights of war and upon such claims declared the blockade of Southern ports, and provided for the capture of vessels and their cargoes attempting to violate it. [If this was a rebellion or an insurrection, this would not be legal.]

> Such captures were made and be judged to be lawful by our Prize Courts. [Under Maritime Law, a Prize Court adjudicates whether vessels captured by the navy or privateers belong to an enemy or neutral nations. The court determines whether the captor's government for losses.]
>
> In the first of these, called the "Prize Cases," decided by the Supreme Court of the United States, the opinion contains one of the two passages which have been relied upon as justifying Congress in considering the States in question [the Confederate States] as conquered provinces [territories captured from a foreign country, not a recovered portion of the United State].
>
> Supreme Court Justice Nelson confirmed, in cases whether the Southern states were in or out of the Union, that the United States Congress legally treated the Confederate states as foreign states, and their inhabitants as alien enemies.

The Antietam Campaign and Its Aftermath

August 1862: After Robert E. Lee defeated Union General John Pope at the second Manassas battle, he was determined to carry the war into the North, into Maryland. Southerners hoped the invasion would "capture" the Old Line State. After the secession vote had failed to materialize, Maryland was referred to as "the weeping maiden, bound and fettered, seeking relief." Confederate leaders believed that their move north would rally support in the bitterly divided state.

And so, with high hopes, the Confederate army began splashing across the Potomac River on Thursday, September 4th, 1862, at several fords near Leesburg, Virginia. A Texan, John Stevens, described the chaos:

> Imagine a river, about 500 yards wide, from two or three feet deep, the water very swift. Now, it is just as full of men as it can be, for 600 or 700 yards, up and down, yelling and singing all sorts of war and jolly songs, and in this connection you must find room for eight to twelve regimental bands in the river all at the same time; the drums beating, the horns atooting, and the fifes ascreaming, possibly every one a different aire. Some on "Dixie," and some on "Maryland, My Maryland," and some on "The Girl I Left Behind Me," and some "Yankee Doodle." Cavalrymen swam with their horses. A few musicians lost their drums, much to the amusement of their comrades, who watched as their instruments floated downstream toward Washington. Teamsters had no trouble crossing with their empty wagons. Men in the infantry stripped to the bare essentials, wrapped their ammunition in their trousers and held it

above their heads. Those who had shoes hung them around their necks. Barefoot, they waded into the current. One soldier, who stumbled on a rock, and went under water, wondered if all the good residents of western Maryland had emptied their icehouses into the river the night before.

John Stevens paused on the bank to cook a pumpkin he had found, and wondered if he alone was uneasy:

> I could not suppress a feeling of sadness as I beheld the vast concourse of humanity wading into the river, so full of music, and for so many of them, never once thinking that their feet would never press the soil on the south side of the Potomac again. [1]
>
> Two months earlier the Union army had threatened Richmond. Now it skulked near its own fortifications around Washington. The toughened Southern veterans were ready to finish the job, and reaching the Maryland shore was significant. "There were few moments, perhaps," wrote a cavalryman, "from the beginning of the war to its close, of excitement more intense, of exhilaration more delightful."[2]

On September 8, Robert E. Lee issued this proclamation to the people of Maryland, announcing that the Army of Northern Virginia would come among them to "assist you in the power of its arms in regaining the rights of which you have been despoiled...The army will respect your choice, whatever it may be, and while the Southern troops will rejoice to welcome your natural position among them, they will welcome you when you come of your own free will."[3]

It was a diminished band of cavaliers that crossed the Potomac. Some balked at the idea of invading the North; some of them disappeared before the crossing. Stragglers, too hungry and ill-shod to keep going, were left at Leesburg. Political ideology and exhaustion robbed the Southern army of about 15,000 men before they reached the river.

The hoped-for crowds of cheering civilians waiting on the northern shore were not in sight. One veteran recalled:

> The coldness of the water was more than equaled by the frigidity of the welcome extended. Not even the dulcet strains of "Maryland, My Maryland" evoked from the half submerged instruments of the bands aroused the enthusiasm of the people; no arms opened to receive us, no fires burned to warm, and no feast waited to feed us, as wet,

1. John Stevens, "Reminiscences of the Civil War" (Hillsboro, Texas: Hillsboro Texas: Hillsboro Mirror Printing Co., 1902) p. 66.
2. Heroes von Borcke, *Memoir of the Confederate: War for Independence* (Edinburg, Blackwood and Sons, 1865) Vol. 1, p.185.
3. Gary W. Gallagher, editor, *The Antietam Campaign* (Chapel Hill and London; University of North Carolina Press) p.32

> shivering and hungry, we stepped out of the water and set our feet on Maryland's soil.[1]
>
> Throughout the countryside, many Unionists expressed their political sentiments with stony silence and locked doors. For the Southern men with money to spend and empty bellies, the reception was galling. "I visited nearly a hundred farmhouses during the day," one soldier wrote his father, "and did not succeed to buy a pound of meat or a bushel of corn. It is true that a number of houses were deserted, but where I found the owners at home, they all told me they had nothing to sell. It is perfectly evident that the people in this section of the state are as hostile to us as if we were north of the Mason–Dixon line."[2]

But fear of retaliation certainly factored into the lukewarm reception.

Secessionist citizens knew that with all probability the Southern army would quickly be replaced again by federal troops. They had already seen too many friends and neighbors arrested and imprisoned because of their loyalties. It was a tense, dangerous time for secessionists. "They seemed much constrained in manner," wrote an infantryman, "as if feeling certain that Union men were in their midst, taking notes of all actions or expressions, and ready to divulge names at future opportunities." [3]

September 5th: Robert E. Lee entered Frederick. It seemed his objective was Baltimore. On September 10, he divided his army, sending Stonewall Jackson to capture the large Union garrison at Harpers Ferry, to clear his communication lines through the Shenandoah Valley. With the remainder, Lee marched northwest toward Hagerstown, near the Pennsylvania border.

General George McClellan learned of Lee's intention; Lee's plan of attack was lost, and Union soldiers found it. McClellan realized that Lee's forces were under strength and he moved to attack.

Between Frederick and Hagerstown is South Mountain. On September 14th, McClellan advanced into the gaps in that mountain, defeated Lee's rear guard, and took the passes. The Confederates fell back to the town of Sharpsburg, nine miles west of South Mountain. His position lay behind Antitank Creek.

September 15th: The Harpers Ferry garrison surrendered to Jackson, who raced to join Lee before McClellan went on the offensive. The two sides clashed on the 17th. Initially, assaults on Lee's right flank were bloody but ineffective, and McClellan failed to press the slight Union advance with his available reserves. In the afternoon Burnside's corps crossed Antietam Creek over the bridge on Lee's right and drove the Confederates back. But A.P. Hill's

1. Kathleen A. Ernst, *Too Afraid to Cry* (Mechanicsville, PA, Stackpole Books, 1999), p. 39.
2. Ibid., p. 57.
3. An English Combatant, *Battlefields of the South, from Bull Run to Fredericksburg* (New York: John Bradburn co. 1861) p. 467.

Southern division arrived from Harpers Ferry and repulsed the offensive. The battle from both sides was not renewed.

Of the 74,000 Union soldiers involved, 12,400 were killed or wounded. Of the 40,000 Southerners, 10,700 became casualties. This was the bloodiest day in American history, including the First and Second World Wars, Korea, Vietnam, and the Mid-Eastern conflicts.

Lee's men remained in their positions for another day to demonstrate that they had not been defeated or driven from the field. On September 18–19, Lee re-crossed the Potomac into Virginia. To this day the battle is considered a draw.

Later, Lee told the Confederate Secretary of War: "I regret that the stay of the army was so short as to prevent our receiving the aid I expected from the state." Summoning a measure of forced optimism, he went on to say: "Some recruits joined us, and others are finding their way across the river to our lines."[1]

Aftermath of Antietam for Civilians

Besides the immediate impact of combat at Sharpsburg on the civilians, the residue of military activity left its mark during the period following the Antietam battle. The presence of more than 120,000 Southerners and Yankees, along with 50,000 horses and mules, generated tons of waste; a tremendous health hazard in and of itself. The threat of disease was further exacerbated by thousands of dead men and animals rotting in the warm September sun, and the many more wounded, left behind to be cared for in field hospitals. Evidence shows that scores of civilians became sick and many died when they returned to what was left of their homes.

Combat and disease were not the only threats posed by this large battle. Economic devastation loomed. At Sharpsburg, soldiers from both sides raided farms and homes, carrying off valuables, destroying property, and confiscating livestock and crops as food for the armies.

In some cases, refugees who fled the Sharpsburg area prior to the battle returned to find themselves in economic ruin, a scenario that was to be repeated hundreds of times throughout the corridor of the war.

As the two armies converged, a correspondent wrote, before the battle began, "Hagerstown is filled with refugees and soldiers," "the roads are jammed with civilians scrambling to get out of the way of the advancing armies, toting babies and pushing carts and wheel-barrows piled crazily with baskets of food and prized china. Hotels and private homes overflow with refugees, and field edges take on a gypsy air as the less fortunate make makeshift camps along the road."[2]

1. Gary W. Gallagher, p. 32.
2. Kathleen K. Ernst, p. 25.

The shopkeepers in Hagerstown locked their doors and sent merchandise to Pennsylvania. City officials were among those who fled, trundling public records with them for safe-keeping. The Hagerstown Bank collected all banknotes not in circulation and burned them. A new set was issued when the crisis passed. This was a pattern that would be repeated. Silver and gold coins disappeared almost immediately, hoarded away and kept out of circulation throughout the war.

The Antietam campaign sputtered to a conclusion. The strategic frontier remained along the Potomac, with Lee maneuvering in the lower Shenandoah Valley, gathering food and fodder from that region, and striking at the Baltimore and Ohio-Railroad.

Despite Lincoln's efforts to prod McClellan into action, he mounted no major effort to get at Lee. This was largely the result of Antietam, where his army was decimated and so many officers killed that it had to be re-organized from the ground up.

On October 13th, Abraham Lincoln wrote the following letter to McClellan, which reflects the President's delusion that he was a military expert. The reality was that Lee, not encumbered with all the materiel of war, could move quickly and outmaneuver the slow, overburdened Union armies.

This letter was the result of Lincoln visiting McClellan at his headquarters to ascertain the actual condition of the army. McClellan complained that he lacked everything and gave constant excuses for not moving. Lincoln found an army of 100,000 in satisfactory shape. On October 6th, Lincoln ordered McClellan to cross the Potomac and drive the enemy south. It was his failure to do so, together with his former inaction, that called forth this letter:

> My Dear Sir: You remember my speaking to you of what I called your over cautiousness. Are you not over-cautious when you assume you cannot do what the enemy is constantly doing. Should you not claim to be at least his equal in prowess, and act upon that claim? As I understand, you telegraphed General Halleck that you cannot subsist your army at Winchester unless the railroad from Harpers Ferry to that point be put in working order.
>
> But the enemy does now subsist his army at Winchester, at a distance nearly twice as great from railroad transportation as you would have to do, without the railroad last named. He now wagons from Culpepper Court House, which is just about twice as far as you would have to do from Harpers Ferry! He is certainly not more than half as well provided with wagons as you are. I certainly should be pleased for you to have the advantage of the railroad from Harpers Ferry to Winchester, but it wastes all the remainder of autumn to give it to you, and, in fact, ignores the question of time, which cannot and must not be ignored. Again, one of the standard maxims of war, as you know, is to operate "on the

enemy's communications as much as possible, without exposing your own." You seem to act as if this applies against you, but cannot apply in your favor. Change positions with the enemy, and think you not, he would break your communication with Richmond within the next twenty-four hours? You dread his going into Pennsylvania; but if he does so in full force, he gives up his communications to you absolutely, and you have nothing to do but follow and ruin him. If he does so with less than full force, fall upon and beat what is left behind, all the easier. Exclusive of the water-line, you are now nearer Richmond than the enemy is, by the route that you can, and he must, take. Why can you not reach there before him, unless you admit he is more than your equal on a march? His route is the arc of a circle, while yours is the chord. The roads are as good on yours as on his. You know I desired, but did not order, you to cross the Potomac below, instead of above, the Shenandoah, and Blue Ridge. My idea was that this would at once menace the enemy's communications, which I would seize if he would permit.

If he should move northward, I would follow him closely, holding his communications. If he should prevent our seizing his communications, and move toward Richmond, I would press closely to him, and fight him if a favorable opportunity should present itself, and at least try to beat him to Richmond on the inside track. I say "try"; if we never try, we shall never succeed. If he makes a stand at Winchester, moving neither south or north, I would fight him there, on the idea that if we cannot beat him when he bears the wastage of coming to us, we can never do it when we bear the wastage of coming to him. This proposition is a simple truth, and it is too important to be lost sight of for a moment. In coming to us he tenders to us an advantage which we should not waive. We should not so operate as to merely drive him away. As we must beat him somewhere or finally fail, we can do it, if at all, easier near to us than far away. If we cannot beat the enemy where he is now, we never can, he again being within the entrenchments of Richmond.

Recurring again to the idea of going to Richmond on the inside track, the facility of supplying from the side away from the enemy is remarkable, as it were, by the different spokes of a wheel extending from the hub toward the rim, and this, whether you move directly by the chord or on the inside arc, hugging the Blue Ridge more closely. The chord-line, as you see, carries you by Aldie, Hay Market, and Fredericksburg, and see how turnpikes, railroads, and finally the Potomac, by Aquia Creek, meet you at all points from Washington; the same, only the lines lengthened a little, if you press closer to the Blue Ridge, part of the way.

The gaps through the Blue Ridge I understand to be about the following distances from Harpers-Ferry, to wit: Vestal's, 5 miles; Gregory's, 13; Snickers, 18; Ashley's 28; Manassas, 38; Chester, 45; and

> Thornton's, 53. I should think it preferable to take the route nearest the enemy, disabling him to make an important move without your knowledge, and compelling him to keep his forces together for dread of you. The gaps would enable you to attack if you wish. For a great part of the way you would be practically between the enemy and both Washington and Richmond, enabling us to spare you the greatest number of troops from here. When at length running for Richmond ahead of him, enables him to move this way, if he does so, turn and attack him in the rear. But I think he should be engaged long before such point is reached. It is all easy if our troops march as well as the enemy, and it is unmanly to say they cannot do it. This letter is in no sense an order. [1]

Again, this is all a layman's theorizing and does not account for the reality of R.E. Lee's far greater maneuverability and speed. McClellan realized that the Southern army could run circles around him.

In November, Lincoln replaced McClellan with Ambrose E. Burnside, and the war in the eastern theatre took on a more active character. By then, the results of the Maryland campaign had become evident. The surrender of 12,000 Union troops at Harpers Ferry cheered the South. The vicious tactical statement at Antietam took on the nature of a Union victory when Lee retreated.

Lincoln's Emancipation Proclamation

On September 22, Abraham Lincoln determined that the ambiguous results at Antietam justified the issuing of the preliminary Emancipation Proclamation.It would free the slaves only in those states "in rebellion," where it would have no legal impact. Yet it would have enormous consequences for the future direction of the war.

When Lincoln issued the Proclamation, General McClellan was horrified. At issue was the doctrine of state sovereignty. He said: "I cannot make up my mind to fight for such an accursed doctrine. It is too infamous...I find it almost impossible to retain my commission and self-respect at the same time."

Another traumatic result of Antietam was Lincoln's September 24th suspension of the Writ of Habeas Corpus throughout the entire United States. McClellan said: "At one stroke of the pen, the Republic has been rendered into despotism."[2]

Union General Fitz John Porter said that the Emancipation Proclamation was "ridiculed by the Army; caused disgust, discontent, and expressions of

1. John C. Nicolay and John Hay, Vol. vi, p. 140.
2. Gary W. Gallagher, p. 53.

disloyalty to the views of the Administration, and amounts, I have heard, to insubordination."[1]

This disillusionment was due to the fact that most Northerners believed that the objective of the war was to bring the South back into the Union and not to transform its social institutions.

Horatio Seymour speaks on "False Emancipation Proclamation"

New York's Governor, Horatio Seymour, made his annual address to the New York State Assembly on January 7, 1863. In this speech he addressed the twin issues of state sovereignty and the Emancipation Proclamation:

> Not only must the national Constitution be held inviolate, but the rights of states must be respected, as not less sacred. There are differences of opinion as to the dividing line between state and national jurisdictions, but there can be none as to the existence of such separate jurisdictions...A consolidated government in this vast country would destroy the essential home rights and liberties of the people. They can never be given up. Without them our government cannot stand.

Then Mr. Seymour turned to the Emancipation Proclamation and its relation to state sovereignty:

> The President has already signed an Act of Congress, which asserts that the slaves of those in rebellion are confiscate. The sole effect of this proclamation, therefore, is to declare the emancipation of slaves of those who are not in rebellion, and who are therefore, loyal citizens. It is an extraordinary deduction from the alleged war powers, that the forfeiture of the rights of loyal citizens, and bringing upon them the same punishment, imposed upon insurgents, is calculated to advance the success of the war, to uphold the Constitution and restore the Union. The class of loyal citizens who, above all others, are entitled to the protection of government, are those who have remained true to the flag of our country. And yet, the sole force of this proclamation is directed against them. May not this, so clearly impolitic, unjust, and unconstitutional, and which is calculated to create so many barriers to the restoration of the Union, be misconstrued by the world as an abandonment of the hope or the purpose of restoring it; a result to which the State of New York is unalterably opposed, and which will be effectively resisted.
>
> We must not only support the Constitution of the United States: maintain the rights of States, we must restore our Union as it was before the outbreak of the war. The assertion that this war was the unavoidable result of slavery is not only erroneous, but has led to a

1. Stephen W. Sears, *George B. McClellan: The Young Napoleon* (New York: Tickner and Field, 1988), p. 320.

> disastrous policy in its prosecution. The opinion that slavery must be abolished to restore the Union creates an antagonism between the Free and the Slave states which ought not to exist. If it is true that slavery must be abolished by the force of the Federal Government; that the South must be held in military subjugation; that four millions of Negroes must, for many years, be under the direct management of authorities in Washington, at the public expense; then indeed, we must endure the waste of our armies in the field, further drains on our population, and still greater burdens of debt. We must convert our government into a military despotism. This mischievous opinion, that in this contest the North must subjugate and destroy the South to save the Union, has weakened the hopes of our citizens at home and destroyed confidence in our success abroad. [1]

Lincoln: Emancipation Proclamation is Unconstitutional

Abraham Lincoln wrote this letter to A. G. Hodge on April 4, 1864:

> You asked me to put in writing the substance of what I verbally said the other day in your presence, to Governor Briolette and Senator Dixon. It is about as follows: "I am naturally anti-slavery. If slavery is not wrong, nothing is wrong. I cannot remember when I did not think and feel so, and yet I have never understood that the presidency did not confer upon me the unrestricted right to act officially upon this judgment and feeling. It was in the oath I took, that I would, to the best of my ability, protect, preserve, and defend the Constitution of the United States. I could not take the office without taking the oath. Now it is my view that I might take the oath to get power, and break the oath in using that power.
>
> I understood too, that in ordinary civil administration, this oath even forbade me to practically indulge my primary abstract judgment on the moral question of slavery. I had publicly declared this many times, and in many ways. And I aver to this day, I have done no official act in mere deference to my abstract judgment and feeling on slavery.
>
> I did understand, however, that my oath to preserve the Constitution to the best of my ability imposed upon me the duty of preserving, by every indispensible means, that government, that nation, of which the Constitution was the organic law. Was it possible to lose the nation and yet preserve the Constitution? By general law, life and limb must be protected, yet often a limb must be amputated to save a life; but a life is never wisely given to save a limb.

1. Albany *Argus*, January 8, 1863.

> I felt that measures otherwise unconstitutional might become lawful, by being indispensible to the preservation of the Constitution, through the preservation of the nation.
>
> Right or wrong, I assume the ground, and now avow it. I could not feel that, to the best of my ability, I had ever tried to preserve the constitution, if, to save slavery, or any minor matter, I should permit the wreck of government, all together.
>
> When early in the war, General Fremont attempted a military emancipation, I forbade it, because I did not then think it an indispensible necessity. When, a little later, General Cameron, the Secretary of War, suggested the arming of the blacks, I objected, because I did not yet think it was an indispensible necessity.
>
> When, still later, General Hunter attempted military emancipation, I again forbade it, because I did not yet think indispensible necessity had come. When, in March and May and June 1862, I made earnest and successive appeals to Border States to favor compensated emancipation, I believed the indispensible necessity for military emancipation and arming of the blacks would come. They declined the proposition, and I was, in my best judgment, driven to the alternative of either surrendering the Union, and with it, the Constitution, or laying a strong hand upon the colored element. I chose the latter. [1]

Josiah Gorgas, the Confederacy's ordnance chief, initially considered the Emancipation Proclamation worthy of note only "as showing the drift of opinion in the northern government." A few days later, however, he recorded that Lincoln's action triggered "marked opposition in the North and was denounced by the Democrats generally." [2]

The Democrats were advocates of state sovereignty. Unhappiness in the Union army relating to emancipation also impressed some Confederates as particularly noteworthy. The Northern press served as a primary source for information about the topic in September and October 1862. "George McClellan has issued a general order cautioning troops against political discussion," observed a man who relied on Union newspaper accounts. "It is a very significant production and goes to corroborate the report that great trouble exists in their camps on account of I the war becoming one for the abolition of slavery." [3]

The following editorial in the Richmond *Whig* has more than a grain of truth to it. "The Emancipation Proclamation indicates a current of distract swelling

1. John D. Nicolay and John Hay, editors, vol. 8, p. 41
2. Gary W. Gallagher, editor, "The Antietam Campaign" (Chapel Hill, the University of North Caroline, 1999) p. 84.
3. Gary W. Gallagher, p 40

even to desperation. Lincoln has surrendered the government into the hands of the Abolitionists, suppressing the last lingering hope of a restoration of the Union, even on the part of those who sustained the Administration under the honest belief that Lincoln was endeavoring in good faith to accomplish that end." [1]

Maryland and the Battle of Gettysburg

June 1863. Robert E. Lee once again sent his troops into Maryland. Federal troops in Frederick retreated from the town. Advancing Confederates pushed toward the west. This time Lee led his men through the western panhandle into Pennsylvania.

Smoke from Gettysburg could be seen from Frederick. The destruction of the Harpers Ferry bridge meant that Lee's men had to be funneled through Washington County.

When the first Confederates limped back to Williamsport, in Maryland, with a vulnerable wagon train of several thousand wounded, 2,000 fit soldiers, 10,600 draft animals, and almost no food, they found the Potomac ten feet above fording level. It was "the highest water level ever known."

Williamsport's river banks became a hospital camp. Local women fed the wounded. Some of them had not eaten in 36 hours. Lee's army was trapped. Local residents felt this would be another Sharpsburg. There was continual skirmishing in the outskirts. Jeb Stuart's cavalry blocked the Union advance using tactics they learned the year before.

Lee's army was close to being annihilated. There were a dozen small battles between July 5th and the 14th, as this rear guard held off attacks and Lee tried to cross the Potomac. There was fighting in Hagerstown. George Custer led Union troops. The Confederates held Hagerstown until the 12th. Their cavalry formed a perimeter protecting Boonsboro, Sharpsburg, Williamsport and Clear Spring.

General George Mead's Union soldiers were too exhausted to aggressively pursue Lee, allowing the Southerners to finally cross successfully over the Potomac, even though it took more than a week to accomplish.

Third Invasion of Maryland

July 6, 1864. The Confederate plan: strike east to threaten Washington, to relieve pressure on Virginia's Petersburg which guarded the southern approach to Richmond and was the only approach route for supplies to reach the capital.

Sharpsburg was occupied again, as well as Williamsport, Boonsboro,, Hagerstown, Jefferson and Middletown. The townspeople in these

1. Richmond "Whig," October 2, 1862.

communities cringed, not knowing what this campaign would bring. They built secret camps in the woods where their animals and food were hidden.

All commodities were sold at fantastic prices to both sides. Now the Confederates practiced a retaliatory scorched earth policy, after earlier orders not to destroy private property. Hagerstown was partially burned to the ground. Jubal Early threatened to burn Middletown if a ransom was not delivered.

Marylander Bradley T. Johnson was a major participant, leading 1,500 cavalry. He did not reach his objective but did get close enough to Baltimore and Washington to induce a general panic.

Before this, Early opened the fight for Frederick. Union reinforcements led by General Lew Wallace poured in from Baltimore. By now, Frederick's citizens were used to combat and watched the fighting without fear.

July 8th: The Confederates almost encircled Union forces outside Frederick. The Yankees retreated to the Monocracy River, southeast of Frederick. Lew Wallace commanded 7,000 men.

The Confederates fielded 14,000. Wallace could only hope for delay, not a victory. But his army was routed, with 1,600 casualties. The Confederates: 700.

July 11th: Jubal Early was poised to attack Washington. But Lew Wallace had delayed him long enough for Federal reinforcements to arrive. Jubal Early waited for a day, for psychological purposes, being so close to the capital; then he withdrew into Virginia. He said: "We haven't taken Washington, but we scared Abe Lincoln like hell!"

July 29th: Jubal Early sent two cavalry brigades into western Maryland, then captured Chambersburg, Pennsylvania. He demanded another ransom. When town officials refused to pay, he burned the town down.

Maryland Reconstructed Like the South

When the war ended, Congressional Reconstruction transformed the ex-Confederacy into a colony of the United States. It brutalized the Southern people who were stripped of their citizenship and rights. This began in 1868. The reconstruction of Maryland, under a similar ruthless plan, began during the war, in 1864.

The first phase, in November 1864, allowed those few Marylanders who could still vote to select state legislators who would then form a convention for a new state constitution.

Since 1861 the military had "supervised" the polling places and disqualified thousands of voters who could not pass the iron-clad oath. Now armed intervention accelerated to a more frightening level. Union army Colonel C.C. Tevis issued the following order, clearly indicating that even the few remaining voters no longer had a choice. Only one party could be selected: the Union (Republican) Party.

Tevis said he created this order based on correspondence with Abraham Lincoln:

> Whereas, The President of the United States...has stated that all loyal qualified voters should have the right to vote, it therefore becomes every truly loyal citizen to avail himself of the present opportunity... by giving a full and ardent support to the whole government ticket. [The Union Party]...None other is recognized by the federal authorities. [1]

Modern totalitarian elections allow more latitude than the Marylanders enjoyed. They can indicate "yes" or "no" for a one-party candidate. Old Line Stators could only select "yes."

This is what Colonel Tevis had in mind: "At most, if not all, the polls, were seen soldiers. In some places, citizens approaching to vote were peremptorily ordered to retire, and their right to vote denied and refused. In some places the soldiers were the judges of elections, challenging and refusing voters, illegally and wantonly opening and inspecting their ballots...They were intimidated and driven from the polls. Others kept away through fear of personal injury." [2]

As a result, two thirds of all voters were disqualified, mostly Democrats. This is a higher rate of disenfranchisement than in the worst days of Reconstruction.

The U.S. army controlled which legislators could participate in the constitutional convention. For instance, General Lew Wallace did not feel that a Mr. Kilbourn was loyal enough. In front of a military panel he was forced to confess his sins, admitting that he had voted to recognize the Confederacy. Kilbourn was ejected from the convention and replaced by a loyalist. General Wallace also determined which candidates for elected office was disloyal. They were barred from running.

The constitutional convention began its work on June 7, 1864. It adjourned on the 8th, and reconvened on the 24th. Work had hardly resumed when Jubal Early's raid on Monocracy Junction occurred. This caused a bitter clash between members of the convention.

During Jubal Early's raid there were no regular meetings for ten days. And during the convention a resolution was passed, proclaiming that all sympathizers with the rebellion were "recreant to the faith of the Fathers, forsaken of God, and instigated by the Devil."

In October 1864 the new constitution was placed before the miniscule "loyal" portion of the voting population to accept or reject it. Some of its more undemocratic features were:

1. Harold R. Manakee, p. 12.
2. Ibid., p. 16.

1. The federal government is supreme over state governments. This, once again, destroyed the principle of state sovereignty.
2. Any disloyal person "ought to be forever disqualified and rendered incapable to hold or exercise, within this State, any office of profit or trust, civil or military, or to vote in any election hereafter held in this State."
3. Additional and tougher loyalty oaths were permanently instituted for entirely new categories of governmental, legal, corporate, and professional fields. This made "war measures" a basic part of Maryland's organic law.
4. Governmental, tax-funded schools would become part of Maryland's landscape, just as in the former Confederacy, to teach children the proper respect for "authority."

New Constitution Rejected, Legalized by Military

In the Reconstruction South, laws which the Congressional Radicals or military commanders did not like were overturned arbitrarily. This took place in wartime Maryland.

Those who could vote rejected the Maryland constitution. Even diehard Radicals had serious doubts about it. They realized that if the Democrats ever regained power, they could turn the loyalty oaths against them and maintain their own form of one-party rule. But the Radicals in power had one more ace.

As was the case in New York, Maryland's soldiers were allowed to vote at the locations where they were stationed, even if out of state. This had never been legal before, due to the high probability of ballot tampering by the military commanders. The results were inevitable. The soldiers' vote converted defeat into victory: The constitution was now law and Maryland remained a militarized dictatorship until well beyond the end of the war.

Post-War Maryland

In 1866, the Union/Republican Party split into several factions over the issue of disenfranchisement of the "disloyal." Each wing held its own election convention. The Radicals lost the State Assembly. They appealed to the Radicals in the U.S. Congress for action to stop the rapid turnover of Maryland to the "rebels."

Nathan Haines of Carroll County implored Thaddeus Stevens, the leader of the Radicals in the U.S. House of Representatives, to prevent the calling of another constitutional convention. "I think Maryland needs military Reconstruction as badly as any Southern state, and I do not see any other way for us. I hope Congress will take us in hand...Give us manhood suffrage and we are safe. [This would include the blacks.] My dear friend, the safety of the nation, enjoins it upon Congress to make suffrage universal, to disqualify and impoverish traitors, and confine the ballot to the loyal only." [1]

Congressional interference in Maryland was exemplified in this manner: U.S. representative Ward, of New York, secured the passage of a resolution in the House, to the effect that in spite of disenfranchisement of "traitors and disloyalists" by the new Maryland constitution, it was alleged that in the last election for representatives in the 40th Congress, many disqualified persons had voted, aided by U.S. troops who interfered at the election on their behalf.

But there was still another way for Radicals in Congress to show that Maryland should be taken in hand. That method consisted of refusing to seat the choices of the "Rebel Legislature." This was shown when Senator Phillip Thomas, from Maryland, presented his credentials to Congress. A flaw had to be found in his personal life. He was charged with disloyalty, and thus would be unable to take the iron-clad oath. The reason for his exclusion: he had advanced money to his son to aid him in joining the Confederate army. In doing so, Thomas had aided the rebellion.

The New York *Times* bitterly ridiculed the Senate's attitude: "The whole thing dwindled down to the complaint that Mr. Thomas behaved kindly toward his son." [2]

The Senate judiciary Committee investigated, and on December 18, 1867, expressed no negative opinion against Thomas, preferring to lay the matter before the Senate. They reported it could "find nothing sufficient...to debar Mr. Thomas from taking his seat, unless it found [it] in the fact that the son of Mr. Thomas entered the military service of the Confederacy." [3]

The son, having been called before the Committee, explained that his father tried to dissuade him from going south but finally gave him the $100 to keep him from starving, and to buy a horse.

Mr. Thomas was still refused admission on the grounds of having aided the rebellion by giving his son the money.

The Maryland legislature protested vehemently against such an excuse for refusing Thomas, but in the end, elected William T. Hamilton, who was able to qualify.

Thereafter, once again, the New York *Times* editorialized about Thomas: "The cause of loyalty is more injured than helped by the refusal of the U.S. Senate to admit Mr. Thomas, after the report of the Judiciary Committee that no adequate cause exists for his exclusion. The zeal which brands a man with disloyalty because his opinions are not those of his accuser, may be fashionable in certain circles; but when it undertakes to make the difference a pretext for curtailing the choice of a State, and excluding one against whom no overt act

1. Maryland Historical Magazine, vol. xxviii, December 1933, no 4, p. 312
2. The *New York Times*, February 21, 1868.
3. Senate Report no. 5, 40th Congress , 2nd Session, p. 27

is alleged, it becomes a nuisance, from which the party tolerating it will be the heaviest sufferer." [1]

Thomas Swann, Next Governor of Maryland

From 1866 to 1869, Thomas Swann was governor. He was the last Republican to hold that office for years after the Civil War. He previously had been Baltimore's mayor for two terms. Swann was a Conservative.

Swann learned a lesson from what had happened to Phillip Thomas. During his term as governor he was elected to the United States Senate, but he made the decision to remain as governor because he would have been barred from the Senate, having been accused of purchasing Confederate Virginia bonds. As governor he had the power to appoint judges of elections. He selected reformers who would interpret the oaths and registry laws as liberally as possible to let more Marylanders vote. The Radicals called Swann a traitor.

1. The *New York Times*, February 21, 1868

Chapter 3. Oliver P. Morton, Indiana's War Governor: "I Am The State"

Far too little has been written about the astonishing events that took place in war-time Indiana, headed by the Republican governor Oliver P. Morton, a disciple and clone of Abraham Lincoln. Here the real face of Lincolnian ideology played out, in a dictatorship paralleling the absolutist monarchs of Old Europe but never before witnessed in the history of the Western hemisphere. The 20th century Nazis, Communists, South American dictators and 19th century Republicans had one-party rule, but Oliver P. Morton went much further; one-man rule. He could truthfully brag, "I am the State," a phrase not heard since Louis XIV of France. Morton was serious. He disbanded the State Assembly and the courts. He really was the State. He ruled alone.

Morton's governance included a concentration camp, aptly named Camp Morton, where Southern prisoners-of-war and political and civilian traitors were hurled, to be starved, frozen and shot to death.

His reign included the wide-spread use of the United States military to terrorize the population and close opposition newspapers and imprison their editors.

Whereas most Democrats and many Republicans sought ways to prevent the oncoming fratricide, or when war actually broke out, to create a negotiated peace, blood-thirsty Morton screamed in Lincoln's ear for war. He provided more Indiana troops than his quota required, hoping to ingratiate himself with the President, to prove his loyalty, and to bolster his political ambitions.

Oliver P. Morton refused to recognize the distinction between verbal or printed opposition to the war and criticism of Abraham Lincoln, which was completely legal and moral, and armed resistance to his unconstitutional one-man rule.

Morton's mania to incarcerate all "traitors" led to a Democratic counterattack to overthrow and assassinate him, which ultimately brought about the famed "Indianapolis Treason Trial." This engendered one of the most celebrated United States Supreme Court decisions: *Ex-Parte Milligan*. This trial and its consequences exposed to the nation the magnitude of civilians being convicted unconstitutionally by military tribunals.

Overview of Indiana's Pre-War History

Indiana was a fulcrum between the older industrialized East and the largely agricultural West and South. Pre-war Governor John Wright attributed Indiana's prosperity to its expanding railroad network. This was true of East–West commerce, but if he had looked to the southern section of the state, toward the Ohio River, he would have seen that his assertion was less than accurate. Here were large areas where the railroads had not penetrated, and where men's eyes looked further southward for their prosperity. In fact, there was a significant cleavage which loomed large in regional economic and political interests.

No region was more vitally interested in compromise and the preservation of the Union than southern Indiana. Inhabitants of the river counties felt a warmer friendship with their southern neighbors than they did with their fellow citizens who dwelt north of the National Road. Steamboats built in Evansville and New Albany sent food products down the rivers to the Deep South, and these riverboats returned with sugar, molasses and rice.

Jeffersonian Democrats dominated Indiana politics for years, and they idealized rural, agricultural virtues, yet a new ideal, one of smoke-belching factories and humming machines, was advancing. As it did, a new bonding, linking Indiana with the industrial East, began. The New Albany *Weekly Ledger* editorialized: "It will be a sorry day for the people of Indiana, when they sacrifice the friendship of their Southern neighbors for the cold and calculating Yankees and grasping Wall Street jobbers." [1]

Jeffersonianism also promoted free trade, but the rapidly rising Republican Party, with its constituent base in the industrialized Northeast, advocated Protectionism. Democrats correctly called this "protection for industry," and asked "isn't farm labor American industry?" They added, "Protection should be called discriminative legislation for the protection of manufacturing capital and labor." [2]

Gradually, Jeffersonian agricultural philosophy gave way to Radical 'Republican Industrialism. This changed the flow of commerce from North–

1. New Albany *Weekly Ledger*, August 20, 1856.
2. Kenneth stamp, "Indiana Politics During the Civil War," Indiana Historical Collections, Vol. xxxi. (Indianapolis: Indiana Historical Bureau, 1949) p.2. Bureau, 1949) P. 2.

South to East–West. High tariffs and nationalized banking created inflationary "greenbacks". Democrats said that this would lead to a Northern financial aristocracy, replacing the "slavocracy." Abolitionists had little support.

Indiana, before, and even during the early stages of the war, overwhelmingly opposed interference with the "peculiar institution." Republicans, when they met to choose delegates to the Indiana state convention of 1860, almost unanimously denounced interference with slavery in the Southern states and even advocated the doctrine of new states being able to choose slavery or not.

A local Republican convention at Dearborn, Indiana, resolved that the principle of state sovereignty was "as old as our government, and that the Republican Party, now as ever, is ready to stand and abide by it." [1]

With Abraham Lincoln's presidential victory in November 1860, and then the secession of the Deep South states, there followed a nation-wide commercial crisis which deeply affected Indianans, who were appalled by the absence of Southern trade and the dominance of the "fanatical abolitionists, and the canting hysterical New England states." [2]

Opponents of Lincoln's proposal to coerce the Confederacy back into the Union expressed their conciliatory views in scores of Indiana meetings which assembled during the winter months in almost every community. While Democrats predominated, it was not uncommon for Republicans to participate, and they called for a national convention to settle the differences between the "sections."

Yet, when the war began, and went on and on, with astronomical casualties, and horrifying defeats for the Northern armies, Indiana became increasingly aware that the conflict was reshaping the national philosophy and character. Americans were becoming a "different people," entering upon a "new stage of being." "Verily," exulted Indianas' Radical Republican George Julian, "the days of Conservatism, of State Sovereignty, are over, and the reign of Radicalism has been fairly ushered in." [3]

The sponsors of "Progress" welcomed the revolutionary results of a long, brutal war and pronounced them good. They pictured the conflict as a "refining ordeal" which would develop the "virtues of the American people... From the crucible of war and sacrifice of blood, would come the most perfect civilization that the world has ever seen." [4]

The war unleashed a contradiction of patriotism, avarice, idealism, cynicism, and the revolutionary centralization of political power. In time, the endless stream of mutilated men and coffins lining the walls of the Indianapolis railway depot, and the broken families, led the people to become habituated to all this.

1. Indianapolis *Daily Journal*, February 21, 1860
2. New Albany *Weekly Ledger*, November 21, 1860.
3. Centreville *Indiana True Republican*, June 11, 1863.
4. Indianapolis *Daily Journal*, June 28, 1864

Oliver P. Morton, War-Time Governor

At the 1860 Republican state convention in Indiana, the nominees for governor were Henry C. Lane and the 1856 candidate, Oliver P. Morton. A deal was made: Lane, while running for governor, would be elected to the United States Senate if the Republicans should gain control of the Indiana Assembly. Morton, who was to be the candidate for Lt. Governor, would then automatically become governor. And this is how, in fact, the scenario played out.

In November 1860, after Abraham Lincoln's presidential victory and the secession of the first Southern states, Morton began his rise toward dictatorial power due to the emotional chaos created in Indiana. The following quote is from a book that was favorable to Morton's tyrannical career and rationalized his crimes as "necessary."

> At this critical juncture in the affairs of Indiana Republicans, there appeared a political genius whose realistic mind clearly understood the party's quandary; whose strong will, matchless energy, and boundless ambition, eminently fit him for those revolutionary times. Oliver P. Morton's talents were scarcely appreciated by his contemporaries.
>
> At thirty-seven, his massive frame, rugged black-bearded countenance, piercing gray eyes, and deep sonorous voice, were already familiar to the leading barristers in Indiana. His law practice afforded him a comfortable income. But since 1854, he had abandoned the Democrats to join the Fusionists [a merging of Whigs, Republicans and Democrats]. He had always been an opportunist and never hesitated to shift his views, as the occasion required.
>
> His prime concern was to discover some common ground upon which his Republican Party could make a united stand. As he watched developments in November 1860, he soon perceived, in the disillusion of the Union, the long hoped-for key issue. Accordingly, he boldly scorned the appeasers in his party and quickly took command of those who would make no concession to treason. ["Treason" was a term reserved for those Republicans and Democrats who hoped for a negotiated peaceful solution to secession.]
>
> Morton's first opportunity to express his views came on the night of November 22, 1860, when he addressed the "Lincoln Rail Maulers" gathered in Indianapolis to rejoice over Lincoln's presidential victory. Slowly and deliberately Morton unfolded his position in blunt language. Denying the right of secession, except by successful revolution, he affirmed that coercion was simply the enforcement of the law. Once the right of secession was granted, the nation would be dissolved.

> The West, he insisted, had more at stake in the preservation of the Union, than any other section. It stood in danger of being "shut up" in the interior of the continent, surrounded by independent, perhaps hostile nations, through whose territories Indianans could obtain egress to the seaboard, only by such terms as might be agreed upon by treaty. Shall we now surrender the nation without a struggle, and let the Union go with merely a few harsh words? If it was worth a bloody struggle to establish this nation, it is worth one to preserve it.[1]

Morton's coercionist Republicans stigmatized Democrats as the allies of "traitors." To block peace efforts, Mortonites sponsored scores of prewar meetings. This defeated the peace-makers. Oliver P. Morton began his Executive career as a war governor but Indiana was nearly bankrupt. It had no funds for a massive military build-up. Initially private citizens provided emergency funds.

Even at this early stage, Morton showed his propensity for leading the state with no political opposition. He called the Assembly for a special session and said: "Let us inaugurate the era where there shall be one party; and that, for our country."[2]

The legislature authorized the issuing of State bonds to borrow four million dollars to buy arms, to call up the militia, and "enlist and maintain troops."

Morton did send representatives to a last-ditch peace conference in Washington, as a ploy to allow his opponents to believe he was interested in a peaceful solution. Of course he was not. He informed his delegates that they should "procrastinate." One Indiana delegate admitted, "the principle good of the conference, on the part of the North, was the postponement of hostilities until after the inauguration of Abraham Lincoln." Thus the Indiana delegation defeated every significant effort at compromise.[3]

January 11, 1861: President-elect Lincoln came to Indianapolis to speak just before his inauguration. Morton spoke first. He tried to draw Lincoln out about the crisis by pledging total support. Lincoln's impromptu words were cautious and evasive. He referred to himself as a "mere instrument... of a great cause," and suggested that national salvation required only the "heart of a people like yours."[4]

Later that day, Lincoln delivered a prepared speech. Now his words were filled with ominous meaning. He asked whether holding the forts and other federal property in the South by the United States army would constitute invasion or coercion; and from what source came the right of a state, a small

1. Indianapolis *Daily Journal*, November 22, 1860.
2. Ibid., April 26, 1861.
3. Autobiography of noted pioneer, *Indiana Magazine of History* 10, March 1914, p. 70.
4. Kenneth Stampp, p. 67.

part of the whole, to break up the nation, and play tyrant over the rest. He implied there was an important difference between "coercing" of a foreign State and "enforcing the law."[1]

Immediately afterward Morton prepared for war, since it was clear now that it was inevitable. Men began to volunteer for the state militia in case of a federal call-up. Morton went to Washington and pledged 6,000 soldiers, although Indiana's quota was only 4,000.

April 12: The firing on Ft. Sumter. Morton went even further and supplied 10,000 men for federal service. Once again, this was to impress Abraham Lincoln with his commitment to the President. Morton believed that the war would be short and this would be the last call-up, but with the shocking defeat at Bull Run, and later the near annihilation of the Union armies as they failed to take Richmond, Lincoln required hundreds of thousands of additional troops. The Republican newspaper, the Indianapolis *Daily Journal*, editorialized: "There is a universal feeling of despondency, not to say discouragement."[2]

Morton wrote Lincoln: "I trust this is the last call-up to complete the crushing out of the present rebellion."[3]

Soon, recruiting offices came under attack by civilians. Morton called the attackers "traitors" and said that Indiana had reached the brink of revolution.

Lincoln and Morton Compared

The following description of both men is from the same pro-Morton biography previously quoted:

> Oliver P. Morton was brought up by old-fashioned Scotch Presbyterian aunts until he was fifteen years old. He was strong, earnest, logical, reading widely, and devouring the Bible along the way; revolting from the narrow religious cults then prevailing, and becoming an independent, as indicated by the well-known term, "non-professor." At some sacrifice, being intensely studious, he obtained a legal education, even attending school after his marriage. Morton was eloquent by his strength; a powerful and successful advocate...Of unflinching courage and energy, skillful in handling men, and above all, clearly a natural chieftain in the crisis.
>
> By contrast, Abraham Lincoln learned by heart six books, and these included Euclid, who furnished his penetrating and overwhelming logic. Not one, not even Webster, exceeded him in the grasp of a perplexing question and lucid power of statement. Morton, on the other hand, had the advantage of schools, substantially good, and their culture.

1. Indianapolis *Daily Journal*, February 12, 1861
2. Ibid, November 5, 1862.
3. Ibid, June 25, 1862.

> It is strange, that Lincoln and Morton bred virtually the same way, although Morton was more favored in education, should have differed so much in their conceptions of the constant power required to subdue a rebellion. Morton, in himself, by his own superior foresight, and tremendous executive energy, had the power of the occasion.
>
> The minds of these men differed, and Morton's method was cyclopedic. A voracious reader, he was fully armed, and could shatter his opponents position with a single stroke. His own argument was not so succinct. He gathered material in heaps, and did not build up a case in architectural development. Although the matter was exhausted when he finished an argument, he did not leave the hearer entertaining a new and positive thing, an actual creation in place of antecedent matter.
>
> This engrossment in his subject reveals a strong phase of his character. He was not self-conscious, but was absorbed in the work of the moment, in the doing, and not standing without exploiting the matter, for statement or otherwise. This faculty made him the great executive that he was; and if Abraham Lincoln had something of the Napoleonic power of action, it would have been a great boon to the American Executive.
>
> President Lincoln, instead of doing the matter simply, generally stood outside when he was making a case, which he handled before the American people, in a masterly manner. Sincere in patriotic intent, he hardly ever lost himself in the force of creative action, whether maneuvering for a contention or lying plans for Congressional legislation. In the largest executive sense, the creative spirit, immanent crisis, did not enter into him and would mold him to the work. Morton said, to an immense multitude, on January 22, 1861: "I am not here to argue questions of state equality, but to denounce treason and uphold the cause of the Union."

Oliver P. Morton wrote one of the chapters of this biography, entitled "I am the State," proclaiming to the world the true vision of his supreme power.[1]

Morton Fuses Military with Politics for Dictatorship

Oliver P. Morton was blunt, ruthless, and completely lacking a sense of humor. He refused to tolerate opposition and harassed his critics to complete distraction. Publicly, he spurned politics, but quietly created a Republican machine under his complete control. Those Republicans out of favor made violent attacks against Morton and his nest "of political speculators in

1. William Dudley Foulke, *Life of Oliver P. Morton* (Indianapolis: the Bowen-Morrill Co. 1899) vol. 2, p. 252.

Indianapolis." Morton's puppets made the citizens believe that he was the only one in government who did anything to save Indiana.

Many politicians hoped to become officers in the army, to advance their governmental careers, but Morton never forgot his Republican enemies. With few exceptions, he barred them from the military since he alone had the power of appointment. He prevented others from securing high-ranking offices from President Lincoln. Such appointments, Morton explained, "would be mortifying to me and regarded as an endorsement of their course." [1]

Morton himself requested from Lincoln a high military command, which demonstrated the ego-mania that inflated his sense of his own importance and Indiana's significance as to the outcome of the war. To Oliver P. Morton, the Indiana–Kentucky border was the main theatre of the entire war. Every day he passed on intelligence reports to the President on Confederate military movements. Lincoln's replies were patronizing and calculated to drive the humorless Morton into a fury.

Morton had continual disputes with federal officials, both military and civilian. Beneath the surface, his anger was attributable to an undercurrent of inter-state jealousy and sectional prejudice. He carefully watched other governors to make sure that none of the others ever obtained an advantage from Lincoln or the War Department. One of his main rages came from the belief that the federal government accepted a disproportionately high number of generals from Ohio regiments. "Why this great discrimination?" Morton asked Secretary of the Interior Smith. "Will you not see that justice is done for Indiana?" [2]

In addition, Morton objected to Lincoln that Indiana did not have a single Major-General, and not a fair proportion of Brigadier-Generals. He persuaded the President to accept six additional Indiana brigadiers. That resulted in the governor of Illinois protesting that too many generals came from Indiana! A bitter debate ensued as to which state had been the most neglected in that respect.

Then Morton criticized the Eastern states for not filling their military quotas as swiftly as Indiana. "Where is the patriotism of the East as compared with the West?" [3]

In February 1862, the capture of Fort Henry and Fort Donnellson by Ulysses S. Grant's Western Army marked the Union's first decisive victory. Morton glowed with pride in his deluded belief that the West alone had the zeal to prosecute the war successfully.

1. Kenneth Stampp, p. 86.
2. "Morton to Smith," May 24, 1861, from "Telegraphic Communication,"I:54
3. Indianapolis *Daily Journal*, November 1, 1861

Events Leading to "I Am the State"

Before Abraham Lincoln ordered a national draft, which would cause insurrections throughout the North, the President put into law the involuntary call-up of each state's militias. Indiana inducted 3,000 men into the national army this way, but this caused a major backlash; violent resistance, and more significantly, the Democrats won substantial victories in both Houses of the Indiana Assembly in the fall of 1862.

With the Republican loss of power, Oliver P. Morton became more emotionally unbalanced and saw treason everywhere and expected a revolution at any moment. At the beginning of 1863, Indiana's Democrats voted for peace negotiations with the Confederacy.

Simultaneously, many Republican army officers appointed by Morton resigned their commissions over Abram Lincoln's Emancipation Proclamation and the governor's support of this document which would destroy state sovereignty. Army recruitments dropped alarmingly. Desertions increased.

Morton was unwilling to attribute these events to disillusionment with his policies. Instead he blamed "organized conspirators," meaning Democrats. Under his orders, Indiana soldiers threatened Senator Thomas Hendricks and Daniel Voorhees, both leading Democrats. Then these troops destroyed Democratic newspapers in Rockport and Terra Haute.

Morton's minions openly accused the Democrats of abject surrender to the Confederacy. "This is no longer a secret, confined to the dark lantern halls of the conclaves of midnight assassins, but is openly advocated, talked of, and hinted, in public places and meetings, in the streets, in the Tory organs of the public press." [1]

January 8, 1863: Amidst military failures and malignant partisanship, the Indiana legislature began its bi-annual session. Hysteria ruled. Rumors circulated that the "traitors" waited expectantly to seize the state arsenal, free Southern prisoners-of-war, depose Morton, to take Indiana out of the war.

Morton telegraphed Secretary of War Stanton that the legislature intended to recognize the Confederacy, implying that the federal army's interference was required to arrest the "traitors" in the Assembly, as was done in Maryland.

At the opening of the legislative session, Morton was scheduled to deliver his annual message. The Democrats refused to let him do this. This created political instability. The next day Morton made another attempt to speak. Again, he was blocked. He countered by printing his speech and delivered it to the Assembly. The Democratic Speaker of the House declared that this was unconstitutional. The printed address was returned. This meant that the legislature could not act on Morton's proposals.

1. Indianapolis *Gazette*, December 11, 1862

These conflicts led to a complete disruption of the Assembly and a breakdown of constitutional government, but the situation escalated much further, and ended with a form of Absolutism, as Morton proclaimed with pride, "I am the State."

This extraordinary situation took shape as the Democratic majority went to the next step and sponsored a bill to create an Executive Council composed of the Secretary of State, the State Auditor, and Attorney-General to curb Morton's political monopoly over the selection of Indiana's military officers who would be incorporated into the U.S. army.

The bill provided for the election of company and regimental officers by the rank and-file-soldiers themselves and not by Morton. Brigadier and Major-Generals would be commissioned by the governor but also through the recommendation of the Executive Council. This was already confirmed by Indiana's constitution, but Morton had over-ridden it. Now the governor would lose most of his patronage and control over the military.

Later, Morton wrote in his biography:

> I could have vetoed it, but under the constitution of Indiana, a mere majority can pass a bill over a veto. Every hour that the bill was pending, it endangered the peace of the State. It would cause alarm throughout all the loyal states, and excite the most intense interest on the part of the federal government. I knew that if the bill passed, I could not afford to surrender my authority as governor. I had taken an oath to administer my office according to the constitution, and I knew that the government of the United States would be bound to sustain me. I knew I could hold my position, but it would involve the state in civil war, and our people would be cutting each other's throat, in every county. I knew there was but one way to prevent the passage of the bill; and this was to break up the legislature. Better that the state should be impoverished and unprovided for; that the criminals, the insane, the blind, the deaf and dumb, should be turned out upon the highways than, under the control of the sympathizers of secession, and Indiana should become an ally of the Confederacy. But the operation of the state should not stop if I could help it. I would risk all to keep it going. The Republican members were determined to withdraw from the House. They did not commit the folly of resignation, so that they would not be counted in making a quorum, but quickly got on the train, and went to Madison [Indiana] where they could not be readily arrested. Thus the legislature came to an end. The passage of the bill was defeated. [1]

Now Morton would administer the state all alone. His first problem was to secure the money to rule as a tyrant for the next two years. From

1. William Dudley Foulke, vol 2 , p. 252.

this point on, Oliver P. Morton ignored the constitution and all law and resorted to a number of illegal schemes to obtain money.

He went to Washington, and with Abraham Lincoln's approval collected $90,000 "for ammunition for the state arsenal." The Republican Indiana *State Journal* triumphantly announced that this money would really be used to carry on the functions of the government.

The Democrats insisted that the funds must be placed in the State Treasury; if not, Morton could be convicted under Indiana's embezzlement laws. Morton accepted the risk and refused to surrender the money, and continued to operate the government as if it was his private enterprise.

Governor Morton quickly exhausted these funds. He appealed to sympathetic citizens and Republican county officials. This resulted in another $150,000 in "donations." Still, this was not enough.

Once again he met with Abraham Lincoln, and the President referred him to Secretary of War Stanton. Morton now laid out his financial troubles before the Secretary and asked for his help. The governor told Stanton that Lincoln said that he knew of no law by which he could aid Morton. Stanton replied: "By God, I will find such a law," and he did. An appropriation of 2.3 million dollars had been made by Congress in July 1862 to be expended by the President "to loyal citizens threatened with rebellion," and in organizing such citizens for their own protection against domestic insurrection. (By 21st-century standards, this sum was more like 2.3 billion dollars.)

Stanton laid out the matter before Lincoln, and the President issued an order that the money was to be advanced to Morton, for which the governor was to be held accountable.

When Stanton placed this order in Morton's hands, both men appreciated the great risk they were taking. "If the cause fails, we shall both be covered in prosecutions," Morton said. Stanton replied: "If the cause fails, I do not wish to live." Morton was of the same mind. He took the order and departed. [1]

Realizing that he could not put this immense amount of money in the State Treasury, Morton created his own financial department and kept the funds in a safe on his desk.

Democrats cried out that Morton's delusional Napoleonic ambition had created a personal dictatorship. They recognized that when he said, "I am the State," it was the truth.

Milo Hascall: Morton's Press Dictator

May 5th, 1863, five o'clock in the morning: Dan Van Valkenburg, editor of the Plymouth, Indiana Weekly Democrat, was awakened by the sound of soldiers breaking down the door to his home. Twelve of them entered, forced

1. Ibid., p. 253.

him to dress, and conveyed him to Indianapolis, where he was confronted by Brigadier-General Milo Smith Hascall, the commander of the District of Indiana. Van Valkenburg faced charges of being a traitor and giving aid and comfort to the enemy, because of an editorial he had written in his newspaper. On April 30 he denounced Hascall's "Order No. 9," which stated that any newspaper or public speaker who gave encouragement to those who would resist the "Enrollment Act" (the military conscription law) or any law of Congress which passed as a "war measure" or that endeavored to bring the war policy of the Lincoln administration "into dispute," would be treated as a traitor, and subject to a trial within a military tribunal. Newspaper editors faced suppression or permanent closing if Hascall deemed that their content was disloyal.

The following is Van Valkenburg's editorial which brought on his arrest:

> Brigadier-General Hascall is a donkey; an unmitigated, unqualified donkey, and his bray is long, loud and harmless, merely offensive to the ear. It merely tends to create a temporary irritation... Will Brigadier-General Hascall please inform us why the citizens of Illinois or Kentucky, sister states, are permitted to express their minds freely, and the citizens of Indiana alone are selected for this abject submission. [1]

Van Valkenburg was one of the few lucky Democratic editors who got off easy. From Indianapolis he was taken to Cincinnati, where Major-General Ambrose Burnside, commander of the Department of the Ohio, who was Hascall's superior officer, was informed of his "traitorous editorial." Burnside simply said: "Be more careful in the future as to the manner in which you criticize those in authority." [2]

Burnside had previously been commanding General of the Army of the Potomac. He replaced McClellan after the slaughter at Antietam. But Burnside, a native of Indiana, was in turn humiliated and deposed after he led the disastrous defeat at Fredericksburg. He was reassigned to a desk job as commander of the federal army's "shadow government" in the Midwestern states.

Other opposition editors were not so fortunate as Van Valkenburg. During his brief two month career as press censor for Oliver P. Morton, Hascall closed twelve Democratic newspapers. In several instances he imprisoned the editors in the infamous and aptly named Camp Morton. The prison supposedly held only prisoners of war.

Based on the policies of General Burnside and Governor Morton, Hascall by-passed the First Amendment without hesitation, suspending or shutting

1. Plymouth, Indiana *Weekly Democrat,* April, 30, 1863.
2. Deniel McDonald, "History of Marshall County", Indiana, p. 394

down newspapers by invoking President Lincoln's "privilege to suspend the Writ of Habeas Corpus during times of extreme political emergency." [1]

Thus the President, his military subordinates, and Morton interpreted primary right of freedom of the press as being subject to extra-legal restraints. But the United States Constitution does not say that freedom of the press depends on circumstances.

Indiana's Democratic editors argued that civilian authority had supremacy over the military because war was not taking place in their state. They also pointed out that Thomas Jefferson believed that a free press served as a watchdog over government, to keep it accountable.

Most significantly, the time period when most of the press censorship took place was when the Democrats were making major political gains. Press suppression did not only take place in Indiana. Nationally, over 300 periodicals were closed; all Democratic. In Indiana alone, during the entire length of the war, 69 were suspended.

Milo Hascall had tried several professions before he settled in Goshen, Indiana, in 1847. He was a West Point graduate and a self-taught lawyer. Nothing in his past suggested that he would become infamous by trampling upon journalists rights to print what they pleased. One of his brothers had been a newspaper editor, and would be again, after the war.

Hascall was born in LeRoy, New York, in 1829, but the town was economically depressed and the family migrated to Elkhart County, Indiana, when he was nineteen. Hascall worked in a general store owned by his brother Chauncy. In 1848 Hascall was nominated by a Democratic Congressman to West Point.

Among his classmates were the future Union army general and grandson of John C. Calhoun. Hascall was in the top third of his graduating class. Unfortunately, there were few opportunities for advancement in the peacetime army, so he resigned in 1853, and returned to Goshen. Once again he worked in his brother's store. Then, step by step, he became a teacher, an attorney, district attorney, and country clerk of courts, then he joined the Republican Party and was elected Elkhart Country clerk.

Elkhart County shifted from Democratic to Republican in the late 1850s and Hascall, showing his opportunistic disposition, rode that tide. Then the war broke out. He volunteered for the army, created the 17th Volunteer Regiment, and with his West Point background quickly moved up the ranks.

Late in 1861, a colonel. By the end of that year, commander of a brigade. April 1862, he fought at Shiloh and was promoted to Brigadier-General. Then he commanded a full division.

1. Thomas M. Bulla, *Lincoln's Censor: Milo Hascall and Freedom of the Press in Indiana*" (West Lafayette, Indiana: Purdue University Press, 2008) p. 2.

Then his duties shifted. In the spring of 1863 he was responsible for tracking down deserters as Commander of the District of Indiana. And from May to June he closed twelve Democratic newspapers in the northern two thirds of Indiana.

During this time period Hascall did much more than close opposition press. As a military commander with a long battle record, he used the Union army to terrorize Democrats and all other opponents of the Lincoln/Morton regime. As an example, on May 20, 1863, Indiana's Democrats assembled in Indianapolis for a convention. This brought on one of the state's most dramatic experiences with war-time violence and military control.

Both Hascall and Morton were alarmed by the rumor that the secret society, The Knights of the Golden Circle, planned to convert the convention into a military uprising. Hascall mobilized all available infantry, cavalry, and artillery, placing Indianapolis on a war footing. Cannon covered all the main streets.

Democratic leader Daniel V. Voorhees was President of the convention. He denounced the ever-increasing use of military force and demanded free speech. "I may, at this moment, be talking myself into prison by uttering these ancient sentiments of liberty." [1]

The first violence occurred when troops rushed the speakers' platform and stopped a speech. Over the next four hours, soldiers and citizens engaged in numerous battles. Many Democrats were arrested.

Democratic Senator Thomas Hendricks (future Vice President under Grover Cleveland) began his speech as soldiers advanced on him with fixed bayonets. Cavalry clattered along the streets. Hendricks was actually able to finish his speech despite the chaos.

The Indianapolis *Daily State Journal* commented: "Indiana today is completely under military rule, as in France, Russia, or Austria. A large portion of the people are willingly bowing their necks to receive the yoke of despotism." [2]

Milo Hascall attacked editors primarily in the northern parts of the state; all near his home town of Goshen. He felt he could intimidate Democratic editors from Plymouth, South Bend, Warsaw, Bluffton, Columbia City, Winimac, Huntington, Rushville, Hartford City, Franklin and Knox. This was because he was intimate with the Republican political leaders in these towns. Hascall bypassed Democratic editors in that area's largest city: Fort Wayne. Here, the Democrats were stronger and more sophisticated. Neither did he threaten their editors in Indianapolis, who were equally split. The Republicans held the Executive branch (Morton) of government. The Democrats held the legislature.

1. Kenneth Stampp, p. 199.
2. Indianapolis *Daily State Journal*, May 21, 1863

Although the Republican press defended Hascall's conduct, Governor Morton soon had enough of him. He petitioned for his removal. His motivation was not because Hascall was too brutal. Quite the contrary. Morton wanted to be more in control of the terror tactics. Hascall's loyalty was to the U.S. army and the Lincoln administration. Morton wanted someone who would be totally loyal to him alone. With Hascall in place, General Burnside was also meddling in Indiana's internal affairs.

Camp Morton

In April 1861, shortly after the firing on Fort Sumter, Governor Morton and General Lew Wallace surveyed the State Fair grounds on the outskirts of Indianapolis and determined that it was a good location to construct a military camp where new recruits for the war could be housed and trained before going into combat. Soon, other training facilities were built and Camp Morton was abandoned.

February 1862: With the capture of the Confederate Forts Henry and Donelson, and the taking of a large number of Southern prisoners, Union General Henry Halleck telegraphed Oliver P. Morton to convert the now unused Camp Morton to hold POWs. More barracks were erected. Within days, 3,700 prisoners arrived. By April, 5,000 inmates. By May, 6,500 as a result of the battle at Shiloh.

Not all of the inmates were combatants. Like at Elmira, New York, many were "traitors," those who had the audacity to criticize Morton or President Lincoln.

Morton appointed Colonel Richard Owen as the Commandant of the camp. Even before he arrived, most of the prisoners were either wounded, sick or dying. Most did not have the basic warm clothing for the harsh Indiana winter. Many quickly died.

Colonel Owen was a good administrator, and he tried to make the prison as tolerable as possible, but he did not have the resources or authority to provide winter garments. Owen said that his goal was "to make [the prisoners] less restless in their confinement, and likely, when they return to their homes, to spread among their friends and acquaintances the news that they had been deceived regarding [the character] of Northern men."

Expressing how he felt the camp should be run, Colonel Owen said: "Every endeavor, will be made by the Commandant to give each and every prisoner as much liberty and comfort as is consistent with orders received and with an equal distribution of the means at disposal, provided that such indulgence never leads to any abuse of the privileges ." [1]

1. Hattie Lou Winslow and Joseph R. H. Moore, "Camp Morton, 1861-1865" (Indianapolis: Indiana Historical Society), 1940, p. 15

Colonel Owen allowed the prisoners to obtain clothing and food from home, but the townspeople complained to the governor that his rules were too liberal. Morton cracked down and forbade any aid to enter the camp.

Oliver P. Morton went further; he sacked Owen and replaced him with Colonel David Garland Rose, who hated Southerners and "traitors." He proved to be a cruel and vindictive commandant, but because a prisoner exchange program went into effect in August 1862, Camp Morton emptied out again and Rose was transferred to another assignment. The camp was not deserted for long. The prisoner exchange broke down, and in January 1863, a new wave of POWs flooded the facility.

As was described concerning Elmira, New York, prisoner exchange was abandoned when Lincoln realized that the war was being prolonged by soldiers returning to the Confederacy's ranks.

Now there was another commandant: Colonel James Biddle. He had the same vindictive attitude as David Garland Rose.

John Wyeth, A POW, Reveals Truth about Camp Morton

From the 19th-century war-time period to the 21st century, Indiana historians, government officials, and military leaders have boasted that the prisoners at Camp Morton were well treated, in sharp contrast to the inhuman conditions in Southern internment camps like Andersonville in Georgia.

Camp Morton had been portrayed as a shining model of Christian virtue. That illusion was shattered in April 1891, a quarter century after the Civil War ended. At that point in time a prominent physician, Dr. John A. Wyeth, wrote of his experiences there, in an article in *Century Monthly Magazine.* His story caused a storm of controversy as he presented Camp Morton as a hell of pain, suffering, brutality, and murder. Far from its former image as a kind of Waldorf Astoria of POW camps, Camp Morton was, in fact, where Southern soldiers desperately struggled to survive with little protection against the brutally cold winter weather and searing summer heat. It was a place where the inmates were beaten, tortured, shot, and denied proper food and medical treatment.

Dr. Wyeth was finally motivated to write about his experiences at a time when Northern propaganda pictured conditions in Southern prisons as inhuman, while ignoring the reality of their awn. His article was entitled, "Cold Cheer At Camp Morton."

Twenty-first century historian Bradley Omanson wrote: "Wyeth made it clear, for the first time, how conditions in Northern prisons, particularly at Camp Morton and Elmira, were as inhuman as those in Andersonville." [1]

Wyeth joined the Southern cause in the spring of 1862 when he volunteered for Quirk's Scouts, the advance guard of John Hunt Morgan's Confederate

1. Bradley Omanson, "The Long March of John Wyeth," February 2004, www.worldwarI.com.

Raiders. Quirk thought that the 17-year-old Wyeth was too immature to fight and refused his enlistment, yet allowed him to ride along. A summer of skirmishes matured "Young Johnny."

In October 1862, after months of scouting in central Tennessee, Wyeth, now a bona fide private in Colonel Russell's 4th Alabama Cavalry Regiment, found himself face-to-face with a company of Union cavalry. He was taken prisoner and shipped by train to Camp Morton, and incarcerated for sixteen months.

Wyeth: "I arrived there about ten o'clock at night. No provision had been made for us. We slept, or tried to sleep, through the cold night, in the open air and upon the ground."

Wyeth came to Camp Morton with a developing case of pneumonia, and after a long delay, while the hospital staff waited for others to die, he was finally admitted to the tent that served as a hospital. He survived while a multitude of other sick men died.

Weather conditions during that winter were severe in Indiana. On New Year's day: 20 below zero. A furious snow storm nearly buried Indianapolis. Wyeth said this about the barracks:

> There were wide cracks through which the wind whistled and snow beat upon us. I have often seen my blanket with snow on it when we were hustled out for morning roll call. About two feet of space was given to each man, making about 329 men housed in each shed. As we had no straw for bedding, and men allowed only one blanket, there was little comfort until our miseries were forgotten in sleep. The scarcity of blankets forced us to huddle together, three in a group, with one blanket between us." [1]

There were four stoves in the barracks, but Wyeth said that only the strongest and most aggressive prisoners, those ready and willing to fight their comrades for warmth, could get close enough to gain any benefit. Wyeth wrote:

> To men, the greater number of which had never seen a cold climate, the suffering was intense, when, with such surroundings, the mercury was near zero. A number of prisoners were frozen to death, and many more perished from disease brought on by exposure, added to their condition of emaciation, from the lack of food. I counted eighteen bodies carried out to the dead house one morning, after an intensely cold night. [2]
>
> . . . I know from personal observation that many of my comrades died from starvation. Day after day it was easy to observe the progress of emaciation, until they became so weak, that when attacked with an

1. James R. Hall, "Den of Misery" (Gretna, Pelican Publishing Co., 2006) p. 58.
2. Ibid., p. 58

> illness, which a well-nourished man would have easily resisted, and recovered from, they rapidly succumbed. The entire ration for one day was not enough for a single meal. [1]
>
> The meat rations were often supplemented by harvesting the camp's rat population, and any other living creature, even dogs and cats that happened to venture too close to the prison quarters. Wyeth: "One fat canine was captured by my messmates and was considered a feast. It was boiled and then baked, and I was invited to the dinner. Although the scent of the cooking meat was tempting, I could not overcome my repugnance of this animal, as an article of diet, as to taste it. Those who ate it, expressed themselves as delighted." [2]

Starvation was not the most disturbing aspect of Wyeth's account. A pattern of cruel and blatant physical abuse and even cold blooded murder emerges. One prisoner was shot because he left the ranks after roll call was ended, before the official "break ranks" was commanded. The prisoner was freezing and simply wanted to warm himself at a fire a few feet away. "The guard did not even order the man back to the ranks, but calmly drew his pistol, saying with profanity, 'I'll show you how to leave ranks before you're dismissed,' and deliberately shot him." [3]

On many occasions Wyeth saw prisoners brutally beaten with clubs because they would not move quickly out of the way of a guard or quit talking when an officer passed by. For this offense, Wyeth once witnessed an officer grabs stick of firewood and bludgeon several prisoners on the head, leaving them lying on the ground, unconscious.

Prisoners were regularly required, as punishment, to "mark time" in deep snow, for more than an hour. Wyeth learned that one man lost both of his feet to gangrene as a result of the exposure and later died.

Wyeth wrote that another frequent evening activity practiced by some guards was firing shots into the prisoners' barracks, for no logical reason than sadism. They often hit inmates, wounding or killing them.

Another prisoner, Mitchell B. Houghton, wrote that "slow starvation among a lot of idle men gradually robs them of noble instincts, and transforms them into weak but ravenous beasts. It was curious but tragic to hear prisoners recount the story, daily and hourly, of former feasts, and revive the memory of every ample dinner they had enjoyed in the past...Food became passion, a frenzy, and men only existed to remember what had been." [4]

1. Ibid., p. 60.
2. Ibid., p. 60.
3. Ibid., p. 61.
4. W.R. Houghton and M.B. Houghton, "Two Boys in the Civil War and After," 1912, p. 82.

The Plan to Free POWs and Assassinate Oliver P. Morton

One-man rule, the incarceration of "traitors" in Camp Morton, the terrorizing of citizens by the military, all led to an underground counter-movement to assassinate Oliver P. Morton, release the prisoners and return Indiana to democratic government.

Soon it became evident to Governor Morton that he had a serious insurrection on his hands. The first sign of this was the rise of two secret political organizations: The Knights of the Golden Circle, and the Sons of Liberty.

Democratic secret organizations came into existence in the face of a national clandestine group which was aligned with the United States army: The Union League. Its purpose, from the perspective of anti-Lincoln citizens, was to strengthen the already tyrannical federal government. This led to more than open protests: opposition secret groups based on the Union League model, which were censored for "giving aid and comfort to the enemy."

The Union League proponents believed that organization was intended to protect communities against Democratic secret societies, but the over-zealous partisan spirit of Union League members led to physical violence and murder, inflicted upon Democrats simply because they were Democrats.

The Knights of the Golden Circle and the Sons of Liberty's membership were not limited to Indiana. They were national in scope: in California, New York, Connecticut, New Jersey, Maryland, Delaware, and Pennsylvania.

Clement Vallandigham, a Democratic Congressman from Ohio who had been convicted and deported into the Confederacy by a military tribunal under Lincoln's orders, because of a speech he made attacking the President, was an officer in the Sons of Liberty.

Vallandigham estimated that its total membership was 300,000; 85,000 in Illinois, 50,000 in Indiana, and 40,000 in Ohio. [1]

In June 1861, Oliver P. Morton made his first move against the anti-Republican secret societies when he sent spies to infiltrate the Knights of the Golden Circle. When they reported that military drills were being conducted, the leaders were arrested in May 1862.

With the help of Governor Morton, the Grand Jury examined numerous witnesses and returned many indictments for treason and conspiracy. Its report included a sensational exposé of the "disloyal activities of the Knights of the Golden Circle" and an elaborate description of the society's organization.

In actuality, these jurors had done little more than accept all the current rumors and therefore revealed their own gullibility or possible collusion with the governor. This is confirmed by the report being immediately reprinted

1. *The Southern Bivouac* (Athens, Georgia: University of Georgia Press 2011) vol. 2, p 206. Also see John Chodes, "The Union League: Washington's Ku Klux Klan" (Tuscaloosa, AL: The League of the South Institute for the Study of Southern Culture and History, 1999)

in a Republican Party campaign publication. Its assertion that loyal soldiers were to be "treacherously betrayed in the bloody hour of battle" formed a lurid phrase for campaign oratory. But the reality was that Indiana Democrats were eminently loyal.

The Grand Jury report sounded like it had been written by Morton: "Said Grand Jury has abundant evidence that the membership of the Knights of the Golden Circle banded themselves to resist the payment of the federal tax and to prevent the enlistment in the Army of the United States. In localities where the organization extensively prevails, there has been a failure to furnish a fair proportion of volunteers. The meetings of the Order are held in by-places, sometimes in the woods, and at other times in deserted houses. Its members frequently attend with arms in their hands, and in almost every instance, armed sentinels are posted to keep off intruders. The credulous and unwary are often allowed into the fold of the Order, upon the pretext that it was instituted for no other purpose than the better organization of the Democratic Party." [1]

Sixty indictments were returned; sixteen for treason, eighteen for conspiring to take and possess the property of the United States, and thirteen for conspiring to defeat the operations of the law.

On February 23, 1863, Governor Morton, while speaking in Cincinnati, informed the audience that the 109th Illinois Regiment had recently been disbanded by General Grant because it had been infiltrated by the Knights of the Golden Circle. Morton added that several Indiana regiments were also under its influence.

Colonel Henry B. Carrington, mustering officer for Indiana, and the same officer that Hascall had replaced, reported in a dispatch to Brigadier-General Lorenzo Thomas, Adjutant-General of the U.S. Army, that 2,600 deserters had been arrested, and true to the code of the Knights of the Golden Circle, deserted with their weapons. Carrington said that the Knights' code required the protection of deserters, resisting conscription as a way of stopping the war.

A commission activated by Morton reported that a state of anarchy existed in several Indiana counties as a result of activities by the Knights, and that men all over the southern half of the state were armed against the government.

In Washington County, where the Knights' presence was unusually strong, the slightest rumor of their movement led Republican sympathizers to barricade their homes or flee to safer adjoining counties.

When Abraham Lincoln asserted that the federal government had the right and the power to conscript troops — over the authority of the states — enrolling officers were killed, draft boxes and enrollment papers burned,

1. Mayo Fesler, "Secret Political Societies in the North During the Civil War" (*Indiana Magazine of History*, Vol. xiv, September 1918, no. 3) p. 202.

and committees organized by the Knights of the Golden Circle and the Sons of Liberty to protect men who resisted the draft.

The Order of the American Knights, founded by lawyer Phineas Wright, superseded the Knights of the Golden Circle and was responsible for transforming the American Knights into the Sons of Liberty. Wright's pledge stated: "Whenever the chosen rulers...shall fail or refuse to administer the government in strict accordance with the letter of the established and accepted compact, constitution, or ordinance, it is the inherent right to resist the usurpations of the functionaries, and if need be, expel them by force of arms." [1]

When the Order of American Knights became the Sons of Liberty in Indiana, the Grand Commander was H.H. Dodd. Later he would gain national attention, along with Lambden Milligan, in the infamous "Indiana Treason Trial." This led to the landmark United States Supreme Court ruling against civilians being tried and convicted by military tribunals.

Dodd stated that his purpose was in the service of true Republicanism; the independence of the individual states as secured by the Revolution of 1776. Dodd declared that the great issue was the centralization of power, to which the Democratic Party had been opposed since the formation of the Union. He opposed the liberation of four million blacks by the federal government, insisting that both Lincoln's and Morton's governments were usurpations, under which the people could not remain passive. He "was willing to abide by the decisions of the ballot box in the election of officers but was unwilling to obey them when they exercised undelegated powers." [2]

Dodd devised a plan to free the Confederate POWs at Camp Morton and seize the state arsenal and the State House, along with Oliver P. Morton, and raise a general insurrection. Dodd's ultimate objective: to form a Northwest Confederacy or, possibly, join the Northwestern states to the Southern Confederates.

The Northwest Confederacy

When it became clear that a peaceful negotiated settlement with the South would be impossible, Dodd and many other Democrats understood that the Abolitionists were intent on destroying the South and exterminating Southerners. Thus Western state Democrats began to formulate a plan to also secede from the United States and form a third political entity: the Northwest Confederacy.

The editor of the New Albany *Weekly Ledger* presented a sobering analysis of the dilemma facing the Western states. He said that an economic alliance

1. "Official Record of the War of the Rebellion, etc.", Vol. vii, p 289.
2. Mayo Fesler, p 232.

with the South would allow Indiana to retain the use of the great commercial rivers, "the natural outlet for our commerce, but maintaining its current position as part of the United States, without the South's presence, meant it could only use artificial channels, the railroads, which must always be a costly means of transportation." The West would have to choose between "the low tariff schedules of the Confederacy, or paying a heavy-tax upon the goods it consumed for the support of Eastern manufacturers. Or a third way; political independence." [1]

Earlier, Senator Thomas Hendricks had made the keynote speech at a Democratic convention in Indianapolis. He cried out against the subversion of civil liberties and the ruins "of a violated Constitution," by Lincoln and Morton. He deplored the tactics of the Republican Party which had divided the nation by teaching the North that its interests were opposed to those of the South. Turning his speech toward New England, Hendricks said that he was appalled by the dismal prospect that the Western states would become "the hewers of wood and the drawers of water" for the capitalists of New England. He scourged the Eastern manufacturers who exploited the West with the Protective Tariff. The exorbitant freight rates charged by the railroads placed Western farmers in a position of dependence upon the Southern market and the cheap transportation of the rivers. "A political party that would destroy that market is our greatest foe. The first interest of the Northwest lay in the restoration of the union, but if the folly and the failure and wickedness of the party in power renders a Union impossible, then the mighty Northwest must take care of herself and her own interests. She must not allow the arts and finesse of New England to despoil her richest trade and commerce, and to render her labor subservient to the Eastern, sectional, and selfish policy. We reject the Eastern lust for power, commerce, and gain." [2]

Oliver P. Morton denounced the "wild and wicked" dream of the "traitorous Democrats" who plotted to from a Northwest Confederacy and dramatically announced that his government was compelled to use "strong measures" to suppress secret societies that promoted this idea.

Again, The Plan To Assassinate Morton

In the summer of 1864, Oliver P. Morton learned of H.H. Dodd's plan to free the prisoners at Camp Morton and then storm the State House, to kill the governor.

Morton and General Carrington took no direct action to stop the plan, except to secretly mobilize the militia. Later, Carrington wrote to Felix G. Stidger, the mole who had infiltrated the Sons of Liberty and discovered

1. New Albany, *Weekly Ledger*, April 3, 1862
2. Indiana *Daily Journal*, January, 8 1862.

Dodd's scheme. "We knew so fully their plans that we could make no public demonstration without getting caught in the act." [1]

Shortly afterward, Governor Morton received information that a large shipment of weapons had been sent from New York to H.H. Dodd's printing company in Indianapolis. Four hundred pistols and ammunition were seized, as well as a list of Democratic politicians who were members of the Sons of Liberty.

Finally, Morton acted just before the plan was to be implemented. He arrested Dodd, Lambden Milligan, and several other civilians who were involved. Milligan was one of Dodd's chief lieutenants. His previous main claim to fame: he was runner-up in the July 1864 Indiana Democratic gubernatorial convention.

All this was given sensational treatment in the Republican press. The Indianapolis *Journal* editorialized: "Let everyone stop and inquire where we are tending and what future is before us. The signs of revolution have been visible about us for many months, and today we find ourselves standing upon its very brink. [2]

Indianapolis was in a frenzy. Morton called a meeting of the faithful. He said that learning of the plot and arresting the conspirators was a triumphant vindication of his repeated charge of "domestic treason," and the whole Democratic Party was equally guilty of Dodd's and Milligan's crime.

Morton demanded that the conspirators must be tried by a military tribunal instead of a civil court. Even the usually accommodating General Carrington had grave doubts about the legality of such an action, but Morton was adamant. "An immediate military trial is essential to the success of the National Cause in the autumn election." [3]

Meanwhile, Clement Vallandigham, a major officer in the Sons of Liberty, met with Southern political and military leaders. He made them aware of Dodd's plan to release the Confederate prisoners from Camp Morton and to assault the State House and kill Morton. The ultimate objective was to pull Indiana out of the war.

The Southerners developed a plan to draw Union armed forces away from Indianapolis so that the assault would have a greater chance of success.

July 8, 1864: Confederate Brigadier-General John Hunt Morgan and 2,000 cavalrymen crossed the Ohio River from Kentucky into Indiana to spread panic and diffuse Union army strength around Indianapolis. The city was in a terror.

July 9th: At Corydon, Morgan's horsemen outflanked 450 Indiana Home Guard militia, captured the town as a show of force, then moved on.

1. Kenneth Stampp, "The Milligan Case and the Election of 1864 in Indiana" (*Missouri Valley Historical Review*, No. 31, 1955) pp. 48.
2. Indianapolis *Journal*, August 22, 1864.
3. Kenneth Stampp, "Indiana Politics during the Civil War," p. 246

July 10th: Morgan pressed forward, captured Lexington, Versailles and Paris, Indiana. For six days the raiders caused havoc in the southern part of the state. Then federal troops rushed into that area. Abruptly, John Hunt Morgan headed north, seemingly toward Indianapolis.

This Union force of 4,000, led by Brigadier-General Edward Hobson, pursued Morgan, as Indianapolis remained in turmoil. Oliver P. Morton called for volunteers to defend the city, and 20,000 responded. Morton ordered all businesses to close so that militia employees could join their units.

John Hunt Morgan plundered more towns, seized horses, and burned bridges to slow his pursuers. Terrified citizens fled before him, carrying all their personal belongings.

By July 12, Morgan's cavalry was exhausted. With Hobson closing in, their initial success became a retreat. Morgan sought refuge in Kentucky. Half his men were captured.

When the POWs and civilian inmates at Camp Morton learned of the early victories of the raiders, they were convinced that Morgan's men would fight their way into the prison and free them. Instead, 1,000 of them would end up as "guests of the state" themselves and were treated like celebrities by the prisoners.

The incursion did not succeed. There was no coordinated attack on Camp Morton, on the arsenal, on the State House, or on Oliver P. Morton himself. By the time of John Hunt Morgan's raid, the main members of the Sons of Liberty had been incarcerated. Although Dodd escaped, Lambden Milligan now faced a military trial and the possibility of a death sentence.

Lambden Milligan: The Second Indianapolis Treason Trial

Late October, 1864: The second treason trial began, this one for Milligan. A brief overview of his early life will give us an insight into how he endured what was to follow. He was born and raised in Belmont County, Ohio. At seventeen, already showing strong intellectual ability, he informed his father of his desire to become a physician. His father, who was proud of his son's academic achievements, promised to send him to college. His wife opposed this, insisting that there should be no distinction made in the education of all their children.

Most adolescents would have grudgingly accepted this decision. Instead, Lambden left home "to seek his fortune," despite his parents' threat to disinherit him. Without a dime and forced to live among strangers, he was thrown upon his own resources. All his inner strength of mind and body were exerted to survive, and he succeeded.

Lambden abandoned his dream of studying medicine, and instead trained for and became a successful lawyer in Huntington, Indiana. This despite the suffering and disability due to epilepsy and spinal meningitis.

Up until 1862, Lambden showed little interest in the political realm, but that year he verbally and vehemently opposed every movement that advocated a violent collision between North and South.

In 1863, Milligan addressed a meeting at Plymouth, Indiana, conclusively demonstrating that the war had neither been started nor continued to preserve the Union. He referred to the Republican Party's often repeated declaration of hostility to the Constitution and the many opportunities for compromise which had been spurned. He saw that the war continued for the purpose of breaking down the influence of the agricultural states, to elevate the moneyed and manufacturing interests, so that the Republican Party might control the legislation of Congress.

Detectives hired by Governor Morton attended this meeting, and the Republican press, seething with denunciatory articles, charged Milligan with treason. Later in the same year Governor Morton concocted a scheme where a Dr. Zumro, acting as an undercover informant, would be arrested on a made-up political charge. He would then visit Milligan's law office, asking Milligan to represent him as his legal counsel. The idea was for Zumro to gain Milligan's confidence and to learn of his political objectives. Unfortunately for Zumro, he played his part so poorly that he was easily detected, and the plot failed.

August 14th, 1863: Milligan addressed another large meeting at Fort Wayne. Governor Morton sent another spy, a Mr. Bush, to report on the speech. Morton, who was running for re-election, was incensed when he learned of the tone of Milligan's words, threatening his overthrow. Morton resolved to destroy him.

Then Lambden Milligan became paralyzed in his left leg and was confined to bed. His neighbors expected to learn of his death.

October 15th: At 11 p.m, a group of soldiers commanded by a Captain Chase surrounded his house and arrested Milligan, without an affidavit, warrant, or any form of legal authority. Since he could not walk, he was carried to a train. Captain Chase said to his men that if Milligan made any noise, he should be shot.

Milligan was taken 100 miles from Huntington to Indianapolis and arrived there the following afternoon, where an infuriated pro-Morton mob threatened to kill him.

Milligan arrived at General Hovey's headquarters and was denied bail. Hovey: "You have no rights which a loyal citizen is bound to respect." Then Milligan found himself in a military post prison and placed in an open shed.

He was fed rotten pork, and passed out. When he awoke he was covered with vermin. He was confined there for ten days. All this time the shed was being transformed into a prison cell. The loud construction noise was designed to drive him mad. Drunken soldiers aimed their weapons at him.

"Loyal" citizens paid a fee to see and mock him, as if he was a wild animal in a zoo. From there he was transferred to a cell at the Federal Court House, where another spy was quartered with him. Then he went on trial with fellow "conspirators" William Bowles, Stephen Horsey, Andrew Humphrey, and Horace Heffner.

Milligan pleaded "not guilty." The charges against him were:

1. Conspiring against the Government of the United States.
2. Affording aid and comfort to rebels against the authority of the United States.
3. Inciting insurrection.
4. Disloyal practices.
5. Violations of the laws of war.

Witnesses were bribed to ensure conviction. Milligan objected to the fact that he, a civilian, was being tried by a military tribunal, which was unconstitutional. His objection was overruled.

The trial began. Testimony was manufactured to the morbid relish of the biased and excited public. False and exaggerated rumors were accepted as evidence. Heffner became a victim of his fears, took the witness stand, and swore to falsehoods as men swear when they feel the rope around their neck. Milligan remained collected and exhorted his counsel to be truthful.

Regardless of the consequences, to break his spirit Milligan was transferred from the Federal Court House jail to the Soldiers' Home Prison, a mile away. Despite his paralyzed leg, he was forced to walk, with a crutch, the entire distance. This effort paralyzed his arm.

Milligan was dragged into a small cell next to a pig-pen, where the stench and constant squealing was intended to break his will. There were gaps in the wood cell walls, and the cold wind whistled in. Milligan was not allowed any other clothing than his light prison uniform. Rotten food was provided periodically. Three hundred other "traitors" were incarcerated there. They were freezing and starving as well.

Then there was "the hole," a black pit for those who "deserved additional punishment." Some were taken out alive. Some died in the "hospital," while others expired in the hole. Even a Democratic member of the Assembly was thrown in the hole, where he died.

Those who refused to admit that they were traitors were alternately hung by their wrists for hours, while all the other inmates could hear their cries of agony, then flung into the hole.

Long after his release, Lambden Milligan stated that the worst part of his ordeal was listening to the wails of those being tortured.

"Guilty" was the verdict. Shortly afterward, Abraham Lincoln was assassinated. The public clamored loudly for the blood of traitors. Heavy iron chains were placed on Milligan's legs, and the guard doubled. His sentence: death by hanging.

May 8, 1865: President Andrew Johnson refused to commute his sentence. Milligan was to die on the 19th. On the 10th Milligan filed an appeal to the Circuit Court of the United States. The only result was that the execution was postponed until the second of June. The postponement infuriated the Republicans. Retaliation took on a new and ugly form, seething and surging into an irresistible fury. Governor Morton, knowing that he was the cause of the uncontrollable outrage and perceiving that he would be held personally responsible, took an extraordinary measure to counteract his work and defuse the intensifying unrest that might bring him down.

Morton commissioned Judge J.W. Pettit to meet with President Johnson to reconsider his decision and commute Milligan's sentence to imprisonment for life at hard labor. Andrew Johnson agreed, but Milligan desired the death sentence. He understood the fate that awaited him when placed in the custody of those selected for their cruelty. He wrote his will and awaited the gallows.

Milligan was moved to a cell near where the death sentence would be carried out. It was located directly over the prison's oven, and the coal's noxious fumes could be fatal. After a week there, he seemed to be dying and was transferred to the prison's hospital, where he remained in critical condition for two weeks. When he had sufficiently recovered, he was placed in another horrible cell, where he lost his hearing and sense of smell from the atrocious conditions. He was given food with rat droppings and maggots in it.

Meanwhile, Milligan's plea to be tried in a civil court was deadlocked in the Circuit Court and was elevated to the United States Supreme Court. Many friends and admirers had gone to Washington to have him pardoned, and they visited him in prison to persuade him to withdraw his suit from the Supreme Court in exchange for a presidential pardon. To these pleas, Milligan emphatically replied "No!"

He had not forgotten the response that President Johnson had made when Milligan's attorney previously asked for a respite of his sentence: "What? The very fact of the prisoner resorting to the court upon a technical question of jurisdiction, is a confession of his guilt." Johnson refused clemency. [1]

Those familiar with the perspective of the Supreme Court were convinced that it would uphold the legality of Milligan's conviction by a military tribunal; a ruling in his favor would not only be a direct condemnation of Abraham Lincoln's policies as President, but also of his administration; that the peace of the country required that years of political animosities should be forgotten.

1. John A. Marshall, *American Bastille* (Philadelphia: Evans, Stoddard and co, 1869) p. 83

Despite all this, the High Court decided in Milligan's favor. Justice Davis delivered the opinion of the Court. He wrote, in part: "Military commissions, organized during the late Civil War, in a state not invaded and not engaged in rebellion, in which the federal courts are open, and in the proper and unobstructed exercise of their judicial functions, have not the jurisdiction to try, convict, or sentence, for any criminal offense, a citizen who was neither a resident of a rebellious state, nor a prisoner of war, nor a person in the military or naval service." [1]

The decision struck the shackles from Lambden Milligan so that he was free from the grasp of tyrants and arbitrary power. He had been imprisoned and abused for eighteen months.

A local newspaper reported his return to Huntington, Indiana: "L. P. Milligan comes back to his home, and was the occasion of a demonstration on the part of his neighbors and friends, which all history furnishes but one parallel; that is the ovation of welcome which greeted the immortal Demosthenes upon his return to Piraeus from his exile at Megara. As the great Athenian was received, upon his arrival in that city, by its magistrates and dignitaries and citizens, so was our illustrious fellow-citizen received by the mayor, the Common Council, and all the citizens, with the utmost manifestation of affection and joy, blended with sorrow and indignation at the flagrant wrongs and cruel persecutions to which he had been subjected during the last eighteen months.

Lambden Milligan spoke to the crowd:

> "Mr. Mayor, friends and neighbors, as such I know you are; my sense of propriety calls for an extended response to such an imposing reception, but I have neither the physical or mental ability to give it; but overcome by the spontaneous enthusiasm of the occasion, I can only thank you for so proud a testimonial...What revolutions in government or society have intervened since my seclusion, I know not, but I am, and have always [been] opposed to revolution, believing that seldom, if ever, have the fruits equaled the cost in treasure, blood, and moral retrogression. I thank you, neighbors and friends, for the glowing tribute of esteem, and I would be the more happier recipient of it if I was sure that, through the ordeal which I have just passed, my deportment was worthy of so flattering a token...My friends, I must now leave you." [2]

Conclusion

In 1865, the Indiana Assembly was reconvened for the first time in nearly two years. In 1867, Oliver P. Morton resigned as governor to enter the United States Senate as one of the leading Radical Republicans. Despite a debilitating

1. Ibid., p. 84
2. Ibid., p. 91.

stroke, he became one of President Ulysses S. Grant's chief advisors, where he promoted extremist Reconstruction legislation. The following conversation gives clear evidence that Grant's views of the future of the American republic were similar to, and influenced by, Morton's vision that "I am the State":

> Governor Holden of North Carolina [a carpetbag Radical Republican] said to a Reverend Smith: "General Grant will hold the government of the United States no matter what the outcome of the election of 1872. President Grant desired that he should be Emperor, and that his son should succeed him as Emperor." [1]

1. Stanley Horn, *The Invisible Empire: The Story of the Ku Klux Klan, 1866-1871* (Cos Cob, CT: John Edwards, 1969) p. 17.

Chapter 4. Lincoln's Annihilation of Missouri

Reverend Miller: Witness to Aftermath of Atrocities

Of all the states involved in the Civil War, Missouri's story is the most horrible, brutal, and most misunderstood.

Reverend George Miller had the grisly task of conducting funeral services for the thousands of innocent civilians: the men, women, and children who were executed, then mutilated after they were dead, then dumped into mass graves, by Union forces and guerrilla bands of both Southern and Missourian loyalty. In his book, *Missouri's Memorable Decade*, he wrote that he could ride for days on horseback, going from one funeral to another through a countryside once filled with prosperous towns which had now become one vast wasteland. Only occasional fire-blackened chimneys stood to mark what had been a thriving community.

Here Reverend Miller describes the truth about pre-war Missouri:

> Missouri has never been understood, and her people have been sweepingly condemned, largely from the fact that she was made the national football of the slavery agitation for forty-eight consecutive years. The Missouri Compromise, the Kansas–Nebraska Bill, the border warfare from 1855 to 1860, were the steps that led to an alienation that never ceased to grow until it culminated in the fearful baptism of blood. Missouri stood in the forefront of each stage of this growing strife, not because her people were worse or better than the people other states, but because of her geographical location. Being then related to the causes leading to the conflict, it is natural that Missouri should suffer more than any other state. Two thirds of her people being Southern born, and enclosed on three sides; and by taking sides, soon forced all her people into one army or the other.

> The South contributed more than she ever got credit for, to the antislavery movement and to the maintenance of the Union... After a life-long study of the slavery situation, and the steps leading to our dreadful Civil War, I feel that the harsh and denunciatory methods of the Radical Abolitionists never advanced the anti-slavery sentiment of our nation. I know this is not the popular view, but history proves it to be the true view. The Garrison Party [William Lloyd Garrison, the famed abolitionist and publisher of the "Liberator"] never attained any weight in the North; it only provoked the resentment and anger of the South and forestalled all appeals to reason and truth, and made the sword the only final arbitrator. Slavery was abolished in one after another of the Northern states not so much because it was wrong as because it was unprofitable in that latitude. As late as 1810 there was no more anti-slavery sentiment in the free states than in the slave states. [1]

Reverend Miller's brother, a lawyer who lived in Lawrence, Kansas, wrote this:

> [The slave-holders] have been aided and abetted, sustained and supported by the non-slave-holders of the North, who rival each other in serving the slave-power. This we consider the fountain of American slavery, and a more abominable one than that which prevails in the South. There are more men in the free states who would own slaves, were they able, and the laws permitting them to, than there are actual slave-holders in the South...The Black Laws of Illinois are fully as abominable as anything in the Slave Code of Louisiana. [2]

Reverend Miller outlined the slave population in Missouri by country, to demonstrate that the majority of counties in that state had few slaves:

> The distribution of slave property in Missouri throws much light upon local sentiment in different parts of the state. In 1860, there were, in the entire state, 114,931 slaves. This is no more than 10% of the number of the white population at that time. Fourteen of the 114 counties contained half of the whole number. 64 counties contained less than 500 slaves. 25 counties contained less than 100 each. One county had none. Only one in eight of Missouri's families owned even one slave. [3]
>
> A short growing season limited cotton production. Tobacco, limited to Missouri's southernmost areas, was so unprofitable that relatively few engaged in it. These two products, where slave labor was most advantageous, were ill-suited to Missouri farms.

1. Reverend George Miller, *Missouri's Memorable Decade, 1860-1870* (Columbus, Missouri: Press of E.W. Stephens, 1898) p 44.
2. Ibid., p. 17.
3. Ibid., p 36

Missouri's population did not divide neatly into a contest pitting slavery supporters against anti-slavery advocates. The break proved far less clear. Missourians had grown accustomed to slavery vs. anti-slavery rhetoric. Their political leaders had confronted them with the issue before the 1820 Missouri Compromise. Since then the population had debated slavery with aplomb. Because they could and did argue over the matter, Missourians and their politics proved quite different from the other states of the South. Hence the subject would not split the state. What now threatened the stability of Missouri was the question of "Union or Disunion," and "state sovereignty or a powerful central government". Should they remain loyal to the United States or follow the course of her sister states of the South?

Yet, precisely because they were so accustomed to the slavery debate, most Missourians were able to remove themselves sufficiently from the emotion of the slavery question to assess it more objectively than their Southern brethren. Although many of the state's largest and most powerful slave-owners pressed for immediate secession, most slave-holders feared that, rather than saving that institution, disunion would prove its death-knell.

Most Missourians were conservative and looked to secession as a last resort. They also feared the coercion of the new Republican government, under Abraham Lincoln, whose leadership few Missourians outside of St. Louis endorsed.

In fact, in the 1860 presidential election, 70% of the population supported the moderate candidates, Stephen Douglas or John Bell. Lincoln ran last, carrying only two counties. One of these was St. Louis, which was more like the industrial North. It had the stigma of being a city of abolitionists, an ugly label in Missouri.

After all, Missouri wished to be left alone, Missourians asked nothing of the government at Washington. They did not need its protection, feeling that such protection would be that which the wolf offers the lamb.

Background to the War in Missouri

The Missouri Compromise

When territories desired to be admitted to the Union as states, the question of whether they would be free or slave became very important. In 1819 the Missouri Territory requested statehood.

At that time there were twenty-two states, eleven with slaves and eleven free. Missourians wanted to become a slave state. This would upset the balance.

Maine requested admission as a free state. In a grand compromise, both were made states to maintain the equilibrium, but Congress determined that thereafter, no other Western territory north of a line that ran along the southern border of Missouri would be allowed in as a slave state.

This balance reached a crisis in the 1850s when the Kansas and Nebraska territories, which were along the western borders of Missouri and Nebraska and above the line set by the Compromise, requested statehood status. By the terms of the Compromise, they had to join as free states. This would upset the balance.

In an attempt to maintain stability, Congress repealed the Missouri Compromise and replaced it with the Kansas–Nebraska Act of 1857. Now the citizens of each territory would determine whether it would be free or slave.

Nebraskans thought that their future state should be free. In Kansas, the voters who favored slavery won. Their opponents cried fraud. This produced a political crisis splitting Kansas into two separate governments. LeCompton was the capital of the pro-slavery faction, Topeka for the pro-free constituency. This engendered a bloody, atrocity-filled guerrilla war. Then the federal government side-stepped the Kansas–Nebraska Act, directly intervened, and overturned the citizens' decision — and with no direct evidence of fraud, mandated that Kansas would be a free state,

Instead of resolving the crisis, this exacerbated it, and the atrocities escalated. This was the real beginning of the Civil War.

Governor Jackson: Misrepresented as Secessionist

November 1860. Abraham Lincoln became President. Immediately five states seceded and formed a separate country.

January 3, 1861. Outgoing Missouri Governor Robert Steward delivered his farewell address to the General Assembly. Steward, a moderate, condemned both the Northern abolitionists and the Deep South states for creating the crisis.

Because of her central position, Steward advised Missouri to take the "high position of armed neutrality," to prevent coercion from either side. Steward, a native of New York, sympathized with the South but held to the Union. He acknowledged the wrongs the South had suffered at the hands of the North and the dangers that threatened the country from the intolerant and aggressive spirit of the in-coming Republican Party. Still, he opposed secession on the grounds that it was without warrant of law, since Missouri had no right to withdraw from the Union; it belonged to the United States by purchase. It was formed from part of a territory bought from France.

Governor Steward finished with these words: "I would, in my last official act as governor of Missouri, record my solemn protest against such unwise and hasty action [secession] and my unalterable devotion to the Union so long as it can be made the protector of equal rights." [1]

Steward was implying that if Lincoln did not respect Missouri's right to retain its internal institutions, like slavery, disunion could be an option.

With the fall of Fort Sumter, President Lincoln called for 75,000 soldiers to crush the "insurrection." Missouri's new governor, Claiborne Jackson, responded to this call with this famous comment: "Your requisition, in my judgment, is illegal, unconstitutional, and revolutionary, and its objective, inhuman and diabolical." [2]

Abraham Lincoln viewed these words to mean that Jackson was a secessionist and was preparing to break away from the Union. Thereafter, all of Claiborne Jackson's public statements were misrepresented to demonstrate that he was disloyal. That gave Lincoln the rationale to invade Missouri and hold it by force, to keep it within the United States.

But Governor Jackson did not wish to join the Confederacy. To do so would mean that Missouri would lose its independence, as we shall see. He wished to remain within the United States as a neutral so he would not be forced either to kill fellow American Southerners or to fight off a federal invasion.

The second misunderstanding occurred when Claiborne Jackson assembled the Missouri legislature in a special session, to take "measures to perfect the organization and equipment of the militia and raise the money to place the state in a proper attitude of defense." [3]

This was not secession but a warning to Lincoln that Missouri would fight back if the federal government planned to invade.

Then Jackson backed this up with contradictory statements which were designed to bring Lincoln and his administration into negotiations: "I do not think that Missouri should secede today or tomorrow, but I think it is a good policy that it should be publicly declared." Then he added: "Every man in the state is in favor of arming the state." [4] Again, this was a warning.

January 22, 1861: Claiborne Jackson called the General Assembly to form a state convention to "consider the existing relations between the government of the United States, the people and government of the different states, and the people of the State of Missouri; and to adopt such measures for vindicating the sovereignty of the State, and the protection of the institutions, that shall appear to them to be demanded." [5]

1. Christopher Phillips, *Missouri's Confederate, Claiborne Jackson and the Creation of Southern Identity in the Border West* (Columbia: Missouri University Press) 2000, p. 234.
2. Ibid, p 238.
3. Dennis K. Bowman, "Lincoln's Resolute Unionist, Hamilton Gamble."
4. Christopher Phillips, "Missouri's Confederate, Claiborne Jackson," p. 151
5. Reverend George Miller, p. 49.

Historians glibly call this the "secession convention" but in reality the opposite was true.

Another misrepresentation occurred on January 29th. The convention adopted a series of resolutions that declared that if the Lincoln administration attempted to coerce the Southern states back into the Union, Missouri would aid them in resisting a federal attack. "Aid" is not secession.

Also, most of the convention members were loyal Unionists. Based on the citizen votes for candidates for the convention, most Missourians opposed disunion, even those who were pro-slavery. The minority also had a moderate plan to conduct a "border states convention" which would clarify their interests. Once that was formulated, there would be a national meeting, where these interests would be presented as an ultimatum to the North. If this was rejected, there would be the possibility of withdrawal. But Abraham Lincoln acted as if Missouri would definitely secede, and he prepared to invade.

Former governor Sterling Price was elected president of the convention. Hamilton Gamble became Chairman of the Committee on Federal Relations. Gamble had been the Chief Justice of the Missouri Supreme Court, and his stature made him one of the most influential members of the convention. He was a slave-holder and as such battled with himself over the United States Constitution as ratified by the original thirteen states.

Both Unionists and secessionists agreed that the states were sovereign and could break away from the Union. But Gamble, formerly a Whig and now a Republican, believed in the principle of a strong central government, and that made disunion illegal.

Gamble's solution was that redress was available through the federal courts; amend the Constitution to guarantee slave property and enact into law the Crittenden Compromise. (John Crittenden, a Kentuckian, had been a senator and governor of that state, and United States Attorney-General under three presidents.) Crittenden was one of the foremost figures in attempting to conciliate North and South. He tried to resolve the slavery issue through constitutional amendments.

Gamble wrote a report in which he said:

> The position of Missouri in relation to the adjacent states, which would continue in the Union, would necessarily expose her, if she becomes a member of the new confederacy, to utter destruction, whether any rupture takes place between the different republics. In a military aspect, secession and connection with a Southern confederacy, is annihilation for Missouri. The true position for her to assume is that of a state whose interests are bound up in the maintenance of the Union, whose kind feelings and strong sympathies are with the people of the

> Southern states, with whom they are connected by ties of friendship and blood.[1]
>
> This was not secession but support from the sidelines. The clearest sentiment of the convention was expressed by delegate William A. Hall: "Our feelings and sympathies may incline us to go with the South, in the event of a separation, but feeling is temporary, and interest is permanent."

Gamble and Hall's views were reflections of the majority of the convention delegates. They voted overwhelmingly to place Missouri in a position to mediate the North–South dispute. They also included a provision requiring a state-wide vote by the citizens on any final decision to insure that they were in agreement. This clause would be major factor in the future deceptive relations with the Confederacy.

Finally, on March 9th, the convention adopted a resolution stating: "At present there is no adequate cause to impel Missouri to dissolve her connection with the Union."

Of the eleven slave-holding states that called Union/Disunion conventions, Missouri alone would remain within the United States. The threat of secession was conclusively ended.

Overview of Governor Jackson's Career

Claiborne Jackson would be a major figure in the upcoming war between Missouri and Abraham Lincoln. He was a Kentuckian of Virginia descent, a man of dignified and impressive bearing, a farmer with an independent fortune. He had been a citizen of Missouri for forty years. Jackson was a forceful speaker, a debater rather than an orator, a politician of experience and a man of positive opinions on public questions. He had the courage to act. Jackson had been connected with the politics of Missouri on and off for twenty-five years in a legislative capacity and had been Chairman of the Senate Committee on Federal Relations.

In his inaugural address, Governor Jackson traced the growth of the Republican Party and its anti-slavery platform, showing that it was in violation of the letter and spirit of the Constitution, was inimical to the rights and interests of Missouri and the South, and was a menace to the perpetuity of the Union. Jackson also objected to the Congressional compromise of the existing crisis, as temporary and ineffective. He advocated additional guarantees.

While Abraham Lincoln viewed Claiborne Jackson as a secessionist, the Confederacy itself did not. In its official history of the Civil War, it presents Jackson this way: "The governor's inaugural address was not a strong document. It lacked nerve and decision. It did not meet the requirements

1. Dennis K. Bowman, p 100.

of the times. The people were intensely excited, and knew intuitively that the impending danger was great and the time for preparation to meet it was short. The address went too far as a peace document, and not far enough for a call on the part of the Chief Executive of the State to prepare for war or even put the State in a position to defend itself, if necessary, from encroachment and invasion."

Nathaniel Lyon: Lincoln's Agent Provocateur

Missouri declared itself neutral, hoping to mediate to diffuse the crisis. But this dream was shattered by a demented Union Army general, Nathaniel Lyon, who was selected by Abraham Lincoln to take charge in Missouri, at the point where negotiations had already been agreed to, for maintaining the peace.

Nathaniel Lyon, rabidly anti-slave, made the decision on his own, to make war, without any authorization from Lincoln or the military high command. In doing so, Lyon accurately reasoned that Lincoln would be forced to back his actions, or else he would look incompetent.

Lyon's long record in the army gives a clue to his irreversible decision in Missouri. As a lower-ranking officer he had been court-martialed several times for beating, torturing, and starving to death troops under his command. He did all this to cure disobedience. Once he said to his men: "I know you all hate me, and if we should ever go into battle, I would get the first bullet, but as long as I command, I will make you toe the mark." [1]

After moving up the ranks due to his successful role in the Mexican War, in the late 1840s, he was assigned to a post in the territory of California that had been ceded to the United States as a result of that war. When Indians in that region killed several American settlers, Lyon led a column to exterminate the entire tribe. He trapped and killed over one hundred warriors. Then he turned his hatred on the women and children. His sense of revenge was boundless. His men murdered 240 of them. The children were shot and bayoneted and thrown into a lake. The women drowned themselves rather than to be tortured and raped. The Indian camp and the dead were burned. Still not satisfied, Lyon found where another hundred warriors were hiding, on an island in the lake. Again, no mercy. It soon became a perfect slaughter pen. Lyon received a commendation for his actions.

Lyon was next assigned to Fort Riley in Kansas. Dr. William Hammond was the post-surgeon there. Later, Hammond became the Army's Surgeon-General. After the Civil War he wrote some very revealing comments about Lyon's mentally unstable character; "I have never, in the course of my life, met a man as fearless and uncompromising in the expression of his opinions, and at the same time, so intolerant of the views of others, as he was. If he had lived 400

1. Christopher Phillips, *Damned Yankee: The Life of General Nathaniel Lyon* (Condon and Company, 1990) p. 87.

years ago, he would have been burned at the stake as a pestilent and altogether incorrigible person, whose removal was demanded in the interest of society."

Hammond recalled that Lyon dominated conversations, not allowing the listener to express his views. Lyon liked "nothing so much as a good listener. His ideas flowed with surprising rapidity, and his words uttered at a rate of speed that would have kept the most skillful stenographer in full action." Hammond continued: "He was so intolerant of opposition, unmindful of the many obligatory courtesies of life; prone to inject the most unpopular opinions at times and places, when he knew they would be unwelcome, and enforcing them with all the bitterness and vehemence of which he was capable; easily aroused to a degree of anger that was almost insane in its manifestations; narrow-minded, prejudiced, mentally unbalanced, and yet, with all this, honest to the core." Lyon's opinions made him enemies on all sides. [1]

In Kansas, Lyon found a target for his animosity-laden personality; slavery. The Kansas–Nebraska Act outraged him. He accused President Pierce and Stephen Douglas (who originated the Kansas–Nebraska Bill) of "subservience to the slave interests" and "prostitution to the demands of the slave power."

In his anger, Lyon lashed out at Southerners for their crimes against the nation, committed in the name of slavery. "It is the greatest of evils. If it were in my power to break up our relations and Union, with .a power that does not regard its promises and pledges, in its blind avarice to propagate and extend its blighted curse and degrading sin, I would do so at once, and declare our glorious Union at an end." [2]

As violence, guerrilla war and atrocities accelerated in Kansas. Lyon, who originally had been a Democrat, became a Republican. In June 1860, he contributed twenty-four political essays to the "Western Star Express," a newspaper that supported the Republican Party. These articles represented Lyon's first public announcement of his unequivocal support for Abraham Lincoln. These pieces caught the eye of leading Republicans, including Lincoln, and led to his advancement within the military.

General William Harney, the new commander of the West, was Lyon's superior-officer, both in Kansas and during the Mexican War. In Kansas, he ordered Lyon to capture James Montgomery, the anti-slave guerrilla who was committing atrocities. Lyon pretended to obey, then tipped Montgomery off, allowing him to escape.

When South Carolina seceded, Lyon was ordered to St. Louis to reinforce the garrison at that city's arsenal. This was the moment when Nathaniel Lyon took center stage in the coming annihilation of Missouri.

1. Ibid. p 83
2. Ibid. p 84

He was overjoyed at his new assignment. Now he could fight against the "evil secessionists."

On the steamer bound for St. Louis, Lyon wrote down his intentions, which proved to be prophetic: "I shall not hesitate to rejoice at the triumph of my principles, although this triumph may involve an issue which certainly I expect to expose, or very likely, to lose my life. We shall rejoice though in martyrdom, if need be" [1]

St. Louis' huge federal arsenal was filled with rifles, artillery and ammunition. A handful of United States troops guarded it. The commander was Major Bell. All sides in the developing conflict viewed the arsenal as a great prize.

Within days of arriving in St. Louis, Lyon met Frank Blair, who had been a state Assemblyman and a United States Congressman, and headed the national Post Office Department. His brother, Montgomery, was a member of Abraham Lincoln's Cabinet. It was Blair who read Lyon's political articles in the *Western Star Express*, and he specifically requested Lyon's transfer to St. Louis. Lyon and Blair were similar. Both possessed acerbic wits and were easily provoked to violence. "When Blair goes in for a fight, he goes in for a funeral." Frank Blair was famous for his duels and fist fights. Once he shot a man in a tavern during an argument. So, immediately, Blair and Lyon hit it off.

Nathaniel Lyon learned that Blair had organized 1,000 "Wide-Awakes," mostly pro-Lincoln Germans, for the defense of St. Louis. They were mercenaries, Blair's private army, not part of the state militia. Their goal was to take the arsenal.

Blair had successfully asked local businessmen to donate money for weapons, but he needed more. Lyon endorsed everything that Blair was doing, but could not supply him with more arms, unless Blair gave him command of the arsenal. Lyon was convinced that Major Bell was disloyal and planned to give the arsenal's stockpile to Claiborne Jackson's militia, to defend against the U.S. army.

January 8, 1861: Anti-Lincoln "Minute Men" held a meeting to block the "Wide-Awake" plan. Winfield Scott, the highest ranking officer in the United States army, saw the confrontation coming. He ordered 40 federal soldiers from Newport Barracks, Kentucky, to guard the federal sub Treasury in St. Louis, which held millions of dollars in gold and silver.

The crossing of a state line was legally an invasion. The presence of this detachment caused great agitation in St. Louis. The citizens believed that these troops were the vanguard of a much larger federal coercion of Missouri.

January 20: Daniel Frost, Claiborne Jackson's envoy, who was a Brigadier-General in the Missouri militia, visited Major Bell at the arsenal. Frost

1. Ibid., p 133.

convinced Bell that according to the doctrine of state sovereignty, Missouri had the right to claim the arsenal, since it rested on her soil. Bell agreed not to defend the arsenal if the state government was determined to take it.

January 22: Bell refused to allow volunteers to enter the arsenal for its defense. Blair was furious. He telegraphed his brother, Montgomery, urgently requesting Bell's removal. Montgomery followed through the same day, replacing him with Brevet-Major Peter Hagner.

Then Lyon marched into the arsenal with a company of regular U.S. troops and immediately began a confrontation with Hagner. Lyon said that since he out-ranked Hagner, he should take over the arsenal. Hagner disputed this claim and refused to abdicate his position.

Lyon wired General Harney to force Hagner to step down, but Harney, aware of Lyon's mental instability, refused his request. Without being in command of the arsenal, Lyon could not legally distribute its weapons to Blair's Wide-Awakes.

So, Lyon went over Harney's head and telegraphed the War Department, insiisting they install him. General Winfield Scott denied his request, and Lyon demonstrated his paranoid personality when he said that Scott had shown "his sordid spirit of partisan favoritism to pets, personal associates and toadies." [1]

Lyon was not yet beaten. He prompted Blair to contact Lincoln, this time to replace the "disloyal" Harney and Hagner with himself. Blair was partially successful. Lincoln over-rode Scott's decision. Finally, Lyon was put in charge of the arsenal, but Hagner and Harney remained.

Via the army's chain of command, it was Harney who would have to give the order for the promotion, but he desperately wanted to get rid of Lyon due to his long history of fanaticism, cruelty, and insubordination. Harney found a way to push him aside, at least temporarily.

Months before, at Fort Riley, a private under Lyon's command had starved to death. Negligence charges were brought against him, stating that it was his action while the soldier was in the stockade that caused the tragedy.

This was yet another in a long series of brutality charges against him. Harney ordered Lyon to Fort Leavenworth, to stand before a military Court of Inquiry. Later the charges were dropped, but this did delay his promotion.

Then Harney used another stalling tactic. He interpreted Abraham Lincoln's orders, involved in Lyon's new role, to the letter. Lincoln wrote that Lyon should take over the arsenal's "defense." Harney took that word at its literal meaning. Lyon would only control the infantry defending the arsenal. Hanger would be in charge of their weapons. This would diffuse Lyon's power.

1. Ibid, p 143

Blair was infuriated, and once again asked President Lincoln to replace Harney; once again saying he was disloyal, mostly because his wife was a Southerner.

Lincoln was cautious about this act, so he called Harney to the Capital. Once together, the President demoted him, putting Lyon in total command of the arsenal. But Harney made a strong case against that action, convincing Lincoln that he was a true Unionist. Lincoln backed down, returning Harney to his post. Yet, as a compromise plan, Lyon was now co-commander.

Now Blair and Lyon prepared for war. They armed the Wide-Awake mercenaries without authorization from the army or the President. In one week, 5,000 of them were equipped for combat from the materiel in the arsenal. One regiment elected Blair as their commander. But the news leaked out and his home was attacked by outraged citizens. Blair quickly moved his family into the countryside.

To legally receive federal weapons and officers, the Wide-Awakes were renamed the "Home Guards," meaning that they were part of the state militia, but this was not true.

Quietly Lincoln gave Lyon a bigger promotion: Commander, Department of the West. Harney was out once again. Lyon's official notification read: "The President of the United States directs you to enroll in the military service of the United States, the loyal citizens of St. Louis and vicinity, for the purpose of maintaining the authority of the United States...You will, if necessary, proclaim martial law in the city of St. Louis." This would be completely unconstitutional, as no rebellion or insurrection existed there.

General Scott wrote at the bottom of the dispatch, a note that acknowledged the illegality of martial law, but he accepted it: "These are revolutionary times, and therefore I do not object to the irregularity of this." [1]

The Camp Jackson Massacre: War

Governor Claiborne Jackson observed how Nathaniel Lyon was building up his military strength. Jackson called up his state militia. The Militia Act of 1857 allowed him to call them into camp, once a year, for a week of drills.

David Frost headed Missouri's militia. He ordered the troops to occupy the hills overlooking the arsenal, but Lyon beat him to it, with infantry and artillery.

Then, St. Louis' city officials allowed Frost to use Lindell Grove, a field on the western side of the city, for his "militia camp of instruction." 900 men pitched their tents there, and re-named the location as "Camp Jackson," in honor of the governor. Hundreds of spectators watched the men drill.

1. Ibid., p. 168.

Nathaniel Lyon sent spies into Camp Jackson, convinced that it was filled with traitors. He believed the militia-men posed an immediate threat to St. Louis. His 8,000 federalized Home Guards vastly outnumbered the state militia.

Although Claiborne Jackson had every legal right to place the militia in the grove, Lyon made another unauthorized, illegal, and spontaneous decision to capture the "traitorous camp" and all those in it. Nathaniel. Lyon clearly understood the gravity of his decision. He could be court-martialed for his action. Although he was empowered to declare martial law, he had no permission from Washington for any offensive military operations, especially against a legally sanctioned group.

Lyon took another illegal step; he met with Governor Yates and former Governor Koerner, both of Illinois. Koerner was the leader of the German community there. Most of the Home Guard were German. An arrangement was made to deploy Illinois troops in Missouri to reinforce Lyon. From Claiborne Jackson's perspective, this was an invasion.

Nathaniel Lyon made a third illegal move. He was an officer in the United States army. Against army regulations, most of his junior officers were civilians who were given fake commissions. Under military law they were "irregulars," but had assumed roles analogous to official ones.

These men on Lyon's staff tried to dissuade him from attacking Camp Jackson. They understood that it would be a criminal act. Lyon responded that he knew the consequences but "the supremacy of the Union" reflected a higher .law.

May 10th: David Frost saw Lyon's Home Guards advancing on three sides of Camp Jackson, through heavy rain and mud. He sent one of his staff with this message for Lyon: "Sir, I am constantly in receipt of information that you contemplate an attack on my camp. While I understand that you are impressed with the idea that an attack on the arsenal is intended on the part of the militia of Missouri, I am greatly, at a loss to know what could justify you in attacking citizens of the United States, who are in performance of duties devolving upon them, under the Constitution, in organizing and instructing the militia of the State." [1]

Lyon refused to read the note. His columns were already at the perimeter of Camp Jackson. Mobs of civilians watched. Some had weapons to help Frost's men, but Lyon's troops blocked the way. Then Lyon sent this note to Frost. Most of his assessments were false or misleading: "Your militia is evidently hostile to the Government of the United States. It is, for the most part, made up of secessionists who are openly hostile to the General Government, and have been plotting at the seizure of its property and the overthrow of its authority.

1. Ibid., p. 186.

You are openly in communication with the so-called Southern Confederacy, which is now at war with the United States; you are now receiving at your camp, from said Confederacy, under its flag, large supplies of the materiel of war. These extraordinary preparations plainly indicate hostility to the General Government and cooperation with its enemies... I hereby demand of you an immediate surrender of your command." [1]

Frost tried to negotiate. Lyon gave him ten minutes to surrender or his men would open fire. Frost surrendered. Now, Lyon had to bring his prisoners back to the arsenal into a civilian crowd that was increasing in size and hostility.

Once the Camp Jackson soldiers had stacked their weapons, Lyon told them that if they took a loyalty oath to the United States, they would be pardoned. Only ten men took it. Most felt that they had already done so, and taking it again would imply that they had committed treason. They opted to be taken prisoner.

Considering the size and antagonistic temperament of the growing crowd, Lyon must have realized the great potential for violence. His military training had taught him to avoid, at all costs, an armed confrontation with civilians in such an emotionally charged atmosphere.

Lyon chose to ignore his training, and instead, used the capture to make a strong public statement. In a grandiose display of deluded might, Nathaniel Lyon marched his captives through the streets of St. Louis, into the heart of the crowd. Rather than avoiding a confrontation, he marched squarely into one.

Lyon placed his long line of prisoners between two columns of Blair's regiment. By 5:30 p.m., the march to the arsenal began. Bands played. United States flags flew. The sidewalks' were packed with on-lookers. Those adverse to the federal army jeered and insulted them. Soon rocks, bricks, and other objects pelted the soldiers. At this explosive moment the column halted to allow the rear units to catch up. A drunken man attempted to push through the column to get to the other side of the street. He was thrown down by the Home Guard. He arose and fired a pistol at them. Several Home Guards fired over the heads of the crowd.

Troops near the incident held their fire, but those near the rear received direct gunshot wounds from the crowd. Their Captain was killed. His men fired into the crowd. Most of the civilians panicked and ran. But those who stayed exchanged shots with the soldiers.

After several minutes, Lyon managed to cease the firing, but not before 28 civilians were dead and 75 wounded. This would be referred to as "The Massacre." Five of Lyon's men were killed.

1. Ibid, p 186.

In a public statement published in the newspapers, Lyon refused to take responsibility for the massacre: "If innocent men, women, and children, whose curiosity placed them in a dangerous position, it is no fault of the troops." [1]

This incident produced a wild state of alarm in St. Louis. Again, citizens filled the streets, listening to prominent politicians speak out against Lyon and Lincoln and their "blood lust."

Oriel Wright, one-of the strongest opponents of secession at the recent convention of federal relations, suddenly saw the reality of Lincoln's intentions: "If Unionism means atrocious deeds as I have witnessed in St. Louis, I am no longer a Union man." [2]

Ten thousand civilians fled St. Louis. Saloons, restaurants, and businesses closed, as crowds of armed men roamed the streets. Police guarded major intersections. At midnight, in Jefferson City, the Capital, Claiborne Jackson ordered the city's church bells to ring, as the signal to call an emergency session of the General Assembly. The legislators arrived, armed and fearful. Within fifteen minutes both Houses passed the much debated new Militia Bill, which gave the governor sweeping military powers to "suppress rebellion and repel invasion." Claiborne Jackson ordered his State Guard troops to burn the Osage River bridge to block an attack by federal troops, but they did not appear. General Harney met with Frank Blair, intending to disarm his Wide-Awakes and Home Guards. Blair refused, saying that Abraham Lincoln had authorized his plan to capture Jefferson City. But Lyon's attack on Camp Jackson and the slaughter of civilians that followed galvanized the population. Now they saw that Lincoln's policy was coercion and the military occupation of Missouri. One St. Louis resident said: "We are so bound down by a military despotism here...that we can hardly say that our souls are our own. The city is as silent as a grave. We are bound, hand and foot, under slavery worse than Egyptian."

Newspapers reported that Governor Yates' Illinois troops were poised directly across the border, waiting for the signal to invade. One reader wrote:

> Frank Blair is a dictator; he has assembled troops from all parts of Illinois...All within an hour's ride, and if the slightest show of resistance is made, we will all be crushed out.
>
> ...While chaos and fear reigned in S. Louis, in the rural interior, the opposite was true. Thousands of men flocked to recruiting stations to join Claiborne Jackson's State Guard. One volunteer said: "My blood boils in my veins when I think of the position of Missouri; held in the Union at the point of a bayonet. I feel outraged. But the sullen

1. Ibid, p 192.
2. Ibid, p 197.

> submission of downtrodden men will be avenged the more terribly in the days of uprising. May I live to see that day." [1]

Former Governor Sterling Price, the president of the recent federal relations convention, and many other prominent men, hastened to Jefferson City and offered their services to Claiborne Jackson. The new Militia Bill authorized Jackson to appoint eight brigadier-generals to lead the state militia men from eight military districts. He appointed Price to be a Major-General, over, all the other officers.

Sterling Price was from an old Virginia family, studied law, and moved with his father's family to Missouri and settled on a farm in Charlton County. He was elected to the legislature and chosen Speaker of the House. He owed this position to his family tree rather than to his knowledge of parliamentary law or the business of legislation. Yet he filled the role admirably. Four years later he was elected to the U.S. Congress. Shortly after taking his seat, war was declared against Mexico, and he resigned, returned to Missouri, raised a cavalry regiment, and was assigned to lead it.

In that war he took possession of New Mexico and Chihuahua, and participated in other battles that were won by the United States, chiefly the one at Sacramento. That victory was instrumental in giving the USA possession of the territory out of which California, Utah, Nevada, Arizona, and New Mexico were formed.

Enter Sterling Price

At the war's close, Sterling Price returned to Missouri, was elected governor and served four years. In 1861 he opposed secession, but when Nathaniel Lyon ruthlessly killed those civilians in St. Louis, he modified his position, not toward disunion, but to defend the state against Lincoln's invasion.

One day after the massacre, General Harney issued a proclamation stating that civil order must be maintained, although he approved of the capture of Camp Jackson. Frank Blair felt that this proclamation did not allow for stronger federal action. Once again he sent an aide to Abraham Lincoln to remove Harney. The President signed the removal order, and then had second thoughts. Lincoln was now concerned about the firings. He wrote Blair: "We have a great deal of anxiety about St. Louis. I understand that an order has gotten out from the War Department to you, to be delivered or withheld at your discretion, relieving General Harney from his command. I was not quite satisfied with the order when it was made, though on the whole I thought it best to make it; but since then I have become more doubtful of its propriety. I do not write now to countermand it, but I say, I wish you to hold it, unless in your judgment, the necessity to the contrary is very urgent. There are several

1. Ibid., p 198 .

reasons for this. We had better have him as a friend than an enemy. It will dissatisfy a good many who otherwise would be quiet. More than all, we first relieve him, then restore him, and now relieve him again. The public will ask, 'Why all the vacillation?' Still, in your judgment, it is indispensable, let it be so." [1]

Blair was convinced that it was. So, Lincoln sacked Harney one more time and promoted Lyon to Brigadier-General of Volunteers. But the notification was sent by letter and it took time to reach Harney's desk. In that time interval Harney made a major political agreement with the Claiborne Jackson government.

Harney-Price Agreement

May 20: Harney, still unaware that he had been fired, contacted Governor Jackson to prevent further confrontations between the civilian population and the federalized forces.

Claiborne Jackson was afraid to meet Harney since Abraham Lincoln had ordered a warrant for his arrest. Sterling Price volunteered to go in his place. Harney accepted Pride because he had "honor, purity of motive, and loyalty to the Union."

When they met, both Price and Harney agree that Lincoln's policy of coercion was wrong. Both wanted to continue Missouri's neutrality. They believed that as long as Missouri's government assumed responsibility for keeping the peace, Harney would take no military action to provoke conflict. In addition, Lyon would not be allowed to search civilians or boats for weapons, and U.S. regular army officers could not lead Wide-Awakes (or federalized Home Guards).

Blair and Lyon were livid over what they saw as Harney's "submission to the secessionists." To them, the agreement was illegal, since Harney had already been stripped of his authority, and the pact was nothing more than a ruse to buy time for Claiborne Jackson to get arms to make war on Washington.

Sterling Price and Jackson realized that with Nathaniel Lyon in complete control, he would initiate a full-scale invasion to topple Missouri's government. But Claiborne Jackson made one last desperate bid for peace. He requested a meeting with Blair and Lyon in St. Louis, while still facing arrest. Grudgingly, Lyon guaranteed the governor's safety.

The four men met at the elegant Planter's House Hotel. All were dressed with formal splendor. Price wore his Mexican War ceremonial uniform; ostrich-plumed hat, sash, sword, and tall cavalry boots.

Claiborne Jackson said he wanted strict neutrality for his state in the war. Jackson was willing to disband his State Guard and guarantee the rights of all citizens, regardless of their political position. He agreed to stop requesting

1. Ibid, p 205

arms from other states and the Confederacy. In return, Jackson demanded that Blair and Lyon disarm their Wide-Awakes and Home Guards, and not occupy localities other than those currently held by them. Jackson also pledged adherence to the Harney-Price Agreement.

Lyon listened for half an hour, nervously puffing on his cigar and pulling on his beard. Then he stood up and dominated the proceedings. Lyon could not suppress his deep hatred for those he considered secessionists. He grilled Jackson on what he believed were inconsistent statements. He asked, without a State Guard, how could Jackson protect residents, when he couldn't do it with them? And how could Jackson punish criminals against the federal government without the means to do so? And, most importantly, to Lyon, the idea of stopping the requests for Confederate arms from entering the state was an admission of disloyalty, and sympathy for the seceded states.

Lyon then stated the true point of his harangue; he would follow Abraham Lincoln's policy that had begun in Maryland: to insure loyalty by force rather than allow the possibility of secession. He refused to accept any limit upon federal authority or any restriction on his own omnipotence. Lyon said he would never make peace with secessionists. He would punish them. He inferred that God was in him.

Then, without consulting with Lincoln or the War Department, Lyon personally declared war on Missouri; "Rather than concede to the State of Missouri the right to demand that my government shall not enlist troops within her limits, or bring troops into the State whenever it pleases, or move its troops at its own will, into or out of or through the State, than concede to the State of Missouri for one single instant, the right to dictate to my government in any manner however unimportant, it would be better sir, far better, that the blood of every man, woman, and child within its limits should flow, that she should defy the federal government. This means war." [1]

Lyon turned, strode out of the room, his sword clattering. All the others sat in stunned silence.

Claiborne Jackson and Sterling Price hurried back to Jefferson City. Jackson called for 50,000 Missourians to drive Lyon's army out of the state. Meanwhile, Lyon began his march on the Capital. Claiborne Jackson realized that his militia was badly outnumbered, since there had not been enough time to recruit more than a few thousand men. He abandoned Jefferson City without a fight, along with most of the legislators, and proclaimed a "government-in-exile."

Jackson and Price moved the state's official paper and public records to Boonville, a town where their supporters and militia volunteers were located.

1. Ibid, p 213

Jackson's plan was to block and stall Lyon at Boonville, giving him time to make a more determined stand at nearby Lexington.

Lyon arrived at Boonville with 1,700 men and slowly pushed Jackson's men back into the town. Lyon outnumbered the Missourians by four-to-one. His army regulars had artillery. The raw militia men had no big guns. Jackson's men panicked and deserted Boonville.

Although this confrontation was little more than a skirmish, Lyon called it a great Union victory, since the Missourians were compelled to abandon the defense of the Missouri River, which meant the cutting off of recruits from the north side, to reach Jackson, who was on the south side.

Price and Jackson fell back to Lexington but there was no safety there, as Lyon advanced from one direction, and more U.S. army men closed in from the other side, from Fort Leavenworth in Kansas, to encircle the Missourians. All looked bleak. Then came the first good news for Jackson and Price.

One thousand German Wide-Awakes, commanded by the German Fritz Sigel, were camped near Carthage. Under the cover of night, 350 Missourian State Guards made a forced march, caught the Wide-Awakes by surprise, killing or wounding or capturing about 600. Sigel was routed and the remaining men retreated until they had put forty miles between themselves and the Missourians.

This was a great psychological blow against the federal invasion, and showed the population that they were not hopelessly subjugated. Also, Sigel's crushing defeat made Lyon more cautious and he returned to Boonville.

The United States army, from Fort Leavenworth, still drove forward, dividing into three groups to encircle Price and Jackson at Lexington. Price remained there to fight, and Jackson crossed the Osage River in a flatboat, moved into Neosho, in southwest Missouri, where he set up a government-in exile. Once established there, his legislators voted to secede; not to join the Confederacy, but to transform Missouri into an independent republic. Secession, whether as a republic or to join the South, was not legal, because the convention to determine Missouri's relation to the federal government had written into law that citizens of the state had to vote on the convention's decision, to accept or reject secession or to remain in the Union. But the majority of the voters had now been over-run by federal armies and no such action could take place.

In addition, when the remnants of Claiborne Jackson's General Assembly gathered at Neosho, that body was nowhere near a quorum. Jackson spent a week securing proxies from members but failed to get the required number. So their decision to secede was doubly illegal.

Claiborne Jackson never had any intention of joining the Southern Confederacy. To do so would thwart all his aims. Jefferson Davis, the President of the Confederacy, did not want to help Missouri. He wanted Missourians to help the South, where they could be shifted to any theatre of the war, particularly to Virginia, where huge armies on both sides attempted to take the other's Capital.

Governor Jackson wrote a letter to Jefferson Davis and simply asked for aid. Davis' reply was realistic from the Confederacy's point of view, but unacceptable to Claiborne Jackson. Davis said he looked forward to the time when he could extend aid, whether in men or supplies, but that could only come about when Missouri's troops were integrated into the Southern armed forces.

Simultaneously, Sterling Price crossed the Arkansas border into Confederate territory. There he met General Benjamin McCulloch at forlorn Cowskin Prairie. Price asked for military assistance and received the possibility of getting it. Here the situation was different. If the federals crossed into Arkansas they would be invading C.S.A. land. If Price could lure them across the border, Jefferson Davis would accept that Missouri, was helping the South, and might send troops.

Without McCulloch's reinforcements the Missourians faced annihilation. But McCulloch was not anxious to join the fray. He viewed Price's men as "a rag-tag rabble."

McCulloch had explicit orders to fulfill for a specific mission, which did not include Missouri. He was to protect the "Indian Territory," which included part of Arkansas. John Rose, the Chief of the Cherokee Nation, was in the process of signing a treaty of cooperation with the Confederacy, giving the South manpower, with the promise that if the C.S.A. won the war, his people would no longer be captives of the United States; forced to live on reservations. They would once again regain their former status as an independent nation.

As such, McCulloch was restricted to Arkansas. LeRoy Pope, the Confederacy's Secretary of War, wrote this to McCulloch: "Give assistance to Missouri as will serve the main purpose of your command." Walker explained why Missouri was such a low priority, even though it was strategically critical: "The position of Missouri, as a Southern state, still in the Union, requires, as you will readily perceive, much prudence and circumspection, and should only be, when necessity and propriety unite, that active and direct assistance should be offered by crossing the boundary and entering the state before communicating with this Department." [1]

McCulloch, a Texan, was one of the most colorful soldiers of the South. Flamboyant, head-strong, intelligent, coarse, sometimes brutal, usually profane, he had served under Sam Houston during the Texas Revolution. He

1. Robert E. Stalhop, *Sterling Price; Portrait of a Southerner* (Columbia MO. University of Missouri press, 1971) p. 169.

had distinguished himself for gallantry at San Jacinto. As a Ranger, he fought Indians in Texas and Mexicans in the Mexican War. For his outstanding valor, President Franklin Pierce appointed McCulloch United States Marshal of Texas. Later, he served as Peace Commissioner to Utah during the Mormon Rebellion and was considered for the role of governor of that territory.

At the outbreak of the Civil War he was promoted to Brigadier-General in the Confederate army and was sent into Arkansas with orders to organize the troops there. McCulloch believed in discipline, organization, and scientific planning for battle. That is why he saw Sterling Price as "an old militia general leading a half-armed mob."

Union forces edged toward Arkansas. McCulloch was now willing to help Price. Together they fielded a force of 11,000 men. McCulloch coordinated three separate attack columns; his Arkansas soldiers, led by their own officers, Price's contingent, and Claiborne Jackson's State Guard, who were suddenly cut off by Sigel. Using only swift-moving cavalry, all three groups turned on Sigel, and once again, crushed him.

When the Missourians first saw McCulloch they cheered. One of them said: "We were all young then, and full of hope, and looked with delighted eyes at the first Confederate soldiers we had ever seen. Their men all dressed in sober gray and McCulloch, resplendent with golden braid and stars of gold." [1]

The Missourians were confident that the Confederates had come to liberate their state, but as usual, McCulloch was not impressed with them. The Missourians had no uniforms, and their rank was designated by pieces of colored cloth tied around their arms. Many had no weapons. Few understood the basics of military discipline.

Now that Price and Jackson were safe for the moment, McCulloch stunned them all by marching back into Arkansas. But he did tell Price that he was prepared to assist again if Lyon moved toward Arkansas.

McCulloch added one more proviso. He would only return if Price agreed to subordinate himself to the Confederate forces. Price, a man with a big ego, regarded no man as his equal. But this time he backed down. Clearly, without McCulloch, he had no chance to whip Lyon.

Lyon advanced for another attack, but a week of torrential rain made the roads impassable for the federals. On July 3rd the weather improved. Lyon continued on. Price made one more bid to draw McCulloch into the conflict. They met again at Cowskin Prairie. McCulloch hesitated once more. But Union forces rapidly approached the Arkansas border. McCulloch felt he had the right to make a small symbolic strike. Lyon was stopped. McCulloch withdrew.

1. Ibid., p. 171.

Lyon withdrew to strategic Springfield, still near the Arkansas border. From there he sent officers to St. Louis and Washington, demanding reinforcements, but received no attention. To make matters worse, at the same time several of his regiment's three-month enlistments expired, and these men simply faded away. McCulloch re-emerged, and now in complete command, advanced on Springfield. He rested his men, exhausted by the 110 degree heat, at an obscure point on the map: Wilson's Creek.

Nathaniel Lyon, aware that his enemies were closing in and that he was outnumbered, began to show his mental instability. His logical move was to pull back to St. Louis, but his ego would not allow that. The intense heat, and not being able to sleep for days, drove him to the suicidal decision to attack. Then he cancelled the order. Then he prepared for an offensive again. His indecision affected the morale of his troops.

A subordinate officer made an impassioned speech that strengthened Lyon's resolve. He said that to even think of retreat would give this entire region to Price and McCulloch. They would boast of their easy victory and terrorize loyal Union residents, and they would lose their resolve. This would lead to the desertion of Lyon's men. The officer ended with: "Let us eat the last of the mule flesh and fire the last cartridge before we think of retreating." This gave Lyon new conviction. When asked if his army would retreat, he snapped: "Not until we are whipped out!"[1]

Price and McCulloch maneuvered as if to attack, probing with skirmishes, but they bided their time. This made Lyon more anxious. He called a meeting of his officers and made a final illogical decision: "Gentlemen, there is no prospect of being reinforced. Our supply of provisions is running short. There is a superior force in front of us. It is evident that we must retreat. The question arises, what is the best method of doing it. Shall we endeavor to retreat without giving the enemy a battle beforehand, and run the risk of having to fight every inch along the line of our retreat, or shall we attack him in his position, and endeavor to hurt him so that he cannot follow us? I am decidedly in favor of the latter plan." Lyon's hatred of the secessionists made him lose all sound military judgment.

Lyon divided his smaller force. Half would make a frontal assault, half would circle behind Price and McCulloch's camp and create mass confusion. It began to rain heavily and Lyon said to one of his officers: "I have a feeling that I will not survive this battle...I will gladly give my life for a victory." [2]

Dawn, August 10th: Lyon's army went on the offensive. Initially, Price and McCulloch's men were pushed back. They were reinforced and Lyon's troops gave ground. His encircling soldiers had better results. They surprised Price's

1. Christopher Phillips, *Damned Yankee: The Life of General Nathaniel Lyon.*
2. Ibid., p. 240.

men who were not prepared to fight. Unnerved, they ran. It seemed they were routed, but re-grouping, they counter-attacked. The fighting was intense, hand-to-hand. Lyon's troops were devastated, and fled back to Springfield.

Lyon saw his gamble falling to pieces. He galloped to the front to rally his men. He was wounded in the leg. His horse was killed. A mini-ball grazed his head. Bleeding badly, he mounted another horse to lead one last charge. "Come on, my brave boys, I will lead you forward!" At that moment Lyon was shot in the chest and died in minutes. His men staggered back to St .Louis.

Once victory was assured, McCulloch disappeared back into Arkansas.

Without him, Price desperately needed to put his "rag-tag mob" together as an effective fighting force, to have any hope of success. Price spent a month at Springfield drilling his men, and then, with 4,500 militia and volunteers, he moved toward Lexington and the Missouri River, which was held by Illinois troops and Wide-Awakes.

September 12th: Price drove the Union men back to their last line of defense, the Masonic College building, then applied siege tactics, so the federals could not reach drinking water; but they refused to surrender. Price then devised a plan to break the deadlock. He took bales of hemp that were stacked on the docks and soaked them in the river so they would not burn. His men rolled them in front, as cover, while they advanced on the college.

The federals realized the futility of further resistance and flew the white flag. Price took 3,500 prisoners but his victory at Lexington proved untenable. He did not have the men or weapons to hold off the 40,000 Unionist reinforcements heading toward him. He retreated to Neosho, where Claiborne Jackson's government-in-exile had assembled.

From there Price issued a proclamation to the people of Missouri, assuring them that his army "organized under the laws of this state, for the protection of your homes and firesides," would continue to remain in the field to prevent "subjugation and enslavement by the usurpers in Washington."

Three weeks later, Price led 10,000 men once again toward the Missouri River, and once again toward Lexington, hoping to start a general civilian uprising. Although he forced the surrender of the Union garrison there, the insurrection failed to materialize.

In February 1862, 12,000 federals, under General Sam Curtis, drove Sterling Price out of Missouri. With the exception of a few probing attacks, and one major and unsuccessful incursion by Price in 1864, the state remained largely in Union hands.

Missouri Not Legally Admitted To Confederacy

A week after the battle at Wilson's Creek, the Confederate Congress passed a bill formalizing an alliance with Missouri, but not drawing that state under the Southern government: "That the Congress of the Confederate

States recognize the government of which Claiborne Fox Jackson is the chief magistrate of the legally elected and regularly constituted government of the people and the State of Missouri; and the Present of the Confederate States be, and is hereby empowered, at his discretion, at some time prior to the admission of the said State, as a member of this Confederacy, to perfect and proclaim an alliance, offensive and defensive, with the said government, limited to the period of the existing war between the Confederacy and the United States." [1]

Then on November 5, 1861, Claiborne Jackson, in trying to draw the Confederacy into defending Missouri, pretended to join the Southern government without actually doing so, by stating the loophole that made it clear that such a union was not legal. He sent this document to Jefferson Davis:

> I have the honor and the pleasure of transmitting herewith, "An Act declaring the political ties heretofore existing between the State of Missouri and the United States of America, dissolved"; also "An Act ratifying the Constitution of the Provisional Government of the Confederate States of America." These two acts were passed with almost perfect unanimity by the General Assembly [in exile]...If, in the opinion of the Confederate Government, anything further is required on the part of Missouri to complete and perfect her admission...The Executive of the State is directed and authorized to perform all other acts which heretofore become necessary to secure the admission of the State. This clause of the Act was inserted, not because the General Assembly deemed it at all necessary to secure the admission of the State, but in their abundance of caution, it was considered safest to provide any and all contingencies that might arise. [The following was a basic requirement by law to secede and become an independent republic or part of the Confederacy.] But some of the members thought that the Confederate Government might require the Act to be ratified by a vote of the people [of Missouri] before the admission of the State. [As we shall see, both Jefferson Davis and the Confederate Congress recognized this truth.] On this point it is proper to say that the Act would at once have been submitted to a vote of the people but for the reason that the State is invaded by the federal army to such an extent as to preclude the possibility of holding an election at the present time.

Here, Claiborne Jackson acknowledges that, as it was, the document did not make a legal connection to the C.S.A. "I am sure that four-fifths of the people desire an immediate and unconditional connection with the Southern Government, and I pray that it will soon be consummated.[2] Jabez Curry, an Alabamian, was a member of the Confederate Congress. Here, he expresses

1. *Journal of Congress of the Confederate States of America, 1861-1865*, (Washington : Government Printing Office, 1904) p. 363.
2. Ibid., p. 695.

why, later on, Missouri's pseudo-admission and pseudo-representation had no legal basis:

> Bills were introduced into the Confederate Congress providing for the admission of Missouri into the Confederacy. Robert Toombs, and other prominent Congressmen favored its admission and the measure was enacted into law. I opposed them ineffectively, and almost alone, on the grounds that Missouri's admission would be in utter contradiction to all the principles underlying our secession and the formation-of the Confederacy; that the majority of the people in Missouri were not in sympathy with us, and that the representatives would have no constituents. My predictions were all too faithfully verified. Missouri was soon in complete control of the federal army; and those who sat as representatives of that State owed their pretense of any election to the votes cast by soldiers in the Confederate army who were from Missouri. With some honorable exceptions, the representatives were worse than useless. [1]
>
> Two months after the supposed absorption of Missouri into the Confederacy, which would have given the Southern War Department control over all the armed forces in that state, Jefferson Davis, in a message to Congress, demonstrated that, to his chagrin, Missouri still had an independent army not subject to Southern authority. This is yet another indication the Missouri was not legally part of the South: "All the troops now in service in the State of Missouri, are state troops, commanded by state officers, which have never been tendered or received," since Claiborne Jackson had not complied with the basic military laws of the Confederacy; supplying muster rolls so that they could be incorporated into the nation-army. Jefferson Davis was looking for a general for the Western theatre, and considered Sterling Price, but rejected him when Missouri troops were not transferred to Confederate service.

Hamilton Gamble, Provisional Governor

When Claiborne Jackson abandoned Jefferson City as Nathaniel Lyon's forces converged on the Capital, he set up his "government-in-exile" in Neosho. Then the Unionist members of the Federal Relations Convention set up a rival nonelected government. The convention gave itself sweeping legislative powers, unconcerned about the legality of their actions. Roger Wilson, the presiding officer, wrote this report: "We find the capital deserted by the governor and other officers of the State. We find that our governor has, upon his proclamation, incited the people of this Commonwealth to armed

1. Jabez Curry, *Civil History of the Government Of The Confederate States, With Some Personal Reminiscences* (Richmond: B.F. Johnson Publishing Co. 1911), p. 781

opposition to the laws and government of the United States, and that he is in open rebellion against that government."[1]

The convention declared that the office of Governor, Lt. Governor, Secretary of State, and the legislators were all vacant, and that elections would be held to fill those posts. But the elections were conducted by the convention, not the citizen voters. Hamilton Gamble was "elected" by the convention as Provisional Governor.

Gamble immediately stated that a regular election by the voters, all eligible Missourians, would take place in one year; in August 1862. But by October 1861, Gamble told a more truthful story. Voting would actually take place in August 1863 because, he said, of the magnitude of the fighting throughout the state. Then, in June 1862, Gamble ordered the unelected Provisional Government to continue on until August 1864, although Missouri was much more secure.

Hamilton Gamble was a well-known political figure. He had been in the State Assembly, was Missouri's Secretary of State, and Chief Justice of its Supreme Court. He gained national attention when his court weighed the fate of the slave, Dred Scott. In 1834, Scott, the servant of Dr. John Emerson, a U.S. army surgeon, was taken by his master from Missouri to Illinois, a free state. After Dr. Emerson's death, in 1846, Scott sued Mrs. Emerson for his freedom on the grounds that his residence in Illinois ended his bondage.

Gamble's court ruled against Scott, determining that Mrs. Emerson had the right to retain ownership of him even when she went into a free state. On appeal, the case became a landmark decision before the US Supreme Court. Their decision also went against Scott, further enflaming the sectional complaints between North and South.

Hamilton Gamble's personal attitude toward slavery was complex and influenced by contradictory factors. Raised in Virginia, he disliked Northern criticism of that institution, although he never adopted an extreme proslavery position. Earlier in his career, as a lawyer, he had represented both sides, slaves and owners, in freedom suits.

In Virginia, the dominant political philosophy was state sovereignty advocated by the Democrats. Gamble went against this doctrine and became a Whig, a party that advocated a strong central power, which restricted the independence of the states. When the Whigs faded, Gamble joined the Republicans who also championed Washington's authority.

Before a career in state government, when Gamble first moved to Missouri, he practiced law in the circuit courts of the First Judicial District, which

1. Dennis K. Bowman, *Lincoln's Resolute Unionist, Hamilton Gamble* (Baton Rouge, LA: Louisiana State University Press 2006) p. 114.

encompassed most of the central and northwestern part of the state. He also argued cases before the Missouri Supreme Court.

At that time, judges and lawyers traveled together on horseback from county to county, covering thousands of miles each year. Unable to carry anything but the barest necessities, and a law book or two, the men shared the hardships and tedium of their journeys, filling the monotonous hours with conversation, debates and practical jokes.

One of these legal fraternities later complained to Gamble that after his departure from law to politics, the lawyers no longer enjoyed the "pleasure and joy which we used to have, traveling this laborious circuit. Indeed, there is not the warm-hearted fellowship with us now, as when you and I traveled together." [1]

Hamilton Gamble formed a law partnership with his brother-in-law, Edward Sates, who, years later, would become a member of Abraham Lincoln's Cabinet. This would become a significant factor to Gamble as Provisional Governor.

Gamble was respected more as a moderate statesman than a political ideologue. As a Supreme Court Justice, his opinions did not reflect his own point of view but the more lofty principle of "precedence." He rarely overturned lower court decisions, believing it better to let an improper ruling stand once it had become a settled matter of law.

Gamble described his judicial doctrine: "It is only when we are satisfied that an error has been committed in the decision of our predecessors, which must be corrected before it becomes a rule, that we feel willing to interfere with previous adjudications. In our state, where the tenure of the judicial office is but for a short time [judges were elected, not appointed], it is of the utmost importance that great delicacy should be observed in overruling or shaking the authority of previous decisions. If, in the change to which the Court must be subject, the spirit of innovation, and disregard of precedent, shall find place, the administration of the law shall be uncertain, and too dangerous to the rights of the people to be endured." [2]

Gamble's Supreme Court did not actively legislate from the Bench to promote prosperity or to serve ulterior political motives. Gamble believed that judicial activism or political bias would make the judiciary part of the legislative branch.

However, Gamble's principles of judicial statesmanship were tested in the Dred Scott case, which was the most controversial of its time. At stake, to prevent disunion and war, it was absolutely necessary for the North and South to compromise on the slavery issue. Gamble was forced to make his

1. Ibid., p. 6.
2. Ibid., p. 45.

decision against Scott based on those kind of political considerations, not just its legality.

After serving three years of Missouri's High Court, Gamble resigned, in October 1854, for health reasons. In his youth he had been a heavy drinker, and the affects remained with him all his life. He was now fifty-five and had made a sizable fortune as a successful lawyer and could retire comfortably. It was the war that brought him back into the limelight.

Convention Above Constitution

The only way to make the Provisional Government a legal body was to impeach Claiborne Jackson and his legislature-in-exile. This was the constitutionally correct method but Gamble, reversing his usual cautious, moderate reading of the law, became a revolutionary radical. He proclaimed that the on-going convention did not derive its powers from the state constitution. It was an "extra and supra constitutional body," in all respects. It held the same authority as if "all the people were gathered together in one vast plain," and it alone could depose Claiborne Jackson. Gamble then asserted that the convention could make legal decisions without the consent of the people and could abolish or replace the current constitution at will.

Those who disagreed with this view found themselves in jail. Uriel Wright, a legislator and convention member, who had not followed Claiborne Jackson into exile, had the audacity to say that the Provisional Government did not have the legal authority to say that the Provisional Government did not have the legal authority to depose Claiborne Jackson. He also said that Abraham Lincoln, through his unconstitutional call for federal troops, was most responsible for the state and national chaos. Wright was arrested and expelled from the convention.

A factor which supported Uriel Wright's claims, was that the majority of Missourians still considered Claiborne Jackson the true governor. Further, most citizens believed the convention had greatly exceeded its original mandate to define the state's relation to the federal government and nothing else.

Radicals Declare War On Gamble

Simultaneously, Hamilton Gamble was both a conservative and a radical. As such, he ran afoul of his more extreme Radical supporters. As a Radical, he believed the convention was above the law. As a conservative, he did not believe that the federal government had the legal right to interfere with the institution of slavery. Yet many Radical Republicans felt that the abolition of slavery was the highest priority. Abraham Lincoln's Emancipation Proclamation, enacted in late 1862, was a "war measure," and extended only to the seceded states, where it had no legal authority.

Earlier, in the summer of 1861, the Unionist Home Guards believed that slavery was the cause of the war, freed them whenever they could. As yet, this was not part of Lincoln's policy. Some federal units aided in the escape of bondsmen, then executed the owners and looted their homes. Hamilton Gamble tried to stop this but the federal officers would not obey him.

Because of these atrocities, Gamble actually moved closer to Claiborne Jackson's original position of raising a Missouri army to prevent a federal presence there.

As noted before, elections for the major state officials were pushed far into the future but this created new problems for the machinery of the Provisional Government. Without a real legislature, fiscal issues could not be properly addressed. Without elections, there could also be no new representatives admitted to Congress. Missouri lurched toward bankruptcy, incapable of paying the militia's salaries or equipping them.

This forced the federal officers to resort to confiscating the property of slave-holders or the disloyal to sell at auctions, to generate cash to finance their troops. This also became a crude form of abolition. Upon confiscation, the slaves were freed. Gamble publicly opposed all that. Missouri's Radical Republicans put increasing pressure on Gamble. They saw him as being lenient with anti-Union sympathizers. They felt that the escalation of guerrilla war and its atrocities was due to Gamble's insistence that only the state militia should defend the state. The Radicals wanted a vast increase in federal troops to do the job. The Radicals launched a full-scale smear campaign against Hamilton Gamble. In August 1862, a committee of Radicals went to Washington to convince Abraham Lincoln that Gamble had failed miserably and should be replaced by Union General Sam Curtis. He had become notorious for his atrocities against Maryland's civilians when he was in command there.

Lincoln hesitated, fearing that radicalization of the state government would mean the loss of conservative support for the war effort. To mollify the Radicals, Lincoln appointed Curtis to direct military operations in Missouri. But Gamble and Curtis had totally opposing views on the conduct of the war. Neither would cooperate with the other. Gamble believed that Curtis was too close to the Radicals. Even when Lincoln stepped in to reconcile their differences, the President was unsuccessful. Some of the points of disagreement were wheher the "disloyal" should be forcibly banished from Missouri (as Curtis insisted), and who controlled the various militia units — Gamble and the state of Missouri, or Curtis and the federal government? Then, in December 1862, Curtis initiated General Order No. 45. This greatly expanded the Military Provost Marshal law system. These marshals could gather private information on those called disloyal and interrogate them with violence. They could arrest and detain indefinitely those they called "guerrillas. Although both classes were civilians, they were unconstitutionally, convicted by military tribunals.

All this took place as more of Missouri returned to peace. Even Lincoln asked Curtis to rescind General Order 35, and restore civil law. Curtis refused. He convinced the President, at least for the moment, that only martial Law could maintain peace. Hamilton Gamble recognized the long-term consequences of General Order 35. It completely usurped state, Congressional and national judiciary powers. Finally, Gamble prevailed upon Lincoln to remove Curtis.

All this put further pressure on Hamilton Gamble to make concessions to the Radicals, who were becoming increasingly militant, particularly on the issue of slavery. He re-convened the convention, requesting a bill that would abolish slavery by 1870. This was much too slow for the Radicals. They increased their attacks on him, insisting on immediate emancipation. They portrayed Gamble as either a fool or a Machiavelli; insisting on total war against "anti-Unionists". Gamble saw this would lead to disaster. He wrote Lincoln: "When office the Union men were oppressed and outraged all over the state. Now they are organized and feel that the strength is with them. In these circumstances there has arisen a desire for revenge, which however natural it may be is utterly hostile to good government and would desolate the state. It would be easy to go with this current, but doing so requires that I endeavor to moderate or restrain the inductiveness which would ruin a class, many of whom are no doubt criminal, without benefitting any other class permanently." [1]

The rift was enlarged by the Radicals to the-point where Gamble's loyalty was questioned. These Accusations, he learned from his brother-in-law and U.S. Attorney-General, Edward Bates, undermined the confidence of Edwin Stanton, the Secretary of War, and the top army officers. Gamble was called a "suspected person" which weakened his ability to govern by "belittling him before his own people." Bates said "This could only lead to anarchy in Missouri, and calamity and Shame in the nation." Only Lincoln had no doubts about Gamble's loyalty. [2]

Charles Drake and the Rise of the Ultra-Radicals

By the summer of 1863 the most extreme Radical Republicans formed their own political organization; the Radical Union Party. Leading them was Charles Drake, a St. Louis attorney whose political views had undergone a complete metamorphosis since the beginning of the war. Drake was a skilled opportunist and demagogue. He had studied law under Hamilton Gamble, and had moved, according to the political winds, from a Whig to a "Know-Nothing"

1. p. 187.
2. p. 202.

(American Party) to a Democrat. In 1860, he had supported Claiborne Jackson, and spoke out strongly against anti-slavery agitation. However, during the following winter Drake experienced a profound conversion; suddenly believing that slavery was the root cause of all of Missouri's difficulties. By the spring of 1862, he had become an ardent abolitionist.

Drake assumed control of the Radical/abolitionist cause and vowed to unseat Hamilton Gamble by all means, fair or criminal. By September 1863, when all legal means had failed, Drake planned a coup to overthrow the Provisional Government and install a military regime.

Abraham Lincoln learned of this and placed Union General John Schofield as a buffer between Gamble and the Radicals. Earlier, Schofield had been Chief of Staff to Nathaniel Lyon. But even Schofield ran afoul of the Radicals. He knew of their plan to violently topple Gamble and he issued a proclamation instituting more extreme martial law against anyone promoting insurrection among the troops or civilians.

Schofield took this action based on a letter he received from Lincoln, in which the President seems to waver between radicalism and moderation.

> You must not give the state and its representatives in Congress to the enemies of the Union, driving its friends there into political exile... Under your recent order, which I have approved, you will only arrest individuals and suppress assemblies or newspapers when they may be working palpable injury to the military in your charge ...With the matter of removing certain individuals from time to time who are supposed to be mischievous in certain counties, I am not now interfering; but I am leaving to your discretion.[1]

To counter any and all preparations to stop attempts at a coup, the Radicals once again sent a delegation to Washington, this time to persuade Lincoln to replace Gamble. Charles Drake headed this group. He demanded that General Benjamin "Beast" Butler should take over as-military dictator in Missouri.

In October 1863, Hamilton Gamble countered the Radical attack against him by issuing a proclamation warning the public that a revolutionary faction was conspiring to overthrow him and his government. He did not name the specific leaders. Until this moment, Gamble had deliberately ignored the threats made against him, but now he felt compelled to answer the charges.

But on December 16, Gamble was seriously injured when he slipped on the icy steps of the governor's mansion. He died of pneumonia on January 31, 1864. He was replaced by the Radical Republican Thomas Fletcher, who had previously commanded a Missouri regiment. Before the war, Fletcher was

1. John G. Nicolay and John Hay, editors, *The complete works of Abraham Lincoln* (New York: Tandy-Thomas Co., 1905) p. 283.

a Democrat, opposed to slavery; then he became a Republican in 1856, and progressively became more radical as the war went on.

Now the Radicals dominated Missouri's government. They viewed all others who were at odds with their program as disloyal. Through skewed loyalty oaths they barred the opposition from taking part, or from voting. A one-party dictatorship was achieved.

The Guerrilla War

The war in Missouri was very complicated. One needs a scorecard to tell who was fighting who, and for what reasons. At first it was the federal army, supplemented by Unionist state militia men, battling Sterling Price's and Claiborne Jackson's anti-federal militia. Later, Confederate troops aided by militia from other border states helped both Price and Jackson.

Then, Price was partially grafted onto the Confederate army and led Southern troops against Lincoln's forces. In addition, as the fighting became more intense, and as Sterling Price was driven out of Missouri; small, fast-moving units, loosely fighting, for him, but not under his direct command, continually harassed and bloodied his slower moving Union army. The federals, in turn, countered with their own small groups, who also existed as semi-independent guerrillas. Not under close scrutiny, all sides committed atrocities in revenge for the other side's outrages.

In addition, there were the "ordinary citizen" guerrillas who fought to defend their home areas against those forces they perceived as the enemy or invaders. These guerrillas were not part of any of the contending sides. They stole their weapons and supplies from any of the warring parties, including neighbors.

Last but not least were the marauding guerrillas who adhered to no side but saw in the chaos an opportunity to loot and pillage. All the guerrilla bands rarely took prisoners.

William Clarke Quantrill led one of the biggest and most famous guerrilla groups in Missouri. Initially he fought with Claiborne Jackson's State Guard and was a combatant under Sterling Price at Wilson's Creek. But he chafed at taking orders and soon formed his own irregulars.

Anyone who wanted to join his band was asked only one question, "Will you follow orders, be true to your comrades, and kill those who serve the Union?" [1]

Quantrill was born in 1837 at Canal Dover, Ohio. He became a school teacher but was dissatisfied with his life and felt he was a failure. Looking to be a "somebody," he turned to gambling and petty theft.

1. James McCorkle, *Three Years with Quantrill* (Norman, OK and London: O.S. Barton Co., 1992) p. 19.

The political turmoil and murder in "Bloody Kansas" motivated him to do something of significance. He believed the citizens of each state had the right to maintain their own institutions and way of life without interference.

Quantrill and his younger brother started out from Maryland, bought two wagons and eight mules in Missouri and continued on into Kansas. On their first night there, they camped near Fort Leavenworth. At midnight, thirty "Red Legs," men who intended to keep slavery out of Kansas by murder and atrocities, fired on the sleeping brothers. Their leader was Jim Lane, who would make a national reputation for his brutal acts against civilians. Anti-slavery men like Lane were also called "Jayhawkers."

Thinking that the Quantrill brothers were dead, the Red Legs took their wagons and mules and departed. William was shot in the thigh but played dead. His brother was killed instantly. In the morning William buried him, then crawled across the prairie until he was found by an Indian who took him to Fort Leavenworth.

Quantrill spent several months there recuperating but never regained full use of his leg. Near Leavenworth, he once again became a teacher, then went on to California and taught there. But he could not stop brooding about the fate of his brother and was determined to return to Kansas for revenge. And he did, by joining the Red Legs and, one by one, killing them with a single bullet to the head.

This led Quantrill to be a vigilante, single-handedly murdering cattle and slave rustlers. When he told a group of Union soldiers what he had done to the Red Legs, they fired point blank at him, but he still killed them all without receiving a scratch.

After the battle at Wilson's Creek, 24-year-old Quantrill went out on his own and commanded guerrilla operations. At first he spared the lives of prisoners, except Jayhawkers. He said, "A Jayhawker is just a bandit with abolitionist leanings." [1]

Then he learned of an order by Union general Henry Halleck, on December 22, 1861, instructing Union army officers that whenever captured, guerrillas were to be "immediately shot." From then on, Quantrill also adopted a no-prisoner policy.

Quantrill showed great ability as a leader but his brutal methods of fighting, like taking no prisoners, repelled many Missourians. When Quantrill captured the town of Independence, he gained great notoriety, but his actions caught up with him.

In November 1862, he traveled to Richmond, the Capital of the Confederacy, in the hope of getting an official rank and larger command under a new law that had been passed by the Southern Congress: the Partisan Ranger Act.

1 Ibid., p. 4.

Like with Claiborne Jackson, Quantrill's request has been misrepresented to mean he was a member of the Confederate military, but this is also untrue.

The Act authorized the organizing and supplying of "Rangers," partisan or guerrilla groups not connected to the Confederate military, in "any of the states west of the Mississippi River." Some of these states were within the Union.

The Ranger Act tried to loosely delineate standards of war-time conduct, like reducing or ending atrocities, but it had no authority to enforce them. Quantrill's crimes preceded him to Richmond, and he was denied a larger command. Officially he was designated "Captain, commanding Partisans." This was not a title in the Confederacy's military system.

The Southern leadership believed in more traditional ideals as to the code of conduct in warfare. They considered themselves Christian gentlemen, fighting for lofty principles, who would rather lose than wage unrestricted war.

Reverend Miller, who earlier in our story officiated at the mass grave-sites of civilians, met Quantrill during the war. Miller said: "He did not look like a desperado. He was clean-shaven and neatly dressed in civilian clothes. He had a gentleman's bearing." But he was still seen as "little more removed from that of the wildest savage."

The Sack of Lawrence, Kansas

Quantrill's most famous raid took place on August 21, 1863, when he devastated the town of Lawrence, Kansas. The town's population was militantly anti-slavery and pro-Lincoln. Lawrence was also the home of two of the most notorious Union guerrillas; the same Jim Lane who had shot Quantrill near Leavenworth, and Jim Jennison.

Quantrill and 350 of his raiders spent three hours in Lawrence, battling and killing 180. The Governor of Kansas, Thomas Carney, said that "No fiend in human shape could have acted could have acted with more savage barbarity."

The sack of Lawrence gave Quantrill the unchallenged reputation as the "bloodiest man in American history." Yet there is another side to this story. For months before the Lawrence raid, Union military authorities had been arresting women suspected of aiding the anti-federal guerrillas. They were imprisoned in an abandoned building in Kansas City.

Among those taken were Mrs. Charity Kerr and Mrs. Nannie Harris McCorkle, the sister and sister-in-law of James McCorkle, who was one of Quantrill's most trusted officers. They spent most the war fighting side by side.

As an old man, McCorkle wrote his autobiography, *Three Years With Quantrill*. In it he said:

> At this time [August 1863] the federal soldiers in Kansas City were under General Ewing [infamous for his Order No. 9, which depopulated several counties in Missouri] who was guilty of some

> of the most brutal and fiendish acts that ever disgraced a so-called civilized nation. My sister and sister-in-law went to Kansas City in a wagon, with a load of wheat to exchange for flour. When they produced the flour, and were ready to start home, Anderson Cowgill, a neighbor, who had known these girls all their lives and the men, who refused to speak to me when we paroled him at Independence [Cowgill was taken prisoner when Quantrill captured that town], saw these girls and reported to the authorities that they were rebels and were buying flour to feed the bushwhackers [anti-federal guerrillas]. They were immediately arrested and placed in jail with some other girls who had been arrested.

McCorkle then quoted an article that appeared in the May 22, 1912 *Kansas City Post*:

> There were nine of these girls in the prison when it fell. One of these was Josephine Anderson. [This was the sister of "Big Bill" Anderson, another anti-federal guerrilla, who often fought in conjunction with Quantrill.] Her two sisters, Mollie, aged sixteen, and Janie, ten, were also prisoners. It was these three especially that the Union soldiers wanted to kill, because they were sisters of Bill Anderson. These three were killed, including Mrs. Christie McCorkle. Five others were seriously injured, including Nan Harris McCorkle. These girls, none more than twenty years old, had been arrested and held in prison while waiting to be banished [deported].
>
> When the soldiers heard that Bill Anderson's sisters were in their power, they determined to kill them all. The first inkling of the plot was when Mrs. B.F. Duke heard some of the soldiers, who were staying in her house; speak of the progress they were making in tearing down a wall. Mrs. Duke was a cousin of Bill Anderson, but the soldiers did not know it, and told her of their scheme, and how they had removed a large section of the foundation wall of the women's prison. The building did not fall the first day; so more of the wall was removed, and it was at this point that Mrs. Duke learned of it. She was beside herself with rage and ordered all the soldiers from her home. With a number of friends she hurried to military headquarters and begged them that the girls be taken from the building before they were killed. Her pleas were in vain, and an hour later the building fell. In the hours before the building came down, the women prisoners became uneasy by hearing the people on the floor below, moving out their stock of groceries and whiskey, which they took to a safe place. The plaster had been falling all day and the girls were in a panic. Nan Harris and Mollie Anderson had just gone into the hall for a bucket of water, when they heard cries from the other girls that the roof was falling. A soldier guard, evidently repenting at the last moment, carried the two girls to safety. But Janie Anderson, the youngest, tried

> to escape through a window, but a 12 pound ball, that had been tied to her ankle, held her back, and both her legs were broken. The other girls went down with the ruins. There were groans and screams for a long time, and Josephine Anderson could be heard calling for someone to take the bricks off her head. Finally, her cries ceased.

McCorkle then continued his own commentary:

> This foul murder was the direct cause of the famous raid on Lawrence, Kansas. We could stand no pore. Imagine, if you can, my feelings. A loved sister murdered and the widow of a dead brother seriously hurt by a set of men to whom the name of 'assassins, murderers, and cut-throats' would be a compliment. My God, did we not have enough to make us desperate, and thirst for revenge? We tried to fight like soldiers, but were declared outlaws, hunted under a black flag (no prisoners) and murdered like beasts. The homes of our friends burned, and aged sires, who dared to sympathize with us, had either been hung or shot in the presence of their families, and all their furniture and provisions loaded onto wagons, and with their livestock; taken to the state of Kansas. The beautiful country around both Cass and Johnson counties, were worse than a desert, and on action of Missouri every hillside stood the blackened chimneys, and sentinels and monuments to the memories of our once happy homes. And these outrages had been done by Kansas troops, calling themselves soldiers, but a disgrace to the name soldier. We were determined to have revenge, and so Colonel Quantrill and Captain Anderson planned a raid on Lawrence, Kansas, which was the home of the Jayhawk leaders, Jim Lane and Jennison. [1]

Order No. 11

In retaliation for Quantrill's raid on Lawrence, General Ewing issued Order No. 11, which directed federal troops and Kansas Union guerrillas in Western Kansas to depopulate the eastern and southern half of Jackson, and all of Bales and Cass counties in Missouri.

All of the loyal families were compelled to move into military posts where, like the brutal Spanish general Valeriano Weyle (when the Cubans revolted against Spanish rule), he "allowed them to live on Wind and dirt." The disloyal Missourians were deported outside of the United States.

Colonel Jenison, the sadistic Union guerrilla, who narrowly escaped being caught at Lawrence, promised "fire and sword and thunder and lightning," and vowed "not to leave a house standing within 100 miles of Kansas."

Retaliation, with accelerating cruelty, was practiced by both sides. Union General McNeil issued an order that for every loyal man shot, he would take

1. James McCorkle, p. 120.

ten disloyal men and execute them in public. McNeil followed out his plan to the letter. His deeds shocked the nation, yet it varied from the ordinary only that it was done in public, under the formality of a military order. It is strongly suspected that the number of civilians killed in Missouri outnumbered those killed in battle.

Many of these civilians were murdered so secretly that their relatives never knew where or how, only that they never came home again. Human bones and unmarked mass graves were found in out-of-the-way places years after the war ended.

Reverend Miller, who officiated at the funeral services at the mass grave sites, said: "The once populated areas had become a vast desolate cemetery. Not a living thing existed."

The atrocities by Union forces alienated Missouri Unionists. General Halleck mentioned "Lane" and "Jenison" as two Union guerrillas who took no prisoners. These two men turned thousands of Lincolnites into Sterling Price partisans.

Hamilton Gamble wanted Halleck to execute Jenison, but the United States army refused to discipline those who committed atrocities. Related to this, Reverend Miller said: "From every town where a murder was committed by federal troops or Unionist guerrillas, the victim's friends and relatives rushed to Quantrill for revenge or protection. This was a natural and logical result of the senseless and vengeful way in which the war in western Missouri was prosecuted by the federal government. No greater blunder, I feel like saying crime, was committed by Washington in its conduct of the war, than that of sending Kansas troops into western Missouri, who had already been in an atrocity-filled war with Missourians since the days of 'Bloody Kansas' in the 1850s." [1]

In October 1863, Quantrill's men killed 89 of 110 Union troops in a surprise ambush. After they were dead, their heads were pulverized by bullets, then they were stripped and castrated. Thereafter, his guerrillas routinely scalped their victims.

Despite their atrocities and mutilations, Quantrill's men did not view themselves as criminals or barbarians. Their self-image was noble: "Bursting in on the enemy, guns blazing, they saw themselves as heroic knights, cunning and daring, rescuing damsels in distress, saving desperate civilians just in the nick of time. Slaying the foe, avenging wrong, defending the cause of freedom. The cruelty they employed was forced upon them by a barbaric foe." [2]

Torture and mutilation was a "blood sport" which held intense pleasure for the combatants on both sides. This was a game, an absurd, fatal game. Historians and psychologists have wondered how this kind of warfare affected

1. Ibid., p. 72
2. Ibid., p. 19.

the guerrillas when peace came and they returned to the mundane world, of work and family. Jesse James and Cole Younger are often cited, since both fought under Quantrill, and who continued on as nomadic outlaws.

For most of the guerrillas, the transition to civility was astonishingly easy. Most went back to the farm, and raised corn and children. James McCorkle drifted into Kentucky, farmed there, grew homesick for Missouri, returned, married in 1867, became a devout Christian, spent the next forty years tilling his fields, and died in 1918, aged 79.

May 10, 1865. The war throughout the country ended. Near Taylorsville, Kentucky, Quantrill encountered pro-Union guerrillas. He was badly wounded and died on June 6th. He was 27 years old.

The Confederacy's Van Dorn, Price, Pea Ridge

In the fall and early winter of 1861–62, Sterling Price had been forced back toward the Arkansas border again by superior numbers of Union forces. He formed a junction with Confederate generals McCulloch and McIntosh, inside Arkansas, where Jefferson Davis could legally and willingly give Price aid. This would include a major Southern officer. Davis offered this role to Colonel Henry Heth. If he accepted, he would be promoted to Brigadier-General, above Price, McCulloch, and McIntosh. Price's troops objected strongly. They wanted "Old Pap" Price to have that promotion, which forced Heth to decline.

Jefferson Davis tried again with another of his favorites, General Braxton Bragg, who was stationed in Florida, and anxious to get into the main arenas of the war. Yet Bragg wired back: "The field to which you invite me is a most important one, but under the present aspects, not enticing...So much has been lost there, and so little done in organization and instruction, that the prospects of retrieving our ground is most gloomy." [1]

Jefferson Davis tried a third time: General Earl Van Dorn. Both were Mississippians, and had been close friends for years. Before becoming President of the Confederacy, Davis was a Major-General of Mississippi-troops. When his state seceded, he assigned Van Dorn to the Chief of Brigadiers on his staff. Later, Van Dorn wrote: "I was sincerely attached to him," and "without a doubt, a strong friend." Van Dorn accepted the Arkansas–Missouri command.

In the earlier stages of the war, Davis assigned Van Dorn to Texas, where he gained Abraham Lincoln's grudging respect by capturing thousands of Union soldiers who were stationed there. Van Dorn took pride that Lincoln put a $5,000 reward on his head; the same figure that was placed on Jefferson Davis.

Van Dorn knew the West and its type of warfare. He outranked McCulloch, McIntosh and Price and had the authority to keep them from destroying each other.

1. Robert G Hartje, *Van Dorn, The Life and Times of a Confederate General* (Nashville, TN: Vanderbilt University Press), 1967 .

Making his headquarters at Pocahontas, in Arkansas, Van Dorn's plan was to employ the-same strategy as McCulloch; lure the Union army into Arkansas. But Van Dorn was overconfident; believing he could field a force of 45,000 men, using Price's and McCulloch's men, the Arkansas militia, and new recruits he would muster as he advanced.

But it was winter. Many of his troops were sick as they were quartered in crude huts that did not keep out the bitter cold. A small-pox epidemic swept through McCullough's men. The reality was that Van Dorn only had 15,000 fit enough to fight.

On the Union side, the federals had a new leader, Brigadier-General Sam Curtis; the same man who had given Hamilton Gamble such a difficult time. Curtis was a West Pointer and veteran of the Mexican War.

Initially, Price and McCulloch were divided and Van Dorn had 7000 men. Curtis, with twice that number, attacked Price first, and he retreated into Arkansas. This was probably a ploy to lure Curtis to where the Confederates were free to engage without restrictions.

In the snow, Curtis rested his frozen and exhausted troops at a section of a mountain range known as Pea Ridge. This was in Arkansas. Van Dorn, Price, and McCulloch raced to unite. When they did, Van Dorn made the rash decision to attack Curtis before he was properly prepared. McCulloch had serious doubts about the wisdom of such a move. His men were raw, inexperienced militiamen. Curtis had regular U.S. army soldiers.

Van Dorn called for an immediate attack but as he moved forward, everything went wrong. In the tangled woods, artillery could not be moved into position. Units that were to advance in a continuous line became separated, leaving big gaps in between. Still, they had initial success. The Unionists were pushed back. But soon McCulloch's cold and starving men lost their momentum. He rode to the front ranks to urge them on and was promptly killed. Several other senior Confederate officers were also slain.

Leaderless, confused, and exhausted, Van Dorn's army came to a standstill. Curtis' men were in the same condition and incapable of counter-attacking. Night fell and both sides regrouped.

At dawn, March 8, 1862, Curtis went on the offensive, with fresh reinforcements. Van Dorn, seeing that he was badly outnumbered, retreated. Price followed. Curtis' men were too weak to pursue effectively.

Since this battle was fought in Arkansas, and not in Mississippi, Jefferson Davis commissioned Price as a Major-General in the Confederate army. This tied Price personally to the South, but not Miss9uri, nor his soldiers. To gain this rank, Price had to resign from the Missouri State Guard, and join the Confederate army. He urged his State Guard men to do the same, but they would have to sign a form signifying that they pledged to accept being transferred to any theatre of the war that the Confederate War Department required. Many of Price's Missourians would not sign it. They were fighting for their state's independence only.

Sterling Price was immediately transferred to Tennessee to relieve the pressure on hard-pressed General Albert Johnson. It would be two years before Sterling Price would lead another major attack into Missouri.

As for Earl Van Dorn, he would team up with Price several times on other fronts, but in May 1863, he would be killed, not on the battlefield, but at the hands of an irate husband, who caught him with his wife.

Price's Last Hurrah: Corinth to Westport

Sterling Price was ordered by Jefferson Davis to Corinth, Mississippi to reinforce Confederate General Pierre Beauregard. Corinth was a significant railroad junction near the Tennessee border, where vast amounts of supplies and reinforcements were moved to all parts of the South.

Beauregard was greatly outnumbered by Union General Henry Halleck's 100,000 men. As Price arrived there, Beauregard made the wise decision to abandon the city. He withdrew to Tupelo, also in north-west Mississippi.

Then, as Sterling Price had feared, Jefferson Davis made a misleading speech for Van Dorn; that Missouri had not yet been abandoned, but that her soldiers were needed for urgent but temporary service elsewhere. Price believed otherwise. He was furious and went to Richmond to confront the Confederate President, to make him-commander of the Western Theatre, which included Missouri. That would make Missouri a high priority and not simply a side-issue.

Jefferson Davis distrusted Price's arrogance, especially when he heard rumors that Price was planning to depose him. Davis humiliated Price by saying he would give him the second position in command of the West. Price replied that he would resign if he could not have the highest post. Davis refused and accepted his resignation. Later, Davis apologized. Price remained under the Confederacy's orders.

July 1862: Union and Southern strategy shifted away from Corinth toward Chattanooga in Tennessee. Halleck was promoted to Commander in Chief of the Northern forces. Van Dorn and Price were now directed to defend Mississippi with only 30,000 men. Missouri was still on its own. Price, ever the egomaniac, would not cooperate with Van Dorn, who in turn refused to follow Price's orders. But when Ulysses S. Grant, not a significant figure at this point in the war, planned to trap and crush Price, and began an encirclement, Van Dorn finally came to the rescue and defeated Grant's forces, allowing Price to escape. Then the two rivals got together to capture a large supply depot at Inks, near Corinth. Re-equipped, they moved on Corinth. After initial success, where forward elements reached the town, they were trapped and slaughtered. Price and Van Dorn retreated. Van Dorn was relieved of his command.

At this stage, Price's Missourians were almost mutinous. They demanded to fight only in the home state. Price requested permission to once again lead a Missouri Army. Again, his request was denied. Instead, he was ordered to defend Vicksburg.

Sterling Price's discontent prompted new rumors that he planned to abandon the Southern cause and establish an independent confederacy of the northwestern states. They would remain in the United States if they could be guaranteed that slavery would be protected. This rumor proved to be false.

Claiborne Jackson died in December 1862 of throat cancer. Lt. Governor Thomas Reynolds took over his position. Reynolds, another man with a big ego, feared that Price would take over his exalted role.

Reynolds realized that if Price wished to command in Missouri, he must resign from the Confederate army. So Reynolds planned to put officers loyal to him on Price's staff to block his political ambitions.

February 10th, 1863. Jefferson Davis played both ends against the middle as he finally gave Price what he wanted, and yet kept him tied to the Confederacy. Price now headed the Trans-Mississippi Department, but Confederate General Kirby Smith was above him. Further, Price was involved in endless conflicts with Governor Reynolds, who was an officious bureaucrat who demanded fiscal and political stability before he would authorize a military invasion of Missouri. Otherwise, he believed, it would be anarchy; of course Price felt the exact opposite. To Price, harmony was anathema. He continued his mental battles with Jefferson Davis, and added Kirby Smith to his list of enemies. Price believed, or fabricated his belief, that while Smith headed the Trans Mississippi Department, Price himself had unlimited decision-making powers, in the field. Either Price had been deceived, or more likely, he invented that scenario to suit his own inflated stature. In reality, he did not have an independent command.

Battle of Helena

The city of Vicksburg was under siege by Ulysses S. Grant. If that city fell, the Mississippi River would be in Union hands, and communications between the eastern and western sides of the river, lost to the Confederacy.

Sterling Price proposed an offensive move against the fortified city of Helena, Arkansas, as a diversion to force Grant to reinforce that city, -to relieve the pressure on Vicksburg. Helena, on the Mississippi, was near Little Rock.

Victory depended on surprise, but the heavy rains and swollen rivers slowed Price down and surprise was lost. Helena was heavily defended with an inner main fort surrounded by several rings of trenches, interdicting artillery batteries added to its impregnability.

July 4, 1863: Price's Missourians and Kirby Smith's Confederates went on the offensive. The terrain, overgrown, tangled, and hilly, slowed the attack and Separated the units. Initially, Price's men made good progress, cutting through the five rings of Union trenches. They reached the fort in the center of Helena. But the federals encircled them and they were trapped and surrendered.

After six hours of brutal fighting, Price saw it was hopeless and ordered a retreat. The Union men were too exhausted to pursue.

Vicksburg also surrendered on July 4th. The Confederacy was now split in half.

Price fell back to Little Rock, built trenches to defend it, but federal soldiers converged from several directions, and he abandoned the city.

Lincoln and the Last Hurrah at Westport

Some Confederates, and Abraham Lincoln himself, believed that Sterling Price's resolve was weakening. After all, in the beginning he has been against secession and linking up with the South. Lincoln was convinced he could be brought over to the Union cause, if the President gave him a full pardon. After secret negotiations it became clear that Price was as committed as ever in the dream of liberating Missouri.

March 1864: Kirby Smith and Price planned one last great effort-to drive the federal army from Missouri. By using Arkansas as a jump-off point, they could penetrate into Missouri, collecting volunteers as they pressed forward.

Aware of the plan, once again Union armies moved from all directions to encircle and exterminate Kirby Smith and Price: But Price, using only swift-moving cavalry, struck first at one of the slow infantry columns. Kirby Smith, also using horsemen, blunted a second Union column. He then reinforced Price and captured 1,000 federals, forcing the rest to retreat toward Little Rock. Price chased them until they collided in a swamp near Jenkins Ferry. Again, the Union men were crushed and continued their flight to the Arkansas Capital.

Sterling Price was now ready to re-take his home state and keep it independent of the USA and C.S.A. As he marched, he urged Missourians to join his army of liberation. Whenever he met potential volunteers; he told them what would happen if the state remained in the Union. If the Confederacy signed a peace treaty under federal control, the citizens of "Southern birth and blood," who, before the war "had formed a distinct and superior class," would be shut out by their conquerors from all political privileges. They would be "oppressed and impoverished by their greedy masters" and "the fate of the Irish and Poles will be theirs." To Price, nothing could be more wretched. [1]

Governor Reynolds, ever at odds with Price, believed that to give the invasion an aura of permanence, he would have to join Price's army. Without

1. Robert E. Stelhope, *Sterling Price: Portrait of Southerner* (Columbia MO. University of Missouri Press, 1971) p. 257.

his presence the citizens would view the attack as ancillary to the defense of Arkansas, making the invasion temporary, even if successful. That would mean Missourians would not give their full cooperation, for fear of reprisals, once Price withdrew.

Then, in July 1864, Reynolds saw the bigger picture; military intelligence learned that Missouri had been stripped of Union regulars to aid Sherman in his drive through Georgia. Reynolds realized that even if Price's expedition was short-term, it would divert federal troops from the eastern theatre, giving the South an opportunity to win. Reynolds, to placate Price, promised not to join his army unless it made substantial progress.

August 1863: Kirby Smith finalized his plan for Sterling Price's aid. The objective was to capture St. Louis. This led Reynolds, ever ego-driven, jealous and fearful of Price, to change his mind again, and he prepared to attach himself to the drive toward St. Louis. His greatest anxiety was that, if Price was successful, he would head a military government, and he, Reynolds, would be out of power.

August 28, 1863: Sterling Price launched his assault from Camden, Arkansas. Small diversionary attacks were conducted along the rail lines between Little Rock and the White River.

September 13: Price arrived in Pocahontas, Arkansas, the rendezvous point for his 12,000 troops, which included new men who joined along the way. But these were not like the volunteers at the beginning of the struggle. Many men joined to loot and murder their personal enemies. They could not be disciplined as soldiers.

September 19: Sterling Price crossed into Missouri with three widely scattered columns, allowing each to forage and find food. Initially they encountered only light resistance, but two federal columns, one led by Brigadier-General Ewing, of Order No. 11 infamy, were converging to meet Price.

At Ironton, advanced Union scouts clashed with the Missourians but they were pushed back into Fort Davidson. Because Southern civilians were held hostage in the fort, Price refused to use his artillery to pound it into submission. Instead he ordered a frontal assault against its thick walls.

The Missourians, not the high-spirited men of the early years, were easily slaughtered, suffering 1,000 casualties in twenty minutes. As a result, Price saw the reality; the civilians inside would have to take their chances. As he ordered his big guns into position, Ewing did the job for him, blowing up the fort's gun powder, and Fort Davidson, and escaping into the night.

With so many killed and wounded, Sterling Price could not take St. Louis.

He now turned west, toward Jefferson City, avoiding battle, hoping to fill out his thinned ranks with new recruits. Few came forward. The population was too exhausted and demoralized after four years of warfare and atrocities.

Price's circuitous route allowed the federals time to fortify Jefferson City. So he turned again, toward Boonville, northwest of the capital, picking up 2,000 men as he moved. As before, most of them were interested in booty, not liberating Missouri.

Union generals William Rosecrans and Sam Curtis saw that they finally had a real opportunity to destroy Price once and for all. They converged from opposite directions. Price perceived that the separation was a chance to smash each group in turn. Price positioned himself between the two. Rosecrans and Curtis moved at different speeds, giving Price the time to finish one off before turning on the other.

October 24, 1864: The first contact was made with Curtis, who outnumbered Price. His men had the latest technology; repeating rifles. But they were raw recruits. Price still had many veterans. This made the contest even.

Curtis cracked first, and retreated toward Independence, directly across from Kansas City, Arkansas. There they made a last stand on the opposite bank of the Big Blue River, which presented a serious obstacle for Price.

The second wing, under Rosecrans, moved in behind him. Price had Curtis now, but crossing the Big Blue meant slow movement in the face of withering fire. Then, there was another problem. Price had 600 wagons at his rear, filled with weapons, ammunition, and food. He had to withdraw a substantial number of men to protect those wagons.

The Missourians who tried to cross the river directly in front of Curtis were cut to pieces. Another element successfully crossed downstream and decimated the Union defenders, as they panicked and fled. But night fell before a complete victory could be achieved, and the federals maneuvered around the town of Newport, encircling Price, who had to fall back to the wagons to escape the trap. Somehow he managed to withdraw into Kansas.

October 25: Curtis and Rosecrans pursued and destroyed the rear of the Missourian's column. The main body of men became unnerved. Price rode among them to stop the rout. Yet his cavalry stunned and stopped the federals at least for the moment. The only way to escape was to burn hundreds of wagons, to move with greater speed. Still, Curtis constantly harassed Price.

October 29: Facing extermination, Price received the first piece of good news. Rosecrans recalled most of the Union troops from Missouri for duty in the East, leaving Curtis with only 3,500 men to continue the chase.

November 7: Sterling Price crossed the Arkansas River, just west of Fort Smith. The remnants of his army were frozen, exhausted, and completely demoralized. Later that month they limped into Laynesport, Arkansas, and stopped dead. They could go no further. After an incredible march of nearly 1,500 miles through Union territory, they had finally reached the safety of the Confederate domain.

This long ordeal would be the last gasp to wrest Missouri from federal hands. Beyond this point to the end of the war, the only resistance would come from the guerrilla bands.

After the War, Missouri "Reconstructed" Like the Confederacy

Despite the fact that Missouri was never a Confederate state, when the war ended, it received the same brutal treatment, as if it was part of the hated enemy.

Andrew Johnson became President upon Abraham Lincoln's assassination. At first it seemed he would be a brutal tyrant over the shattered South. His original plan was to humiliate and destroy the slave-holders, but he soon had a flash of reality. He proved to be a moderate, insightful President.

His plan was "restoration;" bringing the South back into the Union in the shortest time, with the least amount of harsh military rule. This was not "Reconstruction," which implied a long-term radical alteration of the minds, social framework and economy of the South.

Andrew Johnson was committed to the principle of State Sovereignty; internal political matters should be left in the hands of the Southern states. Individual "traitors" should be punished, but the South had never legally seceded or surrendered its rights to govern its own affairs.

As the first step toward normalcy, Johnson appointed provisional governors. Several of them had fought for the Confederacy. Johnson also had to fill thousands of patronage jobs, which inevitably required picking many secession politicians and Southern soldiers. This brought "disloyal" men closer to power soon. Johnson accepted that reality.

Congressional Reconstruction

Andrew Johnson's moderate restoration policy infuriated the Radical Republicans in Congress. They counter-attacked and gradually drew the President's powers into a desire for permanent revenge against the South: "Congressional Reconstruction."

Thaddeus Stephens was the Radical Republican leader of the House of Representatives. His hate-filled ideas became the goal for the next decade: the "Conquered Province" concept. The "law of war" alone would rule the actions of Congress, even though the war was over. The Northern victors must treat the South as "conquered provinces and exterminate or drive out the present rebels as exiles from this country." [1]

Stephens demanded that every inch of Southern soil must be confiscated to pay for the costs of the war and the pensions to wounded Union soldiers. For Stephens, secession had been successful. The South was out of the Union. The Constitution was a "bit of worthless parchment." The South must come back as completely new states or as conquered provinces, under the permanent ascendency of Washington.

Stephens received from Congress the approval to divide the former Confederacy into military districts under a commander who had absolute power and no time-table for the end of martial law. The officers in charge of these districts were only beholden to Ulysses S. Grant, who was now the highest ranking officer in the army, not the President.

Representative Anthony Thornton of Illinois expressed the truth of what all this would mean: "If the states which attempted to secede are dead and defunct states, then the war was a fearful tragedy, resulting in the death of both the Union and the states." [2]

Missouri's New Constitution: One Party Rule

Charles Drake, the head of the Radical Union Party, a splinter group of the Radical Republicans, had his own idea of a "democratic constitution." It would create an oligarchy for himself and his Radical followers, by greatly restricting the power of the General Assembly, so it could not block their plans for a new Utopian social order.

Drake spelled it out: "We intend to erect a wall and a barrier in the shape of a constitution that shall be as high as the eternal heavens, deep down as the very center of the earth, so that the Democrats, conservatives, all who do not share the Radical point of view shall neither climb over it, nor dig under it, and as thick as the whole territory of Missouri, so that they shall never batter it down nor pierce through it."[3]

A constitutional convention was formed, and there were some restrictions placed on the legislative process:

1. It limited the Assembly's ability to make laws and amend the constitution.
2. The Assembly could not make special laws in regard to thirteen classes of cases, where it could before. More specifically, it could not make special legislation where a general law was applicable.

1. Walter Fleming, *Civil War and Reconstruction in Alabama* (New York: Columbia University Press, 1905) p. 347.
2. Congressional Globe, 39th Congress, First Session (Washington, D.C., reprint edition by United States Historical Documents Institute, 1970) p. 1165
3. William E. Parrish, *Missouri Under Radical Rule, 1865-1870* (Columbia, Mo.: University of Missouri Press, 1965) p. 25.

Again, this hampered legislative power.

3. If the two Houses of the Assembly proposed constitutional amendments, these had to be published four months before it could be submitted to the voters for ratification. This dramatically slowed the process.
4. In contradiction to tradition, where the imitative for a constitutional convention to make amendments began from the Assembly; and it could only call for the convention with the approval of a popular referendum. This could stall changes indefinitely.
5. The use of stringent loyalty oaths eliminated most of the Radical's opponents. They called this clause of the new constitution, "Rebel Disenfranchisement." In reality it was a political opposition disenfranchisement.

These oaths required swearing that the person had never committed any one of 86 different acts of disloyalty; taking up arms against the state or the United States; giving aid or supporting the rebellion, contributing money or goods or information to the enemy. These definitions were interpreted with great latitude, so that any activity, however innocuous, could be interpreted as falling under these "disloyal" activities. These oaths were mandatory for voters, candidates for public office, jurors, lawyers, corporate officers, teachers and clergymen.

These oaths could ban the majority of Missourians, because it was retroactive to December 1861. At that time many of the citizens were stunned by the federal invasion of their state, especially when the legislature pronounced its loyalty to Lincoln and the Union. Missourians publicly expressed the righteousness of Claiborne Jackson's calling up of the militia to defend Missouri against this unconstitutional attack.

However, these same citizens, whether from fear or sincere belief, soon publicly expressed their support for the Union army occupation and Hamilton Gamble's government.

Early in the war, Hamilton Gamble issued a proclamation which provided a general amnesty for all who took an oath to the state and Union by December 17, 1861. Regardless of the citizen's previous statements or activities; Lincoln, the army, and the Provisional Government would accept their loyalty.

The post-war oath denied the validity of this and sought to condemn as disloyal or traitorous those who had supported Claiborne Jackson, even before hostilities began.

Charles Drake denied that there was any conflict. He said that the December 1861 proclamation only guaranteed the "repentments' security" in their "person, in their property, in their lives," and nothing more. There was no wording about their rights being protected, like in voting or holding office. His opponent disagreed. One said: "Drake suggests to me, in his violent speech, the code of Draco." Draco was an ancient Athenian politician in the era of 600 B.C. His brutal codification of the law made a death sentence mandatory for even the most trivial offense.

False Atrocity Stories Strengthen Disenfranchisement

The Radicals added another dimension to their all-out effort to label their opponents as traitors, and following Thaddeus Stephens' "Conquered Province" concept, they published false atrocity stories against Democrats, conservatives, and Claiborne Jackson supporters, to disqualify ever more adversaries. And further, via Thaddeus Stephens, they demanded the confiscation of "rebel" property, and bemoaned the fact that all the disloyal could not be hung.

To "protect the suffrage" the constitutional convention required that the General Assembly establish the machinery for the systematic biennial registration of voters. Since the Radicals contended that anyone guilty of the high crime of treason would have few scruples about committing perjury, such a registration system would uncover those who took the oath under false pretenses. The registration officers would be the final judges of loyalty. They alone passed on the validity of each oath-taker.

The Radicals went still further. The convention mandated the re-organization of the judiciary. All such offices, from the Supreme Court down, would be forcibly vacated, giving the governor the power to fill them. The Missouri "Democrat," the Radical's main newspaper in St. Louis, cheered this change to sweep clean the last vestige of Democratic and conservative control over the state government. This was called the "Ousting Ordinance;"Judges and court officers were ejected without charge, cause, or trial. This was so controversial and unconstitutional, it was deliberately not placed before the people as an amendment, and not part of the referendum to the voters.

Acts like this had previously become law under Hamilton Gamble's Provisional Government, when civil law and civil rights had been replaced *by* arbitrary military rule. But now, with peace, supposedly all that had ended. The Radicals countered by declaring that the post-war period was just as unstable, giving them the right to do this without the slightest pretense of legality. Now they had a virtual unbreakable one-party monopoly on power.

As a result, the Missouri Supreme Court was filled with Radicals and they upheld the Ousting Ordinance. The court ruled it was "organic" and no act of the legislature could alter or repeal it.

All these features of the new constitution were passed by the convention. Now it required the ratification of the few remaining voters. One of these who did not agree with the new constitution was William F. Switzer, a delegate at the convention. He said "The constitution was not conceived in statesmanship but in a spirit of malice and revenge; a spirit at war with the wise policy of the times, and unworthy of a victorious and magnanimous people." [1]

Charles Drake tried to go further in the direction of absolutism. He attempted to have the new constitution become the organic law without its ratification by the voters. When this proved impossible, he tried another strategy, as was the case in New York. Drake secured the passage of a special ordinance that required the governor to send ballot sheets to army posts in other states, where Missouri troops were stationed, so they could vote on the constitution. Drake supervised this process. This had been illegal, since tabulating the ballot would be entrusted to military commanders with no civilian oversight. The probability of fraud was very great, which proved to be the case. The results of the referendum remained in doubt for three weeks. There was much opposition to its extreme clauses, and it seemed to be defeated. But then the soldier's votes trickled in, and defeat became victory.

Frank Blair: Radical to Conservative

The ultra-Radical Frank Blair, who had combined with the mentally unstable Nathaniel Lyon, to plunge Missouri into full-scale war, now had an insight, that the end result of Radicalism would be a military dictatorship that would engulf his state and the entire United States.

Blair stunned his fellow Radical Republicans when he became an ally of President Andrew Johnson to promote his moderate policy of restoration toward the South. Blair now opposed the vindictive features of the Drake constitution, denouncing it as "begotten of malice and concocted by a clique destitute of heart or conscience." [2]

Blair, the former hero of the Radicals, was now labeled a "'false Moses, who seeks to lead the rebels back to power." He was also accused of being "a fanatic who would not stop short of perjury at the polls [lying about his disloyalty when taking the oath] or rebellion, if necessary to accomplish his evil purposes." [3]

This was said because Blair intended to test the validity of the oath at the upcoming local election, in St. Louis. He planned to present himself at the polls with his own oath, which simply declared his allegiance to the state and nation. If the election officials refused to accept his ballot and demanded that he take the "iron-clad oath," Blair would say he did not have to, since his record demonstrated his loyalty. He had taken up arms against Claiborne Jackson and gained national fame by commanding one of General Sherman's corps during the final campaign through Georgia and the Carolinas.

1. Ibid., p. 34
2. Ibid., p 57.
3. Ibid., p. 86.

Blair appeared at the polls. The election judges rejected his ballot. Blair brought a law suit against them. If necessary, he was determined to carry his case all the way to the Supreme Court. He sued in the St. Louis Circuit Court, asking for $100,000 in damages. If he won, the conservatives and Democrats would be re-franchised, thus ending the Radicals political monopoly.

The case came to trial in the spring of 1866. Blair's lawyer argued that the oath represented an ex-post facto registration, which made an act criminal, which was not so, when committed. He also argued that Blair had had been disenfranchised without being convicted of a crime by a judicial trial.

The Radicals considered this trial so crucial that Charles Drake defended the election officials. Drake maintained that Missouri's citizens, acting through the constitutional convention, had the power to establish voting qualifications and fix rules for carrying them out without any interference "from any tribunal or authority in the wide world."

The Circuit Court ruled against Blair. He appealed to the Missouri Supreme Court. In October 1866 that court, now packed with Radical judges, upheld the oath.

Then the United States Supreme Court heard Blair's case. Again, Charles Drake appeared, for the right of a state to make its own qualifications. Blair contended that its purpose was to disqualify political rivals, not only the disloyal.

The U.S. Supreme Court stalled on a decision. Finally, it was evenly divided, four to four. This tie affirmed the Missouri ruling that the oath was legal.

Oaths for Clergy: Fusing Church, State, and Military

Another law had passed the constitutional convention, which forced all clergymen to take a loyalty oath. Failing it meant being barred from preaching and voting.

The Roman Catholic Archbishop of St. Louis, Peter Richard Kennick, deplored the oath and hoped it would not be enforced. If the civil powers insisted on exacting its "sacrifice of ecclesiastical liberty," he advised his priests not to succumb.

Catholic Father John Cummings thus refused to take the oath. This made him the target of Radical vindictiveness. He was indicted. His case gained wide notoriety, which led it to becoming of primary importance in the struggle over the oath.

Father Cummings announced that he would defend himself and plead not guilty. The court found him guilty. The judge, before sentencing Cummings, asked if he wished to make a statement. He did, saying that the entire proceeding was an attempt to persecute the Roman Catholic Church and the clergy. He repudiated the right of the state to interfere with his divine calling.

Cummings was fined and refused to pay it, and spent a week in Jail. His lawyer refused to give up. He brought the case before the Missouri Supreme Court, where he lost again. Reverdy Johnson, the Maryland Senator, put Cummings presentation before the United States Supreme Court.

Johnson had just gained national prominence with his Supreme Court victory in the landmark "Ex-Parte Milligan" case in Indiana. Johnson had also been the counsel for Mrs. Emerson in the Dred Scott case.

The Radicals screamed at the possibility of Cummings winning. "No class of people between Heaven and earth or outside of Heaven or Hell, deserve the curse of God more than disloyal ministers, and no class deserves sympathy, less than this class. If they cannot take the oath, they should go and seek a home somewhere else." [1]

January 14, 1867: The United States Supreme Court decided that the test oath constituted an ex-post facto legislation. The decision unraveled the iron-clad oath at all levels. Soon it was dismantled for lawyers. Then for other classes. "Disloyal" voters and politicians crept back into their legitimate roles.

Radical Governor Fletcher and his allies desperately tried to hold on to power. As during the war, Fletcher organized the loyal militia to terrorize the population into staying away from the polls, through atrocities. And once again the citizens continued guerrilla war against Fletcher's militia-men.

As always, with such tactics, in the local and legislative elections, the Radicals won big. They still controlled both Houses of the Assembly by a wide margin, and won seven of nine Congressional seats.

Still, the Radicals were not satisfied, claiming they should have won more Assembly seats, except that in some districts the Radical registering officials were so intimidated by the disloyal, they could not enforce the oath.

Missouri's Secretary of State, Mr. Rodman, arbitrarily refused to accept the conservative and Democratic votes. In a bitter two year battle, the "disloyal" representatives lost, and the radicals gleefully replaced them with their own. More guerrilla war followed these events.

New Constitution Mandates State-Funded Schools

No former Confederate state could re-enter the Union until it had added a public, tax-supported education system clause to its post-war constitution.

This would be controlled by the carpetbaggers. Several Southern states refused to accept such a clause. They understood that it meant a hostile world-view would be forced upon their children. Eventually, all the former Confederate states acquiesced. Otherwise they would remain territories forever.

1. Ibid., p 68.

A similar education clause was grafted onto the Missouri constitution. Its objective was the same. This is an example: "Textbooks and all publications used in public schools should be free from sectarian and denominational and partisan bias in religion and politics." This meant that the state would control spiritual thought as well as Southern and Democratic Party ideology.

In addition, "Studies pertaining to the government of the United States, and the individual states themselves would be taught with a view of creating a sentiment which would foster a love for the perpetual union of our states." [1]

This was at odds with the United States Constitution, based on state sovereignty, where the citizen's primary loyalty was to his state, and that state could voluntarily leave the Union if its rights were infringed upon by the federal government.

Missouri, like many Northern and Southern states, was dominated by the public attitude that tax-supported schools should exist only for the poor. It was a restricted governmental philanthropy. The rest of the population sent their children to church affiliated schools or private academies or had tutors come to their home. Parental responsibility also included the education of one's own children. To tax one man for the benefit of another was considered unjust and unfair.

The Freedmen's Bureau: Educating Ex-Slaves, Rebels, and the "Disloyal"

In 1865 Congress created a new federal agency; the Bureau of Refugees, Freedmen and Abandoned Lands. Its name was commonly shortened to the Freedmen's Bureau. It was placed within the War Department. Supposedly the Bureau was designed to help the former slaves make the difficult transition to citizenship. The noble ideas had a different reality. As part of the army, it took on the coloration of the military's objectives; to turn the former Confederacy into a permanent colony of the victorious North.

The Freedmen's Bureau had two primary missions. Since most Southern whites had lost their citizenship, most could not vote. The freedmen, although generally unqualified, became the majority of voters.

The Bureau's first task was to re-educate them to become loyal Republicans, and elect Radicals to office. The Congress authorized no money for school construction, yet within two years of its creation the Bureau had built 2,118 schools: built with money illegally received by confiscation of immense tracts of land in the South as well as in Missouri. These tracts were sold off at a great profit. Freedmen who refused to be re-educated as Radicals were terrorized, tortured, and killed.

The Bureau's second mission was to re-educate the children of whites. This was a desperate necessity. After all, they were the next generation of the

1. Proceedings of the Peabody Education Trust Fund, Report of the 24th Meeting, 1885, p. 264.

traitors and disloyal who dared to make war and defy Uncle Sam. They had to be trained to be loyal, and above all, docile and obedient.

J. P. Wickersham, a Radical educator, stated this objective clearly: "What can education do for the whites of the South? There are some intelligent men, but the majority are deplorably ignorant. More ignorant than the slaves themselves. It was this ignorance that enabled the rebel leaders to create a prejudice in the minds of these people against the North, and to induce them to enlist in their armies. As long as they are ignorant they will remain tools of political demagogues and therefore be incapable of self-government...They must be educated; the duty is imperative. A republican form of government cannot exist without providing a system of free schools. A republic must have education universal among its people. Ignorant voters endanger liberty. With free schools in the South [and Missouri] there could have been no rebellion. And free schools now must render impossible rebellion in the future." [1]

Charles Sumner, the Radical head of the Senate, added: "You may exclude the rebels from the government, but their children, who are not excluded, have inherited the rebel spirit. The schools and colleges of the South have been nurseries of rebellion. In a republic, education is indispensable. A republic without education is like a creature of imagination, a human being without a soul, living and moving blindly, with no means of the present or future. Such has been the rebel states. They have been for years political monsters. But such they must be no longer. It is not too much to say that had these states been more enlightened, they would have never rebelled." [2]

Missouri was viewed in the same light, and state-funded schools became the dominant means of re-educating the next generation of whites and blacks: . "Republicans notice that where has been the most schooling since the war, the freedmen are surest for our party." [3]

Negro schoolhouses became Republican Party headquarters and the sites for political and military activity. Bureau teachers viewed themselves as "political revolutionaries."

Jabez Curry, the Alabama Congressman and cavalry officer, observed Bureau education first-hand and made this caustic comment: "What kind of schools were established under the Freedmen's Bureau? Some fanatical 'marms' who came down here to 'enlighten' and enflame the ignorant Negroes with all sorts of ideas about his greatness, perpetuated a crime that never has been equaled in the annals of any race. And with their minds filled up with all these ideas, and a little smattering of education, perhaps they would go

1. John Chodes, *Jabez curry and the Re-Education of the Old South* (New York: Algora Publishing, 2005) p. 155.
2. Ibid., p. 155.
3. George Bentley, *History of the Freedmen's Bureau* (Philadelphia: University of Pennsylvania, 1993) p. 95.

out and forage, or rob. But it was not the result of the education they received, but the fault of those human vampires; I wish I had some words, I wish the dictionary would furnish me some other words with which I might express my detestation and contempt and hatred of these acts." [1]

The Reverend John Alvard was the head of the education division of the Freedmen's Bureau. Although he refuted claims by Thomas Carlyle and Southern whites that Negroes were inferior, and would become extinct on their own, his policies treated them as if this theory was true.

This was exposed by Henry M. Turner, the outspoken Methodist Bishop, who accused the Bureau-funded Hampton Institute of perpetuating Negro inferiority: "The graduates sent out cannot be called educated by any means, for they have not the learning given by a respectable grammar school. Besides, I think colored children are taught to remember 'you are Negroes. Your place is behind.' " When Turner inquired about the higher branches, mathematics, science, and classical languages, a white faculty member replied: "Oh, the colored people are not prepared for those studies yet. They are too ignorant; it will take time enough to talk about that, years from this time." [2]

The Freedmen's Bureau Becomes the Bureau of Education

The Freedmen's Bureau was supposed to pass out of existence a few years after the war. In 1867 a small agency within the Interior Department was created; the Bureau of Education. It had only five employees: a supervisor and four clerks. Its mandate seemed innocuous: "To collect such statistics and facts as show the condition and progress of education in the various states and territories."

And yet, within a few years it employed or had access to 12,000 Interior Department personnel, and controlled most Southern schools and many in the North.

A series of amendments to the original Bureau of Education bill allowed it to grow in size and destructive power. One of these amendments permitted it to absorb every one of the Freedmen's Bureau's 2,118 schools, and all of its officers, who were mostly Radical career army men. Now they would become a permanent part of the federal civil service system: "Section 3. The Bureau of Education is hereby authorized to exercise the same powers as those hitherto exercised by the Freedmen's Bureau in its education division... Section 7: All clerks, messengers, and employees of the Freedmen's Bureau shall be transferred to and retained in the Bureau of Education." [3]

1. Fragment of letter by Jabez Curry to unknown person, unknown date, from Curry Papers, Library of Congress, Washington D.C.
2. Robert Morris, *Reading, Riting and Reconstruction* (Chicago: University of Chicago Press, 1970) p. 128.
3. Annual Report of the Commissioner of Education, for the year 1868, Congressional Globe, 41st Congress, 2nd session, p. 2295.

The effect of this was to militarize a civil agency. Thomas McNeely, a Congressional representative from Illinois, spoke of the consequences of this amendment: "The bill, by its title, pretends to discontinue the Freedmen's Bureau, but it does not. On the contrary, it continues under a new name, under different officials charged with duties more expansive, clothed with more authority, more unconstitutional, and without the safeguards thrown around it, that have, with so little success, opposed the abuses heretofore practiced by that bureau...Mr. Speaker, we have reached the time when the Freedmen's Bureau and all that belongs to it, should be abolished. The people expect it. Sir, it has never had a constitutional foundation, and so apparent was this fact, that those that originated it based it upon certain war powers which they claimed in a time of war was superior to and outside the Constitution." [1]

The End of Radical Rule In Missouri

The end of Radical rule begins with the rise of Carl Schurz and his move to the forefront of the Missouri political scene. Schurz came to the United States as a German émigré in the wake of the revolutionary turmoil of 1848. From the outset he assumed a leadership position among his fellow German-Americans, within the fledgling Republican Party.

During the Civil War he rallied the Germans to the Union cause. After serving as a Brigadier-General of Volunteers, Schurz accepted an editorial position at the Detroit *Post*, and traveled the lecture circuit, where his radical ideas found a ready acceptance with like-minded groups across the country.

As Schurz gained power among the Radicals, Charles Drake declined. He became a United States Senator and spent his time in Washington, losing his hold on the Missouri Radicals. It was Schurz who captured them, and over time, as he became more moderate, the Republicans in that state split into factions; Conservatives and Radicals.

Schurz's political transformation began when Emil Pretorius, the owner of the *Westliche Post*, one of the largest German language newspapers in the country, offered Schurz a partnership in that publication. In that position, Schurz saw a wider reality. While remaining a Radical on national issues, he saw that in order for Missouri to prosper, it required reconciliation with Democrats and conservatives.

When Schurz defeated Drake for the U.S. Senate seat, this began the process. The Radicals lost their hold; Democrats became the majority party. Ex-Confederates came into the legislature. In 1872, the Radicals collapsed. For the next 35 years Missouri was Democratic. The era of Radical Republican hate was history.

1. Ibid., p. 2316

Bibliography

Albany Argus, January 8, 1863, October 28, 1864, November 8, 1864. Baltimore *Sun*, April 22, 1861.

Bentley, George, *History of the Freedmen's Bureau.* Philadelphia: University of Pennsylvania Press, 1955.

Bowman, Dennis K., *Lincoln's Resolute Unionist; Hamilton Gamble*, California State University Press, 2006.

Brooklyn Eagle, July 16, 1863.

Brummer, Sidney David, *Political History of New York State During the Period of the Civil War*, New York: Columbia University and Longmans, Green and Company, Agents, 1911.

Bulla, Thomas M., *Milo Hascall and Freedom of the Press in Indiana*, West Lafayette, Indiana: Purdue University Press, 2008.

Butler, Benjamin, *Butler's Book: Autobiography and Personal Reminiscences of Major-General Benjamin Butler*, Boston: A.A. Thayer and Company, 1892.

Caldwell, Luther, *Amended Constitution of the State of New York*, Albany, New York: Weed, Parsons and Company, Printers, 1868.

Carterville *Indiana True Republican*, June 11, 1863.

Chodes, John, *The Union League: Washington's Ku Klux Klan*, Tuscaloosa, Al. The League of the South Institute for the Study of Southern Culture and History, 1999.

Citizens' Association of New York, "The Constitutional Convention of 1867: Alterations in the Fundamental Law of the State," New York: George F. Nesbitt and Company, Printers and Stationers, 1867.

Citizens Union of the City of New York, "The Proposed Constitution: Summary of Important Changes;" Albany, New York, 1915.

Commissioner of Education, Annual Report, 1868, in the *Congressional Globe*, 41st Congress, Second Session.

Cook, Thomas, and Knox, Thomas, editors, *Public Record of Horatio Seymour*, New York: I.W. England, at the office of the New York *Sun*, 1868.

Croly, David, *Seymour and Blair, Their Lives and Services*, New York: Richardson and Company, 1868.

Curry, Jabez, *Civil History of the Confederate States, With Some Personal Reminiscences*, Richmond: B.F. Johnson Publishing Company, 1911.

Davis, Jefferson, *The Rise and fall of the Confederate Government*, New York: D. Appleton, 1881.

Dix, Morgan, *Memoirs of John Adam Dix*, New York: Harper and Brothers, 1883.

English Combatant, "Battle-fields of the South, From Bull Run to Fredericksburg," New York: John Bradburn Company, 1864.

Ernst, Kathleen, *Too Afraid To Cry*, Mechanicsville, PA: Stackpole Books, 1999.

Evans, Clement A., editor, *Confederate Military History*, Wilmington, N.C., Broadfoot Publishing Company, 1987.

Fesler, Mayo, "Secret Political Societies in the North During The Civil War," *Indiana Magazine of History*, Vol. XIV, Indianapolis. September 1918, No. 3.

Fleming, Walter, *Civil War and Reconstruction in Alabama*, New York: Columbia University Press, 1905.

Foulke, William Dudley, *Life of Oliver P. Morton*, Indianapolis, The Bowen-Morrill Company, 1899.

Franklin, Allan, *The Trail of the Tiger, Tammany: 1789-1928*. New York, 1928.

Fry, James B., *New York and The Conscription of 1863: A Chapter in the History of the Civil War*, New York: G.P. Putnam's Sons, The Knickerbockers Press, 1885.

Gallagher, Gary W., editor, *The Antietam Campaign*, Chapel Hill and London, University of North Carolina Press, 1999.

Hall, John R., *Den of Misery*, Gretna, LA., Pelican Publishing Company, 2006.

Hanson, John W., *Historical Sketch of the Old Sixth Regiment*, Boston: Lee and Sheppard, 1866.

Hartje, Robert G., *Van Dorn, the Life and Times of a Confederate General*, Nashville, TN, Vanderbilt University Press, 1967.

Horigan, Michael, *Elmira: Death Camp of the North*, Mechanicsville, PA: Stackpole Books, 2002.

Horn, Stanley, *The Invisible Empire: The Story of the Ku Klux Klan, 1866-1871*, Cos Cob, CT: John Edwards Company, 1969.

Houghton, W.R. and M.B. Houghton, *Two Boys in the Civil War and After*, Montgomery, AL: Paragon, 1912.

Hyman, Harold Melvin, *Era of the Oath: Northern Loyalty Tests During the Civil War and Reconstruction*, Philadelphia, PA, University of Pennsylvania, 1954.

Indiana Magazine of History, No. 10, March 1914, "Autobiography of a Noted Person."

Indianapolis *Daily Journal*, by the state Republicsan Party. 1860–1863.

Indianapolis *Gazette*, December 11, 1862.

Johnson, Reverdy, *The Dangerous Condition of Our Country; The Cause Which Has Led To It, And The Duty of the People*, Baltimore, MD: The Sun Book and Job Printing Establishment, 1867.

Journal of the Congress of the Confederate States of America, 1861–1865; Washington, DC: Government Printing Office, 1904.

Manakee, Harold R., *Maryland in the Civil War*, Baltimore, MD: Maryland Historical Society.

Mandelbaum, Seymour, *Boss Tweed's New York*, Chicago, IL: Elephant Paperbacks, 1996.

Marcotte, Frank, *Six Days in April; Lincoln and the Union in Peril*, New York: Algora Publishing, 2005.

Marshall, John A., *American Bastille*, Philadelphia: Evans, Stoddard and Company, 1869.

Maryland Historical Magazine, "Disenfranchisement In Maryland," Vol. xxviii, December 1933, No. 4, Baltimore.

McCague, James, *The Second Rebellion: The Story of the New York City Draft Riots of 1863*, New York: The Dial Press, 1968,

McCorkle, James, *Three Years With Quantrill*, Norman, OK, and London: O.S. Barton Company, 1992.

McDonald, Daniel, *History of Marshall County, Indiana*, Mt. Vernon, Indiana: Windmill Publications, 1908.

Miller, George, Reverend, *Missouri's Memorable Decade, 1860-1870*, Columbia, Missouri: Press of E.W. Stephens, 1898.

Mohr, James C., *Radical Republicans and Reform in New York During Reconstruction*, Ithaca and London: Cornell University Press, 1973.

Moore, Frank (Ed.), *The Rebellion Record*, New York: Arno Press, 1991.

Morrill, Louis Taylor, "Ben Butler in the Presidential Campaign of 1864," *The Mississippi Historical Review*, Vol. xxxiii, No.4, March 1947.

Morris, Robert, *Reading, 'Righting, and Reconstruction*, Chicago, IL, University of Chicago Press, 1970.

Mushcat, Jerome, *Fernando Wood: A Political Biography*, Kent and London, Kent State University Press, 1990.

Myers, William Starr, *The Maryland Constitution of 1864*. Baltimore: The Johns-Hopkins Press, 1901.

New Albany Indiana *Weekly Ledger*, April 20, 1856, April 3, 1862.

New York *Herald*, March 8, 1863, March 19, 1863, April 3, 1863.

New York *Times*, 1864–1867.

Nicolay, John, and John Hay (Eds.), *The Complete Works of Abraham Lincoln*, New York: Tandy-Thomas Company, 1905.

Omanson, Bradley, "The Long March of John Wyeth," www.worldwarI.com, February 2004.

Parrish, William E., *Missouri Under Radical Rule, 1865-1870*, Columbia, MO:, University of Missouri Press, 1965.

Peabody Education Trust Fund, "Report of the 24th Meeting," 1885.

Phillips, Christopher, *Damned Yankee: The Life of General Nathaniel Lyon*, Columbia, MO: Condon and Company, 1990.

Phillips, Christopher, *Missouri's Confederate: Claiborne Jackson, and the Creation of Southern Identity in the Border West*, Columbia, MO: University of Missouri Press, 2000.

Radcliffe, George L., "Governor Thomas Hicks of Maryland and the Civil War," *Johns Hopkins University Studies in Historical and Political Science*, Series XIX, Nos. 11–12, Baltimore, MD: The Johns Hopkins Press, 1901.

Rakove, Jack N., *The Annotated United States Constitution and Declaration of Independence*, Cambridge, MA, Harvard University Press, 2009.

Sanger, Eugene F., *Papers, from the records of the office of the Adjutant General, Regimental Correspondence, 1861–1865*, Maine State Archives.

Sears, Stephen W., *George McClellan: The Young Napoleon*, New York: Tickner and Field, 1988.

Semmes, Raphael, "Vignettes of Maryland History," Baltimore: *Maryland Historical Magazine*, XL, No. I, March 1945.

Spear, Lonnie R., *Portraits in Hell: Military Prisons in the Civil War*, Mechanicsville, PA: Stackpole Books, 1997.

Stanhope, Robert E., *Sterling Price: Portrait of a Southerner*, Columbia, MO: University of Missouri Press, 1971.

Stampp, Kenneth, "Indiana Politics During the Civil War," *Indiana Historical Collections*, Vol. xxvi, Indianapolis, IN: Indiana Historical Bureau, 1949.

Stampp, Kenneth, "The Milligan Case and the Election of 1864 in Indiana," *Missouri Valley Historical Review*, No. 31, 1955.

Stevens, John, *Reminiscences of the Civil War*, Hillsboro, TX: Hillsboro Mirror Printing Company, 1902.

"Treatment of Prisoners During the War," Southern Historical Society Paper I, No. 4, April 1876.

United States War Department, *The War of the Rebellion: A Compilation of the Official Records of the Union and Confederacy*, Series III, Vol. 2, Washington, DC.: Government Printing Office, 1880-1901.

Von Borcke, Heros, *Memoir of the Confederate War for Independence*, Edinburg, Blackwood and Sons, 1865.

Wall, Alexander J., "A Sketch in the Life of Horatio Seymour," New York: New York Historical Society, 1929.

Winslow, Hattie Lou and Joseph R.H. Moore, "Camp Morton, 1861–1865," Indianapolis: Indiana Historical Society, 1940.

World, November 12, 1865.

About the Author

John Chodes is a writer and a New Yorker in equal parts.

The Civil War and the problems of Reconstruction have been the subject of thirty articles and several books and monographs by Mr. Chodes.

In "The Constitution and State Sovereignty," Mr. Chodes documents the fact that the United States Constitution was only ratified on the condition that secession would be an accepted alternative in case the Federal Government overstepped its mandated powers. The monograph condenses the classic book by Jefferson Davis, President of the Confederacy, *The Rise and Fall of the Confederate Government*.

"The Paradox of Jabez Curry; State Sovereignty to Federalized Schools" was called "a work of universal significance." The related book *Destroying the Republic: Jabez Curry and the Re-education of the Old South* details how an influential Alabamian switched from defending states' rights to promoting public education aimed at eradicating the spirit of rebellion — in the North as well as the South — helping to transform the US republic into an emerging dictatorship in the 21st century.

Mr. Chodes demonstrates that a US federal agency equaled or surpassed the Ku Klux Klan in brutality toward Southern freedmen in his third monograph, "The Union League, Washington's Ku Klux Klan."

Another book, *Horatio Seymour, Governor of New York, Attacks Lincoln's War*, combines the antagonistic letters and speeches between the President and the Governor. This led to two armed invasions of the Empire State and to its military occupation, as seen in the present work.

Articles by Mr. Chodes relating to the history of education and the federalizing of Southern education, culture and property, have appeared in The *New York Times*,

Chronicles, *The Freeman*, *Social Justice Review*, *The New York Tribune*, *Southern Partisan*, and *Southern Events*.

Additional non-fiction books include *Bruce Jenner*, a biography of the 1976 Olympic Decathlon gold medalist, and the award-winning *Corbitt*. This is the biography of the first African-American to compete in an Olympic marathon, who was a mentor to Mr. Chodes. *Corbitt* won the "Journalistic Excellence Award" from the Road Runners Club of American. The *New York Times* rated it as one of the best sports books of the year. On this account Mr. Chodes became technical advisor to Dustin Hoffman in the Paramount Pictures film, *Marathon Man*.

Seven plays by John Chodes have been performed Off-Broadway in New York City.

Mr. Chodes has also written extensively to promote the "free market," with over one hundred articles, TV and radio editorial replies, chapters in four books, and a complete book called *In Praise of the Free Market*, a compilation of much of this material, which has appeared in the *New York Times*, *Chronicles*, *Reason*, and *The Freeman* as well as on CBS-TV, ABC-TV, FOX-TV, and others.

His photographs have appeared in *Newsweek*, *Track and Field News*, *Athletics Weekly* (England), *Long Distance Log*, *Town and Country*, *The Brooklyn Eagle*, and *Brooklyn Record*.

Index

A

B

G

H

I

J

O

P

Q

R

S

T

U

V

W

Printed in the United States
By Bookmasters